GOOD
WRITING

GOOD WRITING

**BY JUDI KESSELMAN-TURKEL
AND FRANKLYNN PETERSON**

FRANKLIN WATTS
New York/London/Toronto/Sydney

Library of Congress Cataloging in Publication Data

Kesselman, Judi R
Good Writing.

Includes bibliographical references and index.
1. English language—Rhetoric. I. Peterson,
Franklynn, joint author. II. Title.
PE1408.K558   808'.042   80–20924
ISBN 0–531–06504–9 (pbk.)

FRANKLIN WATTS
730 FIFTH AVENUE
NEW YORK, NEW YORK 10019

*To Karen and Mike and John and Gini
and Judy and Jill and Margaret and
Bernadine and Phyllis and Linda and
Dave and Jim and Don and Marianna and
Julie and Sally and Sandy and Jeff*

*who forced us to figure out what
we were trying to tell them.*

CONTENTS

UNIT I
HOW TO TELL GOOD WRITING
FROM BAD

UNIT II
SENTENCES: BUILDING BLOCKS OF STRONG WRITING

Chapter 3
Put Strong Words
in Your Sentences   **55**

UNIT III
PAPERS: HOW TO MAKE THEM SERVE YOUR PURPOSE

Chapter 15
How to Develop a Style of Your Own   **348**

UNIT I

HOW TO TELL GOOD WRITING FROM BAD

CHAPTER 1
WHAT GOOD WRITING
CAN DO FOR YOU

Good writing isn't hard;
no harder than ditchdigging.
Patrick Dennis

The authors of this textbook are, by profession, writers. We have written over a dozen books and several hundred articles for magazines and newspapers. In order to keep up with the demands of professional writing, we've had to strip away romantic misconceptions and develop, instead, basic guidelines for good writing. Recently, we have taught our skills to young people and adults who've wanted to write so well that editors and publishers would pay for their words. A large proportion of those students have sold their nonfiction work, so we know that good writing can be learned.

But experience has convinced us that writing is often taught with the wrong emphasis. The traditional method starts by examining, after-the-fact and secondhand, the process that leads up to a finished piece of nonfiction. It relies on tearing apart published writings in an attempt to second-guess how the authors brought their work to that finished state, or it teaches safe topics such as how to outline and how to recognize a metaphor. It emphasizes terminology instead of sharply outlined methodology. Rules of grammar that can be corrected objectively often get more teaching time than subjective criteria for figuring out why somebody would want to read what you want to write.

In this textbook, attention will be given to metaphors, outlines, and grammar rules. But they will be put in the context of the creative process. You'll see actual copies of real manuscripts that only minutes earlier were blank pieces of paper in the hands of professional writers or students like yourselves. Instead of trying to imagine how the polished writing evolved, you'll watch the actual logical metamorphosis take place. We will explain why it took place and how. More important, you'll learn how you can make it happen, too.

1.1 GOOD WRITING
REQUIRES A READER.

In many ways, we look upon this as a brush-up course for you. You might want to view it similarly. You see, you almost learned good writing once before—while you were learning how to speak. If you'd been encouraged then to write as instinctively as you speak, you might not be enrolled in this course now.

Our language is so logical that even an infant can learn its fundamentals by the age of three. Most people speak well by the time they leave high school. Few are destined to be spellbinders like Katharine Hepburn and Martin Luther King, but most express themselves well enough to get across the meaning of complex ideas even though oral rhetoric and public speaking courses are seldom taught in school these days. People learn naturally not only to express themselves clearly but to keep their listeners interested in what they have to say. Good speaking habits become ingrained through consistent positive or negative feedback, mostly in the form of attention from friends when the talk is interesting and clear, and yawns when it isn't.

Good speaking comes about only if there's someone listening, someone providing feedback. Until then it's just noise like those electrical impulses, from distant stars, that scientists haven't been able to decode. Good writing comes about only if there's someone reading it. Otherwise it might just as well be a marked-up surface like Cleopatra's Needle, an obelisk with ancient scratches that only a few people in the world know how to decode.

In order to write well, you must write for readers. That is a basic building block on which the study of good writing has to be built.

EXERCISES:

1. Compare your present speaking habits to your present writing habits. How are they similar? How do they differ? Ask a good friend to compare them objectively.

2. Think back to when you were learning to talk. (If you can't recall that part of your life, think about a time when you observed a youngster learning to talk.) List six rules for speaking that came from that part of your speech development.

3. Now think back to when you were learning to write. List six rules that came from that period.

4. Compare your six speaking rules to your six writing rules. Consider why they differ or are similar. Which of them are still valid at your present level of speaking and writing development?

1.2 NOT ALL WRITING HAS TO BE GOOD.

Is everything you write meant to be read by somebody else? Probably not. In fact, maybe even *you* intend never to read some of it again. Some writing is done for catharsis, such as love letters (or nasty letters) that are torn up or filed away and forgotten. Some writing is done for diversion, like the doodles and scribbles penned during boring lectures. Author Kesselman-Turkel writes lots of lists. They're just a prod for her visual memory, which stores away facts she's seen better than facts she's heard.

When you write for yourself—when you take notes at a lecture, for instance—you don't have to consider whether any other person can understand your handwriting or your mode of expression. You can misspell, make up your own shorthand, ignore punctuation altogether, even leave out whole chunks of information you already know well. But now put yourself in the place of a friend who has missed a lecture and wants to borrow your notes. They'll probably do her little good unless you sit down with her and fill in the gaps. What you write for yourself is of little value to anybody else unless you deliberately rework the notes so they *communicate* to your reader.

Some people write for themselves as a way to focus on fuzzy or complicated information they're thinking about. It's a device very similar to the rough charcoal sketches that artists make to test composition and proportion before beginning complicated paintings. Most people can't focus on their use of the English language and, let us say, economics equally well at the same time. So in order to test their notions of a new economic theory, they hastily sketch out their ideas on paper. They use jargon, half-sentences, misspelled words, abbreviations, sketchy punctuation. They may even invent words to fill temporary gaps in their thoughts. This is all perfectly natural; it's a useful device for *beginning* to decode the cerebral information they want to share with others. It becomes a problem only if the process stops at this point, only if the incomplete thoughts are shared. Here's an example of that:

> Prioritizing goals to include a socially beneficial outcome is going to be difficult under the best circumstances.

The economist who drafted the above phrases was grappling with a tough concept. He got down on paper what he wanted to say, but even though all his words (except perhaps "prioritizing") are standard, simple English, only he could understand exactly what he meant. The words in his sentence might have meant several different things:

- The goals will be listed in rank order and social benefit will be included somewhere within the listing.
- All the goals will have as their priority a socially beneficial outcome.
- It will be difficult to establish priorities for the goals.
- It will be difficult for even the cleverest researcher ("the best circumstances") to include social benefit among the priorities.
- Even when economic times are good ("the best circumstances"), it will be difficult to include social benefit among the priorities.

We spent several minutes discussing the concept with the economist before we were able to translate his notes into English that would communicate his precise meaning to most readers:

Establishing goals that include benefit to society as one of their priorities will be difficult even when the most liberal boards of directors are involved in the decision-making.

EXERCISES:

1. Photocopy a page of your classmate's lecture notes. Study them. Insert an X wherever information has been omitted.

2. Ask your classmate to fill in the missing information. Then rewrite the notes in standard English.

3. Duplicate Exercises 1 and 2 with a page of your own lecture notes.

1.3 WHY GOOD WRITING IS IMPORTANT.

Even at your present level of maturity, your principal goal in every paper you have written until now may have been to get good grades. That goal does not often require good writing. In many classes, the clarity and logical organization of your thoughts has been tested far less than your regurgitative powers and your ability to paraphrase. Vivid language is risky: it calls attention to the facts, which you may, after all, have gotten wrong. Precise language is an even bigger risk, for the same reason. Foggy generalities and pedestrian usage stand a chance of slipping past the harried grader unnoticed. Originality is sometimes misconstrued as a cover-up for not knowing the assignment.

But worse than the poor writing habits you've learned is what you haven't learned. You've never needed to entice your teachers to read your papers. They've been a captive audience, compelled to read (and maybe correct). All this will change. Outside the classroom, the director of personnel will *not* have to read your application. The grants director will *not* have to read your proposal. The vice-president of your department will *not* have to read your report on your brilliant discovery. You need to learn how to lead them to want to read what you have to say. And you need to learn how to say well what's on your mind.

This is an era in which communication counts. Until recently, corporations sent executives to speed-reading courses so they could wade through all the memos and reports that wash onto corporate desks. Now many pay for key executives' writing courses in an effort to wipe out redundant paperwork. As our pace of life quickens, people more and more can't wait for reporters to come and write about the block association's demands for a new stoplight; they have to find a leader who can write effectively on the spot. Aggressive scientific teams can't wait for outside editors to translate their jargon into publishable reports; a competing lab may report first on a similar discovery and gain an edge on the next grant request.

Although it's true that poor writers can hold their own within corporate, government, or academic bureaucracies, good writers have a decided edge. One major difference between Dr. Lewis Thomas and a million other physicians is that Thomas writes interestingly enough so that his collections of scientific papers such as *The Medusa and the Snail* make the best-seller lists. One difference between Theodore Bernstein and a thousand other newspaper editors is that Bernstein's books are fun to read. Here's an example from *The Careful Writer*:

> If Miss Thistlebottom taught you in elementary school
> that **between** applies to two things and **among** to more
> than two, she probably knew what she was doing: She
> was making things easy for herself.[1]

Albert Einstein's scientific and philosophic thoughts are accessible to millions because he wrote with the goal of being understood by everyone. He wrote so well, in fact, that he was asked to write the foreword to the University of California Press's reprint of a major dialogue by Galileo. Of Galileo, Einstein made a statement that every writer would be proud to have said of him:

> His unusual literary gift enables him to address the
> educated men of his age in such clear and impressive
> language as to overcome the anthropocentric and myth-
> ical thinking of his contemporaries. . . .[2]

EXERCISES:

1. In a field in which you'd like to be employed, name one specific job title you would someday like to hold. Then write a paragraph or two about how good writing skills can help you reach that goal. (You may need to interview someone in that position to complete the assignment.) Tape the paragraph to the front of your notebook or this book.

2. Locate the name of someone who is well known in your chosen field. At a library, use the card catalog, *Books in Print*,

Readers' Guide to Periodical Literature, research indexes, and other reference books to find something written by this person. Read it and decide whether writing skills helped him succeed.

NOTES: CHAPTER 1

1. Theodore M. Bernstein, *The Careful Writer* (New York: Atheneum, 1973), pp. 72–73.

2. Galileo Galilei, *Dialogue Concerning the Two Chief World Systems—Ptolemaic and Copernican*, trans. Stillman Drake (Berkeley: University of California Press, 1953), p. 1.

CHAPTER 2
EXACTLY WHAT
GOOD WRITING IS

*The two most engaging powers
of an author, are, to make new things familiar,
and familiar things new.*
Samuel Johnson

In the previous chapter we demonstrated the value of good writing. Now we must define exactly what makes some writing good, other writing bad. If this book were about fine literature, poetry, novels, or creative writing, the definition would have to be as nebulous as human taste in the arts. But here we are limited to factual writing, often called nonfiction, exposition, rhetoric, or reporting. It is neither an art nor so precise that we could label it a science. Most professionals call it a craft. Crafts can be learned, and good craftwork can be defined.

There are six attributes of good factual writing:

- Good writing elicits one main intellectual response from readers.
- Good writing grabs the readers' attention and holds it.
- Good writing says something new.
- Good writing is sensory.

● Good writing builds on ideas already understood by readers.

● Good writing makes every abstract idea so concrete that readers can picture it.

We will discuss each of these attributes in turn so that, by the end of the chapter, you will have a complete definition with which to evaluate all writing—yours or somebody else's. Furthermore, when the writing isn't good, you'll be able to answer these questions: Why isn't it good? What's wrong with it? How can I make it better?

2.1 GOOD WRITING ELICITS ONE MAIN INTELLECTUAL RESPONSE FROM READERS.

A reader can react to a piece of factual writing in a variety of intellectual ways. Most composition textbooks put the responses into four major groups:

1. *Learning* how to do something
2. *Finding out* what happened at some event
3. *Understanding* an idea
4. *Considering* another viewpoint

You may not recognize these groups because we have worded them from the *reader's* viewpoint. Most texts discuss them as tasks faced by writers. We'll turn them around for now so they seem more familiar:

1. To *offer directions* on how to do something
2. To *report* whom something happened to, what happened, why it happened, when it happened, where it happened, and how much of it happened
3. To *explain* an idea

   4. To *persuade* on behalf of a viewpoint assumed to
   be at odds with that of the reader

There are three fundamental problems with trying to build a definition of good writing from these four writers' tasks, which many textbooks call the *purposes* of factual writing. One problem is that such lists are misleading. They suggest that to give directions requires one kind of writing and to persuade requires another kind. You don't need to learn several paths to good writing; one is enough. Master that smoothly, and it will serve you well for all these four purposes and others as well.

   A second problem is that arbitrary lists of purposes lead you into the trap of attacking a writing task with a rigid preconception. Inflexible thinking restricts communication. If you write a paper that says no more than "First you do this, then you do that, and finally you end up with a thingamajig," you've got a paper that gives directions, but directions that only the most highly motivated reader is willing to *receive*. If you approach an assignment in persuasion with the mind-set that you've got to do a bang-up job of persuading, you're likely to overkill. The articles that persuade best are low-keyed; they do not signal that their purpose is to change readers' attitudes. They use carefully selected information, not preachment or provocation, to make their points.

   The third, and most usual, problem is that you forget the one all-inclusive purpose of writing anything when you get caught up in selecting a single goal. It's like the old joke about the doctor who, when asked if the operation was a success, replied, "Yah, indeed it was. I did everything just right. Unfortunately, the patient died." Good writers, like good doctors, concentrate not on performing the operation right but on getting the correct results.

   When you write, it definitely is helpful to have in mind clear subpurposes, which may be to persuade, explain, narrate, direct, or accomplish something else. But most good writing has several purposes at once, and it's important to learn how to write this way. This book, for example, *explains* what good writing is, *offers directions* for mastering the craft, and at the same time attempts to *persuade* you that writing is not as difficult as you may have thought. But the book's one main purpose—the campaign on which we want to use most of our ammunition and get your most consistent reaction—is to get you to write well. We know from long experience in nonfiction writing that if we succeed in our main purpose, we will have succeeded in the others too. But if we let any subordinate purpose get in the way, the main purpose will be diluted and your reaction diminished.

2.2 GOOD WRITING GRABS THE READER'S ATTENTION AND HOLDS IT.

In order to get a reader to react the way you want (the first part of our definition of good writing), you must first get her to *start reading* what you have to say, and then make sure she reads *all the way through*. That may sound obvious, but it is the ruin of writers who forget (or never learned) that they're competing for a reader's attention.

The competition for attention is fierce. Every year in the United States alone, enough paper is covered with factual writing to bury the Empire State Building under a neat stack of paper three blocks long and three blocks wide. Annually our national output is 25,000 new nonfiction book titles, of which 654 million copies in all are printed. We also print 257 million copies of 10,000 different magazines and journals that publish 2.6 million articles made up of over 9 billion words.

But you and your writing are up against more competition than just other purveyors of the written word. You also compete with other media—video, audiovisual, sound tape—that share less information per minute than good writing does, but are newer, more glamorous, and effortless for the receiver. Unless you recognize and accept the fact that you are in competition for readers' attention, you can never be a good writer. Your writing will take its place among the other background noises in the scientific, educational, artistic, and commercial world.

Good writers demand attention. They use explicit *titles* that appeal to the potential audience. They start with *leads* that generate enough excitement to make readers want to keep reading. They present their *bodies* of information in ways that keep readers interested, intrigued, excited, entertained, or in some other way gratified or motivated to read on. They know that otherwise, like the street-corner orator on a freezing day, they'll end up talking to themselves. They recognize that while the orator can simply look around him to learn that he's lost his audience's attention, if they don't keep the reader in mind they may not learn for months that the important report went unread.

2.3 GOOD WRITING
SAYS SOMETHING NEW.

There is one writing purpose that exists, for the most part, only in academia. This is the *summary* of the writing of one or several sociologists, philosophers, political scientists, or other authorities. It presents no new thoughts of the summarizer's own. Some textbooks list and teach *summarization* right along with the other kinds of writing.

Summary papers are usually written with no purpose beyond the pedagogic exercise of showing a teacher that the student has learned how to research and comprehend written information, prepare note cards, and type footnotes. Since the writer's personality, point of view, and generally even intellect are pointedly excluded, only a writer who can do magical tricks with words can churn up a well-written paper from the swamp of pointlessness. In writing of this sort, teachers often give high marks for long and unusual words, farfetched similes, and other verbal pyrotechnics. Many students have been influenced to carry over this flashy style into the rest of their writing. Fireworks are fun to watch, as we're reminded every Independence Day. But even fireworks can bore an audience unless they either keep getting progressively more dazzling or, even better, are seen only once in a while.

Readers who want only to be entertained generally don't pick up factual books or papers. They select novels or collections of poetry, or they flick on the TV. When they turn to nonfiction books or magazine articles, they want to learn something they didn't know before. A chemist reads to find out what other labs have learned about new techniques in pyrolosis. An executive reads to learn what new plans his Detroit sales manager has devised for boosting sales. A foundation officer reads to select the grant proposal with the most originality for his award. A mother reads to learn why Junior doesn't listen. A coin collector reads to find out how much his collection is worth nowadays. A fisherman reads to learn the name of the fish he almost landed. If you expect people to read what you have to say, you'd better tell them something new.

Something new can be new factual discoveries on an old subject, of course. But it can also be a new way of interpreting an old idea. Writers often have to write about old subjects for which there may be no new information: to warn of longtime dangers like forest fires and burglary, to explain illnesses like the cold and the flu. Good writers deliberately locate some new aspect of the old subject. Consider the following:

> 1. Automobile drivers must learn that the green light at the corner means it's safe to go and the red light means they must come to a full stop. If they go on red or stop on green, they are inviting trouble.
>
> 2. A study this year by the National Safety Council has shown that 15 percent of all automobile accidents occur because drivers creep past red lights at intersections or linger at corners after lights turn green. Easy-to-make changes in driving habits will eliminate this significant cause of accidents.

How much of an impact did paragraph 1 have on you? Did you

read any part of it carefully or with keen attention? Was there anything in the paragraph that you didn't already know? Now, what about paragraph 2? Did you read that one more carefully? Did the revelation of new information at the start of that paragraph grab your attention and keep it throughout the entire paragraph— even the parts that reiterated very old information? If not, is there an approach that would have grabbed *you*?

The importance of giving people something new, if you want their attention, is evident in much more than just writing. During the 1970s, the American Cancer Society bogged down in its nationwide drive to convince people not to smoke. For the previous two decades, they'd been able to come up periodically with a new fact, a new statistic, a piece of new evidence that was more startling than the one released the year before. But the impact of shocking facts had worn off. Then educators at the University of Minnesota tested a new appeal altogether. Instead of intellectual data, they tried an emotional inducement on high schoolers: "Smoking isn't cool." It worked, too, until that goad lost its sting.

When you've become a good writer, one of the first questions you'll ask yourself when you sit down to draft a paper, article, book, or report, is, "What's new?"

2.4 GOOD WRITING IS SENSORY.

Telling the reader what the two of you already know is boring, but it's also easy. You don't need to explain anything. Telling something new is a much harder task. How does the good writer share new ideas and experiences with the reader? One important way is to call on five valuable communication tools that they have in common: the senses.

There are few ideas and almost no physical objects or phenomena that cannot be described vividly and tangibly by drawing on words related to sight, sound, touch, taste, and smell. If you stand at a particular place and see a perfectly shaped pine tree growing atop a barren mountain, there is no doubt that another observer standing in that very same place and looking at that very same tree would develop objective mental impressions comparable to yours. (We'll deal with the subjective aspects a bit later.) The same assumption works in writing. If you adequately describe a particular tree from a particular vantage point, your reader will form the same objective impressions you have, even if she's never seen the tree.

This principle can be extended, too. If you describe something other than the tree—let's say the organizational structure of a company—as if it were like that perfectly shaped pine tree, your reader will *still* form the same objective perceptions that you have in your head. In reading, she will relate the company's organization to the same visual image of the pine tree that you thought of while writing.

Let's study the following passage that relies on sensory images:

> Today, huge numbers of books are crumbling into dust in our public libraries, schools, and private collections. In some libraries more than a quarter of the books have deteriorated to the point where it is impossible to turn a page without tearing it. The Library of Congress estimates that more than 40 percent of its collection is too brittle to lend out.[1]

In this example, Eric Stange uses our visual mind-set of *crumbling into dust*, our aural mind-set of *tearing*, and our tactile mind-set of *brittle* to make his point vivid. Less imaginative writers might have said, "Books, these days, are not very well preserved." If you, as a reader, had never seen a poorly preserved book, which passage would tell better what the writer means to say?

Here are several more examples, all from an article about Seattle by Raymond Mungo.[2] First, Mungo lays out a physical description of the land around Seattle:

> Millions of years of **rushing water** have **smoothed out** great boulders.

Much later, Mungo extends this image when he wants to make his readers understand a social phenomenon taking place in Seattle:

> And the city **grinds** us, and itself, down.

At another point, Mungo weaves a tactile analogy and a simple visual image into another comment on social life in Seattle:

> [I] am glad to be back in society—swimming in the human soup—and running from the rain.

As you read the examples of good writing that are sprinkled throughout this book, examine how the writers use sensory clues to explain new devices, new phenomena, even new ideas. Once you've become accustomed to noticing how important the senses are in creating good writing, you'll find examples all around you, in everything you pick up to read.

2.5 GOOD WRITING BUILDS ON IDEAS ALREADY UNDERSTOOD BY READERS.

The five senses are one of the most useful sets of communication devices shared by writers and readers. A set of similar devices is the backlog of images and ideas that your readers have acquired from their previous reading, education, TV-watching, movie-going, and the like.

If you write a paper for advanced philosophy students or professors, you do not have to define metaphysics or existentialism for them. You can assume that those readers already know very well what those words mean. However, if you write for the philosophers about an obscure offshoot of metaphysics, you have to use their existing knowledge of metaphysics as a jumping-off point to explain how the offshoot differs from its parent ideology. If you write for an audience of chemists, you needn't feel obliged to explain nitrobenzene, because it's a basic building block of organic chemistry. If you've added an exotic substance to the nitrobenzene molecule, you can build on their existing understanding of nitrobenzene's properties, explaining only the new properties that the new substance confers.

Assumptions like these are equally valid in writing for readers outside narrow academic disciplines. In fact, they're not only valid, they're vital techniques for making your writing at once explicit and interesting. Let's see how Lillian Smith made use of her readers' store of images and ideas when she wrote the following passage in *Killers of the Dream*:

> Camp meetings and revivals are the South's past, and once were a heroic part of that past. Today, though often cheapened and vulgarized to the point of obscenity, they are still a part of the South's present. Guilt was then and is today the biggest crop raised in Dixie, harvested each summer just before cotton is picked.[3]

To appreciate just how carefully Ms. Smith built this paragraph on knowledge and images that you and other readers share, reread it while you imagine that you are a Laplander who spent your entire life in the snowy wilderness of northern Finland, isolated from books, television, and all other information about the southern United States. Answer these questions from that Laplander's perspective:

> 1. Where is *the South?*
> 2. *Webster's New Collegiate Dictionary* (8th edition) defines *obscene* two ways: disgusting to the senses, and designed to incite lust. Which meaning did the author probably have in mind?
> 3. Where is *Dixie?* Does the term have more connotations than merely geographic?

4. What is cotton? Is it a big or little part of the South's economy and heritage? How, then, does *guilt* figure, in Ms. Smith's mind, as part of the South's heritage?

But Lillian Smith wasn't writing her book for Laplanders. She was writing it for you and us, and she could assume that we had already acquired certain common notions—subjective as well as objective ones. She not only limited herself to explaining just those things we didn't already know, but she counted on our contributing our stored knowledge to the reading. She knew that *Dixie* means more to us than *the South*: it means the old, conservative, tradition-bound South. She knew that *picking cotton* elicits common images and reactions among most American readers. She could even safely assume that her use of *obscenity* wouldn't bring forth mental pictures of half-naked women preachers at the meetings, but of overemotionalism and theatricality. Knowing all that, she could limit herself to as few words as possible to convey as many concrete images as possible. The better the writer, the tighter the writing and the more weight she freights on each word in leading readers to picture what's in her head.

As you practice writing, you will learn to keep in mind automatically what your readers already know. You won't bore them by explaining facts and notions they already accept. You will utilize their storehouses of images and conclusions to quickly and graphically explain new ideas.

Here's a final example to study. Notice all the facts its author, Scott Jacobs, conveys with his images. See if you can say the same things in as few words, and if you can think of even better images.

The roll-call vote sounded, and he raced down the hall to vote. Minutes later, he came back into the room as if he'd been blown out of a cannon.[4]

. . . when he met with reporters, his mind spun out in tangents and you'd have to reel it back to the topic.[5]

2.6 GOOD WRITING
MAKES EVERY ABSTRACT
IDEA SO CONCRETE THAT
READERS CAN PICTURE IT.

Good writers have to grapple with some of the same problems that good scientists face. When Newton was puzzling over mysterious forces in the universe, legend tells, it wasn't until a very concrete apple dropped onto his head that he was struck with a real solution to his problem—a solution he called gravity. When Albert Einstein noticed the juxtaposition of a beam of sunlight in the town square and a distant church steeple, he was able to make the logical jump that resulted in his theory of relativity. When James Watson and Francis Crick were feverishly searching for the physical structure of the DNA molecule, they chose to painstakingly build a model rather than to sit around doing cerebral exercises.

Psychologist Philip G. Zimbardo explains why gifted scientists—and writers as well—do best when they reduce airy abstractions to concrete symbols:

> Our human capacity to use our minds for solving problems above and beyond the ordinary problems of survival frees us from being slaves to our environment. We can manipulate symbols representing elements of the environment (think), utilize these symbols in solving problems (reason), and conceive new and original ideas (create). Thinking involves images, words, and covert muscular processes. *Images* are "mental pictures" of actual sensory experiences. Most people are strongest in visual imagery. . . . [6]

To find out how intangible and unpredictable abstract ideas can be if writers leave them as abstractions, ask any ten people you know for twenty-five-word definitions of each of the following abstractions, and see how many come up with the same definition:

- democracy
- love
- safety
- insincerity
- ambition

There are two basic ways writers can convert abstract notions into concrete images. One is to relate them to the senses, as Elaine Morgan did in showing how our primate forebears, and we, too, communicate states of mind:

> If the smell of anger comes out of him you will know it; if the smell of fear comes out of you he will know it. . . .[7]

> . . . and some of your most classic facial expressions like the open-mouthed threat face are apt to end in a gurgle and a sputter if you hold them too long.[8]

The other basic way writers pull abstractions down to earth is to relate them to universal images that the chosen audience of readers shares. Jeanie Kasindorf did this in her brief portrait of a woman:

> She made you feel as if you were trapped in a maze of funhouse mirrors. You were never sure which of Erin's faces you were going to find.[9]

Most good writers use all the tools at their disposal. They mix sensory words with shared images. They find their own symbols, or call on familiar similes and metaphors (which are covered more fully in Chapter 4). Here are some examples of mixtures that combine to bring abstract notions down to the concrete level. The first is by William Flanagan, the second by John D. Spooner.

> But the carpeted corridors and luxuriously appointed offices of the executive suite are not ordinary places. This is the land where three-piece pinstripe suits, narrow collars, and cordovan wing tips never went out of style; where black faces are still as rare as black

pearls; where aside from the few success stories and token board members, women still mostly type and fetch coffee.[10]

Granny was one of the Palm Beach matrons who had elderly retainers and lawyers who would fly down in wool suits from Chicago for the day, and relatives who drooled and groveled every time she said, "Time for cucumber sandwiches and some tea."[11]

2.7 LEARN HOW TO TELL GOOD WRITING FROM BAD.

One of the first steps you must take in learning how to write well is to recognize good writing—yours or somebody else's. The reading that you do will help prepare you, but only if you look for the attributes of good writing that we've pointed out. (To guide you, we'll summarize those attributes in a checklist at the end of this chapter.)

When you read in order to learn how to write, there are five pitfalls to avoid:

1. Language changes with the times. What was considered good writing when Thomas Jefferson penned the Declaration of Independence is no longer considered good writing for *today's* readers. Read, for example, the following two selections:

This pure and more inbred desire of joining to itself in conjugal fellowship a fit conversing soul (which desire is properly called love) "is stronger than death," as the spouse of Christ thought, "many waters cannot quench it, neither can the floods drown it." This is that rational burning that marriage is to remedy, not to be allayed with fasting, nor with any penance to be subdued, which how can he assuage who by mishap hath met the most unmeetest and unsuitable mind?

Who hath the power to struggle with an intelligible flame, not in paradise to be resisted, become now more ardent by being failed of what in reason it looked for; and even then most unquenched, when the importunity of a provender burning is well enough appeased; and yet the soul hath obtained nothing of what it justly desires. Certainly such a one forbidden to divorce, is in effect forbidden to marry, and compelled to greater difficulties than in a single life; for if there be not a more human burning which marriage must satisfy, or else may be dissolved, than that of copulation, marriage cannot be honorable for the meet reducing and terminating lust between two: seeing many beasts in voluntary and chosen couples, live together as un-adulterously, and are as truly married in that respect.[12]

General society, as now carried on in England, is so insipid an affair, even to the persons who make it what it is, that it is kept up for any reason rather than the pleasure it affords. All serious discussion on matters on which opinions differ, being considered ill-bred, and the national deficiency in liveliness and sociability having prevented the cultivation of the art of talking agreeably on trifles, in which the French of the last century so much excelled, the sole attraction of what is called society to those who are not at the top of the tree, is the hope of being aided to climb a little higher in it; while to those who are already at the top, it is chiefly a compliance with custom, and with the supposed requirements of their station. To a person of any but a very common order in thought or feeling, such society, unless he has personal objects to serve by it, must be supremely unattractive: and most people, in the present day, of any really high class of intellect, make their contact with it so slight, and at such long intervals, as to be almost considered as retiring from it altogether.[13]

The first selection was written by John Milton in the mid-seventeenth century, the second by John Stuart Mill in the late nineteenth century. The thoughts of both men live today because they were great writers of their times. But if you wrote a factual piece today in the style of either man, you'd have little chance to interest readers in wading through it. Our post-TV, McLuhan-paced culture demands a faster rhythm in its writing, more vividness, less work on the part of the reader, whose other pastimes and professional interests vie for his attention.

2. Many professions promote resistance to change in language. Often it's out of inattention to changing details like the fact that people no longer wear trousers but jeans or pants. Sometimes it's from opposition to more basic changes like the fact that company executives no longer have girls but secretaries and assistants. One of the most steadfast resisters to change in language is the legal profession. Here's a passage from an actual legal brief written in 1979. Only the names have been changed.

> Plaintiff, by her attorney, JOHN SMITH, complaining of the defendant, respectfully shows to this Court and alleges:
>
> FIRST: That at all times mentioned herein, plaintiff was and still is a resident of the State of New Jersey.
>
> SECOND: That on or about the 15th day of August, 1977, the defendant JAMES JONES, obligor, entered into a stipulation of record in the Supreme Court of the State of New York, County of Kings, before the HON. JOHN ROE, whereby he covenanted and agreed to pay to said SUSAN DOE the sum of $20,000.00 by payment of $500.00 on the 1st day of September, 1977, and monthly thereafter in payments of $500.00 on the first day of each subsequent month until said sum is fully paid. That said stipulation expressly provided that the whole of the principal sum together with interest

> thereon shall become due upon the failure of the ob-
> ligor to make an installment payment within 30 days
> of its due date.

The passage translates into modern language this way:

> SUSAN DOE, through her attorney JOHN SMITH, is
> bringing JAMES JONES to court. Ms. Doe has lived in
> New Jersey throughout this action. About August 15,
> 1977, defendant Jones agreed in Judge John Roe's
> open court to pay Ms. Doe $20,000, at $500 per month
> on the first of every month beginning September 1,
> 1977. The agreement provided that if plaintiff is more
> than 30 days late in an installment, the entire amount
> still owed, plus interest, will become due.

Did our translator leave out any vital details? Why then do lawyers persist in writing like this today? Because nobody has made an effort to change. Attorneys used to be paid by the word, so each *whereas* and *wherefore* was worth another penny or two in a day when a loaf of bread cost a nickel. The lawyer who could say things in the most complicated, most redundant way, became the best-paid lawyer in town. Over the years, as beginning lawyers copied the styles of their betters, the redundancies thrived. Nowadays, however, even publications that pay their contributors by the word expect those words to be put together with the conciseness that today's readers expect.

3. Some groups of people deliberately develop their own private "in" words and communication styles. This is often done to foster the feeling that they're members of an exclusive club. When it's done by people with limited education it's called *dialect*, and teachers strive to correct it. When it's done by people with many years of higher education in one field of art or science, their *jargon* is accepted, even aspired to by neophytes as a mark of belonging to the group. However, jargon can be defended only when, in all honesty, it does communicate information or nuance more effectively and efficiently than traditional English. This is rarely the case. For examples of what to avoid we'll borrow from two great minds in fields most choked by jargon:

- Psychologese:

    Because the Self-image is an evaluation of the Self in relation to the environment, we can for convenience distinguish two modes of variation: differences in the evaluation of the environment and differences in the conception of the Self, as such.[14]

- Translation:

    Because a person's self-image is his evaluation of himself in relation to his environment, there are two ways his self-image can change: in the way he evaluates his environment, or the way he sees himself.

- Educationese:

    As with most complicated social problems, these matters depend very much on commitment and leadership, but one cannot escape the impression that a massive increase in funding is a critical necessity. New levels of expenditure will surely be rationalized in legitimate educational and economic terms, but the basic goals are social and the motivation is political. It seems not at all a simple question of massive funding in order to meet quantitative demand and to carry on the development of an increasingly expensive enterprise, but rather resources that will be required to achieve the metamorphic transition of higher education into a rather different social institution.[15]

- Translation:

    These matters, like most complicated social problems, depend very much on commitment and leadership, but a massive increase in funding seems to be critically necessary. The greater expense can be blamed on education and economics, but **actually** the basic goals

> are social and the reasons political. Massive funding
> to pay for increased numbers **of students** and an in-
> creasingly expensive enterprise **may not be sufficient**
> without proper resources that can change higher ed-
> ucation . . . (**?**)

Notice the portions in bold type in our translation of this educationese. For those parts, we lacked sufficient information to
make sense of the language. In fact, the entire concluding sentence leads readers to feel that the author suggests that higher
education has to change, but we omitted the begging phrase,
"into a rather different social institution" because it doesn't tell
us a thing. Do you agree or disagree?

**4. Some people deliberately write badly, hoping to disguise
what they really mean.** They do it to confuse the reader, or to
puff up the writer's own image with big, empty catchwords. In
politics, this kind of writing has become an art encouraged by
even the most well-meaning legislators.

● Politicalese:

> On September 12, the House defeated the proposal to
> require 18-year-old males to register for the draft be-
> ginning Jan. 1, 1981. However, the militarists need
> a draft to fuel the military machine they are building.
> They will be back and we must be prepared to face
> the issue of registration and a peacetime draft again
> in coming years.

In the above example, taken from a "Bob Kastenmeier Reports"
newsletter, the first and third sentences are perfectly well written.
They seem to say what they mean. But look closely at that second
sentence; it makes us wonder whether the writer is confused or
trying to confuse the voters. The sentence is a classic example
of the art of graceful obfuscation. Which militarists does it refer
to? The Pentagon brass? The heads of corporations making money
on munition sales? The senators and representatives who voted

for registration? And what about that military machine they are building? At the time the newsletter was written, the United States already had a sizable military machine. Was there something new we didn't know, or was the staff writer in Representative Kastenmeier's office simply dazzling us with fancy verbal footwork? Politicalese is insidious. It seems to say a lot until it's read closely.

5. You can't learn factual writing by studying fiction. Most nontextbook readings assigned in school to illustrate fine writing are fiction. Although there is some overlap in technique, it's tough to learn how to write good nonfiction from novels and short stories. The goals and many of the methods are worlds apart.

2.8 WHERE TO FIND
MODELS FOR GOOD WRITING.

In these first two chapters we've already referred to several nonfiction authors whose books and articles are worth studying as models for your own writing attempts. We'll suggest others in the following chapters. Many of the large-circulation magazines can serve as worthwhile models too. *Fortune*, for example, is a literate showcase for business, economics, and technology writing. On scientific subjects, see how *Scientific American* and *Popular Science* attack writing for audiences with different educational backgrounds. Good writing in the social sciences and humanities can be found in the magazines *Psychology Today*, *American Heritage, Harper's, Atlantic*, and *Playboy. Sports Illustrated, National Geographic, Reader's Digest, Good Housekeeping, Redbook, Woman's Day*, and *McCall's* aim for good writing too.

Remember to size up the readers that the various publications attempt to interest, and compare them to *your* intended audience. For instance, although the writing in *Reader's Digest* is generally very good, its subject matter and depth of coverage—

as well as its word choice and sentence structure—are targeted for readers with barely high school educations. If your readership is better educated, you'll be able to show more complex relationships with your writing.

Most of the examples in this book are not literary works of art, but they have been chosen from our home library shelves and our accumulation of consumer magazines because they're good reading—and, therefore, good writing. In addition to fulfilling the other qualifications for good writing, they are all generally alike in three ways:

1. They use words that today's readers are comfortable with. Here's part of a paragraph written by astrophysicist Carl Sagan, who overcame academia's partiality to fancy language and in doing so won a Pulitzer Prize:

> William Wolcott died and went to heaven. Or so it seemed. Before being wheeled to the operating table, he had been reminded that the surgical procedure would entail a certain risk. The operation was a success, but just as the anesthesia was wearing off, his heart went into fibrillation and he died. It seemed to him that he had somehow left his body and was able to look down upon it, withered and pathetic, lying on a hard and unforgiving surface. He was only a little sad, regarded his body one last time . . . [16]

2. They rarely achieve perfection. Few of the examples are perfect; we see words we'd like to change, sentences we'd like to alter, phrases we think should be turned around. Even when we read our own writing in print, we find things we wish we'd said differently. All good writers do.

In your reading, you will reach a point where you'll want to change other people's words to make them better. Do it; then learn to do the same with your own papers. Don't get hung up on the perfect word or phrase or punctutation mark. What's more important is complete communication.

3. The writing looks so simple that novices are likely to conclude it requires little effort. Actually, like a Picasso drawing or a perfect field goal, seemingly effortless prose comes only from years of hard work at acquiring and practicing the skills. But once you know what the skills are and how to apply them, the work will lose its drudgery and frustration. It will always remain challenging, but it will become rewarding. Never forget—good writing can be learned.

EXERCISES:

The illustrations referred to below are at the end of this chapter.

1. Illustration 2/1 reprints part of *Night Comes to the Cumberlands*, a classic work about Appalachia by a small town Kentucky lawyer, Harry M. Caudill.[17] Read the reprint and then evaluate it, using the checklist that follows this chapter.

2. Illustration 2/2 reprints part of Chapter 2 of *The Cellular Basis of the Immune Response* by Purdue University professor of biological sciences Dr. Edward S. Golub.[18] The book is on a subject that another eminent researcher has called "one of the most complicated subjects known to science today." It is intended for advanced students, generally graduate students, in the biological sciences. Read the reprint and evaluate it using the checklist.

3. Illustration 2/3 reprints a complete article written by a student. Using the checklist, she's been able to rework the paper and make it publishable. Suggest improvements you would make, based on the checklist, and defend the parts that you wouldn't change.

4. Find a paper of at least 500 words that you wrote for an assignment that required more than rote retelling of facts. Using the checklist as a guide, try to read it as objectively as you read the illustrations in Exercises 1, 2, and 3. Make three specific suggestions for improvement. (Remember, this is not an exercise in criticizing what you wrote, but in learning how to *read critically* with an eye on improvement.)

NOTES: CHAPTER 2

1. Eric Stange, "From Rags to Ruin," *The Atlantic Monthly*, June, 1979, p. 90.

2. Raymond Mungo, "Blissed-Out in Seattle," *Mother Jones*, November, 1978, pp. 30–34.

3. Lillian Smith, *Killers of the Dream* (Garden City: Doubleday Anchor, 1963), pp. 86–87.

4. Scott Jacobs, "The Last Harrumph," *Chicago*, December, 1977, p. 220.

5. Ibid., p. 141.

6. Philip G. Zimbardo with Floyd L. Ruch, *Psychology and Life*, 9th ed. (Glenview, Ill.: Scott, Foresman, 1975), pp. 228–29.

7. Elaine Morgan, *The Descent of Woman* (New York: Stein and Day, 1972), p. 120.

8. Ibid., p. 125.

9. Jeanie Kasindorf, "Groucho and Erin," *New West*, December 5, 1977, p. 45.

10. William Flanagan, "No Divorce at the Top," *Esquire*, June 19, 1979, p. 8.

11. John D. Spooner, "Smart People, Smart Money," *The Atlantic Monthly*, June, 1979, p. 44.

12. *Complete Poetry and Selected Prose of John Milton* (New York: Modern Library, 1950), pp. 632–33.

13. John Stuart Mill, *Autobiography* (London: Oxford University Press, 1949), pp. 192–93.

14. Ross Stagner, *Psychology of Personality*, 2nd ed. (New York: McGraw-Hill, 1948), p. 172. Used with permission of McGraw-Hill Book Company.

15. Warren W. Willingham, *Free-Access Higher Education* (New York: College Entrance Examination Board, 1970), p. 233.

16. Carl Sagan, "The Amniotic Universe," *The Atlantic Monthly*, April, 1979, p. 39.

17. Harry M. Caudill, *Night Comes to the Cumberlands* (Boston: Little, Brown, Atlantic Monthly Press, 1963), p. 150.

18. Edward S. Golub, *The Cellular Basis of the Immune Response* (Sunderland, Mass.: Sinauer Associates, 1977), pp. 15–17.

ILLUSTRATION 2/1

From
Night Comes to the Cumberlands

At dusk immense black clouds began boiling up on the eastern horizon and rumbles of low thunder sounded from their depths. Lightning flashed and the sullen rumbling grew louder. As the night came on the stars were obliterated and the cumulus piled ever more massively above the mountains. About 8:30 the downpour began. Immediately the cascade of water was terrific, but its volume steadily swelled. By midnight the rain had long since surpassed anything within the recollection of living men, and it pounded rooftops and cornfields with the concentrated power of millions of fire hoses. Water ran down the hillsides in sheets two or three inches deep in places. Hollows, dry a few hours before, roared like Niagaras. Log houses that had withstood the ravages of a hundred years were carried away. Scores of frame houses were washed off their foundations and whirled out onto the bosoms of surging rivers which lapped angrily where gangs of workmen had hoed corn during the afternoon before.

Highway and railroad bridges broke beneath the onslaught. Rows of camp houses were flooded, and people took refuge on rooftops or on the second floors of two-story houses. With hollow roars, mountains of slate crashed into streams, forming dams which restrained the water for a few moments and then released it with even greater violence.

ILLUSTRATION 2/2

From
The Cellular Basis of
The Immune Response

The process of blood cell formation is called HEMOPOIESIS (*hemo* meaning blood, *poiesis* meaning formation). The fact that all the cells of the blood have finite life-spans but are constantly replenished argues that there must be a mechanism for their renewal. Whether each cell type has a separate renewal system or all derive from a common cell is one of the most interesting questions in biology and has obvious implications in medicine. One of the first major clues about the nature of the self-renewal system of blood cells came from studies in radiobiology in which it was found that the hemopoietic systems of an animal could be destroyed by X-irradiation. The entire system could be fully restored by injecting bone marrow or spleen cells from a compatible donor. It was clear from these studies that the bone marrow and spleen were hemopoietic organs, i.e. blood-forming organs. The problem then became how to study the cells in these organs which were responsible for regeneration of all the cells of the blood. One of the major obstacles in studying the cells involved in hemopoiesis was the lack of a good quantitive methodology. Such a method, called the SPLEEN COLONY FORMING ASSAY, was devised by Till and McCulloch in 1961 (Figure 1). The assay is performed by lethally X-irradiating mice and then injecting small numbers of syngeneic bone marrow or spleen cells (syngeneic cells are cells from mice of the same inbred strain). The X-irradiation destroys the animal's own blood-forming capacity, and the mouse becomes a "living test tube" in which the injected cells can grow. After about 7 days the spleens of these injected mice are found to contain visible, discrete nodules. There is a linear relationship between the number of cells injected and the number of nodules or colonies obtained. Each nodule represents a colony of cells which is derived from a single cell. The cell which gives rise to the colonies is called the colony forming unit or PLURIPOTENT HEMOPOIETIC STEM CELL. It is the stem cell which gives rise to the cells of the blood.

Histological examination of the colonies reveals that when they first are detectable (at about 4 days after injection) they are usually composed of one cell type, either erythroid *or* granuloid cells. This would be consistent with the idea that each of these blood cells has its own renewing cell system. However, by day 6 as many as 10 percent of the colonies contain mixtures of erythroid *and* granuloid cells. The number of mixed colonies increases with time until by day 12 as many as 47 percent of the colonies have more than one cell type. Mixed colonies are consistent with the idea that the different blood cells arise from the same cell; in other words, a single stem cell gives rise to erythroid and granuloid cells.

ILLUSTRATION 2/3

Coffee Klatsch

Some call it their A.M. transfusion. For those who feel they need to be catapulted out of the bleary-eyed stages of sleep, that morning cup of coffee can truly be the elixir of life.

But why does coffee seem to make one think more clearly and work more effectively? Caffeine is part of a class of chemicals called xanthines which are also found in tea, cocoa and cola drinks. Once absorbed, caffeine stimulates the central nervous system, producing a more rapid and clearer flow of thought. With the capacity for muscular work increased, simple motor skills, such as typing, can be performed faster and with greater accuracy.

Too much coffee, however, can adversely affect any activity requiring delicate muscular coordination. A noted plastic surgeon for example, gave up drinking coffee because his hands shook minutely and thus interfered with surgery.

Caffeine also affects the circulatory system, causing the coronary arteries to dilate. It produces the opposite effect in the parts farthest from the heart. This is perhaps why caffeine is credited with alleviating headaches and is often included in pain relievers.

A ninth-century Arab physician was the first to record the properties and uses of coffee. While the plant is native to Ethiopia, the Arabs were among the first to promote coffee as a beverage.

Its introduction to Western society three hundred years ago was met with resistance and hostility. A "Women's Petition Against Coffee," published in London in 1674, complained that too much coffee drinking rendered men impotent. In Italy, priests called it the "hellish black brew" concocted by Satan and therefore drunk only by infidels. Pope Clement VIII, however, having tasted the Devil's draught, found it so pleasant that he is said to have exclaimed, "Why this Satan's drink is so delicious that it would be a pity to let the infidels have exclusive use of it. We shall fool Satan by baptizing it, and making it a truly Christian drink."

Frederick the Great of Prussia, who was vastly annoyed by the large sums of money going to foreign coffee merchants, issued a declaration in 1777 saying: "It is disgusting to note the increase in the quantity of coffee used by my subjects. . . . My people must drink beer."

With ubiquitous coffee consumption came the coffee houses, a social phenomenon in itself. In France, coffee houses were credited with having provoked mob spirit and, in effect, generating the French Revolution. In England, their influence was enormous on the political, social and literary life of the times. Newspapers, insurance houses, merchant banks and the stock exchange all began in coffee houses. In America, the colonists were initially tea drinkers until a certain tax, resulting in a boycott and well-known tea party, turned them into confirmed coffee drinkers.

And coffee drinkers they are! The Census Bureau reported that in 1976, per capita consumption was 12.1 pounds of coffee per year, or enough to provide every man, woman and child over ten with at least 2.4 cups per day—over 180 billion cups of coffee a year!

CHECKLIST FOR UNIT I:
GOOD WRITING:

1. Is it written so you can read it? (Is it legible? Are words spelled correctly? Is punctuation in line with what you've become accustomed to reading?)

2. Does it attempt to elicit specific reactions from you? What reactions? Does it try for one main intellectual reaction? Which one? Does it succeed at its tasks?

3. Does it hold your interest throughout? Does it entertain you, challenge you, present new information in an intriguing fashion, or use another device to keep you reading?

4. What's presented that's new about the subject? Are there new facts or ideas? Are there old ones presented in a new way? Are new concepts told in terms of ideas and experiences you already understand? Are they related in terms of ideas and experiences the expected audience probably understands?

5. List some of the more obvious sensory descriptions used by the author. If the subject hasn't lent itself to sensory presentation, did the author compensate by using other devices?

6. Can you understand it easily? (What ideas are offered? Is each idea presented abstractly or concretely? Are there any ideas that you cannot grasp? Should someone at your present level of education be able to grasp them? Should someone at the intended level of the piece of writing normally be expected to grasp them? Do the words make sense? Do the sentences make sense? If there are words you don't understand, are you able to figure them out from the context?)

UNIT II

SENTENCES: BUILDING BLOCKS
OF STRONG WRITING

CHAPTER 3
PUT STRONG WORDS
IN YOUR SENTENCES

Words without thoughts,
never to heaven go.
Hamlet,
Act III, Scene 3

Unit I has turned you into a budding critic of factual writing. But you could read and criticize for the rest of your life and still not learn how to write well. Only through writing—lots of it, done with care—can you learn to be a skilled writer.

In Chapter 1 we suggested that if you'd been allowed to learn to write in the same natural manner that you learned to speak, you'd probably be a fine writer right now. Accordingly, we've organized this book in the same progression you followed as you taught yourself to speak. It's a straightforward, logical technique that's worked for us and for our students.

Children generally attempt first to isolate words from the sentences that they hear adults around them use. They point to something and say: *Light. Car. Mommy. Daddy. Milk.* They learn the nouns that stand for important things in their lives. Almost immediately, they begin to make sophisticated choices among the nouns that mean slightly different things. For example, *car* isn't the same as *truck*, even though both have four wheels. And even though they both taste sweet, *cookie* isn't exactly *cake*.

Pretty soon, youngsters start to learn personal pronouns. Usually they begin with *me* because it's the first pronoun Mom and Dad use: *Come with me. Bring that to me.* Some verbs follow right after: *Me go. Me take. Me want lollie. Me get lollie. Johnny hit me.* Before long they're off and speaking nonstop, filling in other nouns and verbs as they need them along with indicators or modifiers, such as adverbs that show time, place, manner, degree, frequency. They add the demonstrative pronouns *this* and *that*, and adjectives such as *big, fast, bad,* and the like. They listen to their parents, they listen to their TV sets, and they quickly sort out verb tenses and work into their sentences all the little articles (*a, an, the*) and prepositions (*on, under, near, by*). Nobody stops them to say, "Now it's time to learn relative pronouns," or, "This is how you use the past tense of the verb *to be*." They notice that if they say what they mean, they get what they want, but if they don't, frustration results.

This chapter will show how to select the single words or groups of words that say what you mean. Chapter 4 will show how to choose strong ideas in the first place. And Chapter 5 will explain how to put together strong sentences, since the sentence is the basic building block for getting onto paper the thoughts that otherwise stay trapped in your mind. But just as we didn't learn first how to chew and then how to swallow, or first all the nouns and then all the verbs, it's next to impossible to separate the learning of good word usage, good idea representation, and good sentence construction. From chapter to chapter, there will be a great deal of overlap. And when we speak of *words* in this book, we will mean most often *word groups*, because most of the time the good writer chooses words in a group, not one at a time.

3.1 HOW TO FIND WORDS
THAT WORK FOR YOU.

One good picture may be worth a thousand words, but only if those thousand are ineffectual. One short phrase that etches an image in the minds of readers lives longer than a thousand ordinary pictures. William Tecumseh Sherman in 1879 said, "War is hell," and people haven't found a stronger image in over a hundred years.

Good writers don't always have the inspiration to create immortal phrases like Sherman's. Instead, they substitute a little perspiration to find words that mean what they want to say. They take time to think, and because there are so many words, they use a tool, a thesaurus of words.

Why a thesaurus, not a dictionary? Dictionaries are handy when we have no idea of the meaning of a word. But they can't help us pick out the precise word we mean because they concentrate on individual words instead of word families. They collect words alphabetically, and for a writer in search of a way to express an idea, a word beginning with *p* might be as good a choice as a word beginning with *r*.

For serious writers, a thesaurus is indispensable. In the same way that children build their language from words and word groups of similar meaning, a thesaurus displays families of words having similar *but rarely identical* meanings. There are usually as many subtle shades of meaning within word families as there are shades of red in a family of red-headed people. The best way to understand a particular word's real meaning is the way children comprehend: by hearing or seeing it used over and over in many different contexts. To get full value from a thesaurus, read critically, file away in your memory interesting and different words and, to recall them, open the thesaurus.

Here's an entry for *cunning* from *Roget's International Thesaurus* (4th Edition):

cunning
crafty
artful
wily
guileful
sly
tricky
Machiavellian
cunning as a serpent
crazy like a fox
slippery as an eel
deceitful

Notice how the words change slightly in meaning from *cunning* and *crafty* down to *deceitful*. The first two words on the list generally imply no moral judgment. A person can be cunning or crafty in business by simply making smart investments or negotiating well. *Deceitful*, however, has a much more limited application; it denotes a particular kind of cunning.

A thesaurus refers us not only to closely related words, but to distantly related ones. Some thesauruses place them physically nearby. For example, *Roget's Thesaurus* puts the word families *skill* and *facility* right near *cunning*, and lists more than a dozen words in each category. Other thesauruses have *see* references. Our own trained eyes and ears tell us which word from each word family best expresses what we want to say, and practice has taught us to take into account accuracy, precision, vividness, and conciseness. Sometimes these criteria overlap. Often, we can't succeed in satisfying all four goals at once. Then we make choices based on the purpose of our writing.

EXERCISES:

Using a thesaurus, list all the words that are part of the word family of each of the following words:

1. bondage
2. sailboat
3. false
4. nosy
5. dress up
6. dislodge

3.2 CHOOSE ACCURATE WORDS.

It should be self-evident that writers must choose words that say exactly what is meant. Unfortunately our reading—probably yours, too—tells us that this assumption may not be self-evident at all. Inaccurate word choice often results from haste or sloppy thinking. Even published writers are guilty of that, along with all the other writing faults. But since it isn't tactful to criticize our colleagues' work—or wise either, since some of our own published writing had to be done hastily or perfunctorily—we'll stick to students' papers for examples of what not to do. Here are typical examples of inaccuracy:

> While young people are generally aware of the dangers of smoking, their immediate social situations and perceptions appear to counterbalance what they have seen, heard, or read about the dangers.

The word *perceptions* implies seeing, hearing, and reading, so this sentence doesn't make sense. When the author later explained what he meant to say, we concluded that *social pressures* is the phrase he wanted when he grabbed at *social situations and perceptions*.

> People justify prisons by saying that if you punish criminals, you create the fear of repetition.

This sentence sacrificed accuracy for conciseness. *Fear of rep-*

etition is not what's meant, but *fear of reimprisonment, which deters them from repeating the crime.*

3.3 CHOOSE
PRECISE WORDS.

In tackling accuracy, don't forget precision. Many writers overlook the sharp distinction between these two qualities. For instance, *vehicle* is perfectly accurate if you mean a wheeled apparatus for carrying people. But it is precise only if you actually mean a wheeled conveyance of no special type. If that's not what you want readers to visualize, pick a more precise word like *bus, motorcycle, car, Buick,* or *convertible.*

Read these examples of how precision works for or against writers in building strong sentences:

A: 1. You, don't pull the toy here.
2. Johnny, don't lug that heavy fire engine over to my side of the room.
3. Son, don't drag that dump truck on my feet.
B: 1. You hurt your leg when you fell.
2. You scraped your knee when you tripped over the rock.
3. You severed your ankle when you stumbled over the broken glass.

In each of the two groups, the first sentence is perfectly correct. Its choice of words is accurate. But is it the best sentence for the purpose? If you examine sentences 2 and 3 in each example, you may conclude that the first sentence is not good enough; it can mean either 2 or 3. It is imprecise. If the purpose is to give the information contained in 2 or 3, it is not a good sentence.

However, if the purpose of the first sentence in example B is to give fast information, it may contain all the precision that's needed. *Precision* is a relative term. The way to judge whether you have been precise enough is to ask yourself, "Is there sufficient detail in my sentence to make my meaning clear?" Here are some examples from students' papers:

> There is the fear and wish within people that their thoughts might inadvertently turn to actions.

Most of the words here are too imprecise to communicate even the rough outlines of what this author wanted to say. Discussion with her elicited the following:

> Translation: Most people secretly hope their fantasies will come true, yet they're afraid of what that would do to their humdrum but secure lives.

The author of the next sentence was reporting on his problems in researching a local charitable organization:

> Unfortunately, the path back through the history of the Society was often obscured by the passage of time and a lack of complete information.
> Translation: Unfortunately, the Society's archives relied as heavily on officers' memories as on written records, and both have faded over the years.

The student's example below makes an important point, but her imprecise language hides it:

> A variety of laws prohibit discriminatory treatment on a variety of different grounds.
> Translation: No two states require the same kind of evidence to prove you've been discriminated against.

Sometimes imprecise word selection is deliberate. We encounter it suspiciously often in ads and in press releases from political offices.

EXERCISES:

1. Rewrite the following sentence so it is accurate and precise: *Writers should choose words that say what they mean, on the*

theory that inaccurate word-choosing follows after fast or sloppy ideas.

2. Read the following sentence from an ad: *You'll discover how to get people all over your community gladly to lend you their cars and then just as gladly pay you up to $50,000 a year to perform one simple, nonmechanical act with those cars.*[1] Pick out the imprecise words. Suggest three different meanings for each imprecise word group. Consider whether the statement as a whole is accurate. Why do you think imprecise words were chosen?

3.4 CHOOSE VIVID WORDS.

Because visual images are among the strongest mental stimuli available to writers, you must try to make your key words paint a thousand pictures. But don't pack in too many stimuli, or the reader will be so blinded by the images that he won't notice the meaning. And don't load stimuli onto insignificant ideas, or he won't know what you consider important. A good rule is to try for at least one picture for every important idea. For example, consider these two sentences:

> He was even more shocked than before.
> His eyebrows shot up even higher.

The first is accurate, precise, concise. But the second—which actually uses fewer words—is vivid. It paints a picture. The first relies on the abstraction *shock*, whereas the second rests on something concrete (*eyebrows*) and visual (*shot up*). The first converts the writer's image into words, but the words can be converted back into the writer's image by only the most imaginative of readers. The second transmits the picture right from the writer's mind into the reader's; the words serve only as a vehicle.

Generally, images become more vivid as the words that

describe them progress from the general to the specific, or from abstract to concrete. We'll cover this aspect of writing more thoroughly in the next chapter, but here's an example of how the technique increases vividness, all the while retaining accuracy and precision:

> They were brave men.
> They defied danger and coolheadedly stood up to drunken bullies.
> They could kill a rattler or swamp panther or wild turkey with casual accuracy or throw a drunken bully out of their meeting with no more than a comma's pause in their sermon.[2]

It's knowing how—and where—to write vividly that separates great writers from adequate hacks.

There are some word families that don't lead to pictures no matter how hard you try, like the ones containing *how* and *what*. These are direction words. They chart the roads the reader's images should take—the context in which they belong—and should be used for accuracy and precision without calling attention to themselves.

EXERCISE:

Read the following sentence: *His thin black eyebrows shot up bulletlike to an awesome height.* In as few words as possible, express the main idea of the sentence. Compare it to the first two sentences in this section and discuss why it does a better or worse job than they do.

3.5 CHOOSE
CONCISE WORDS.

You can choose accurate, precise, and vivid words and still leave readers guessing what you mean if you inundate them with verbal overkill. Television is the hand that rocked the cradle of today's readers; they demand of their factual writers the same bang-a-minute, tightly scripted, easy-to-ingest pablum they lap up from the tube. You may not approve intellectually of that situation, but defy it and you risk going unread.

Read the following paragraph about English architecture and see if it holds your interest:

> One thing especially continues unfamiliar to the Scotchman's eye—the domestic architecture, the look of streets and buildings; the quaint, venerable age of many, and the thin walls and warm coloring of all. We have, in Scotland, far fewer ancient buildings, above all in country places: and those that we have are all of hewn or harled masonry. Wood has been sparingly used in their construction; the window-frames are sunken in the wall, not flat to the front, as in England; the roofs are steeper-pitched; even a hill farm will have a massy, square, cold, and permanent appearance. English houses, in comparison, have the look of cardboard toys, such as a puff might shatter. And to this the Scotchman never becomes used. His eye can never rest consciously on one of these brick houses—rickles of brick, as he might call them—or on one of these flat-chested streets, but he is instantly reminded where he is, and instantly travels back in fancy to his home.[3]

We expect little argument when we assert that Robert Louis Stevenson was a skilled writer, widely read in pre-TV days. But the pace of Stevenson's loose and wordy 1880s style in the previous excerpt might carry today's typical reader for maybe a line or two before he asked, "Yes, yes, but what's the point?" Still, some people try to use the old classics as their models, which is akin to designing today's bathing suit in an 1880s style.

It's easy to achieve conciseness if the only problem is that you've been using the wrong model. Far too often, wordiness is the result of a rush to get the job done.

Writers who race along often drop words onto paper helter-skelter in the vain hope that if one word doesn't do the job, a second and a third one will. Often, the words stray off the point entirely. This student's paragraph is an example:

> Smoking has become more American than apple pie. I only know one American, my brother-in-law, who consistently bakes and distributes apple pies that the founding fathers would have been proud of—tasty, flaky, tart. I cannot begin to count the number of Americans, at work, at play, at school, at home, who have established smoking as an integral part of their daily routine.

In looking for an image to concretize his point that everybody in America smokes, this student grabbed at what everybody in America eats—apple pie. Then, not certain that he had convinced the reader of his assertion, he tried to explain what he meant and, instead, got hopelessly lost in a tangle of words that had nothing to do with his point. When he returned to the point, he was lacking in hard facts, so instead he again piled word onto word in an attempt to convince the reader.

The smoking-is-like-apple-pie image is a tough one for even an old pro to work with, but here's a shaky stab at one solution:

> Translation: Marlboros have overtaken apple pie as America's symbol of taste pleasure. No red-blooded American at work, school, or play would be caught dead without a cigarette poised casually between his fingertips.

With half as many words, we managed not only to preserve the metaphor, but to make a clear point with it, and we underscored the imagery by adding some other American clichés: *red-blooded American* and *wouldn't be caught dead*. But it took several minutes to make the image work. It would have taken less time to admit the image wasn't working and find another.

3.6 LIMIT YOUR
USE OF LIMITERS.

A reader visualizes best when her view of the important words is unobstructed. If you plant your important nouns and verbs amid a tangle of modifiers or limiters, the reader may miss your point or decide it isn't worth weeding out from the qualifiers.

Depending on where you went to school, you may use the term qualifier, modifier, or limiter for all those adjectives, adverbs, and phrases that are so easily dropped in front of or after important words. Many beginning writers put in excess limiters hoping readers will choose the best ones. But choosing is the writer's job; the reader's job is to react emotionally and intellectually to the well-chosen words. The use of too many qualifiers emphasizes too many images—and too much emphasis, of course, is a contradiction in terms. It boils down to no emphasis at all.

Sometimes adjectives and adverbs sneak in by force of habit; we've seen them so often with certain nouns we forget they don't always belong together: *golden* opportunity, the *right* answers, *wide* world, *a little* better, *quite* sure, *pretty* close, not *really*. At best, these habitually used limiters mean nothing to the readers. At worst, they mean you aren't sure what you're trying to say. Either way, they don't belong in good writing.

Many writers think limiters make their prose lively; in fact, used in overabundance, they deaden it. Here's a student's example:

> When my four-year-old **daughter gently** slipped her mother's cigarette from its **familiar** pack, placed it **jauntily** at the edge of her mouth, and said, "Hey, Dad, howya doin'?" I entered the final phase of a **long, too** drawn out **personal** battle against smoking.

All the words in bold face are extraneous. Read the sentence without them and see for yourself.

Writers often pile on modifiers because they pick imprecise

words to begin with. Here's an example of that, taken from a think-tank report:

> The Investment Board might be categorized as a microcosm of a democratic governmental unit where participants, public representatives, and investment experts converge. Unfortunately, one must not forget that in this equation, the public (and often the participants) become somewhat removed from immediate involvement. The anticipated mingling of viewpoints does not occur because of the increasing complexity of investment decisions and a lack of understanding of the Board itself.

Here's what happens when we strike excess qualifiers and choose more precise words:

> Translation: The Investment Board is a democracy where participants, public representatives, and investment experts converge. Unfortunately the public and many participants are not sharing their viewpoints because of the increasing complexity of investment decisions and unfamiliarity with the Board itself.

Now that the author's meaning is clear, notice how abstract even his important words are. The fact is, he piled modifiers upon qualifiers upon limiters upon imprecise words because he was hedging. He didn't want to offend members of the Investment Board by saying in clear English that it wasn't working the way it was supposed to. But his bucket of extraneous words obliterated his diplomacy. Most readers of muddy writing assume only that the writer is a muddy thinker.

Here is a three-step formula for getting full value from your limiters:

1. Work hard on selecting your nouns and verbs. If you choose the right noun, you cut out a lot of unnecessary adjectives. If you choose the right verb, you get rid of clauses that are otherwise needed to explain what you really mean to say. Read the following, which is as precise as it needs to be:

> The pitcher eyed the ball. He rubbed it, leaned, toed the mound, pivoted, hurled. The missile misfired. It conked the batter. He grinned, flung the bat, sauntered to first.

Except for the little articles and one preposition, all the words in the above paragraph are nouns (or pronouns) and verbs.

2. Use modifiers judiciously to emphasize important images. A few adjectives, carefully chosen for vividness, make stronger pictures than dozens of them strewn in the path of your nouns. A few adverbs, used judiciously, clarify by limiting or strengthening the words they modify. This paragraph by Harry Golden is a good example:

> Not all widows flock to Florida to snatch a new husband. Some of the more imaginative widows settle in the quiet little college towns. And, of course, the naive professors are easy prey.[4]

If any one of Golden's limiters is discarded, the meaning of his ideas is changed.

3. Get rid of every word you don't need. The one action that improves writing most dramatically is ruthless trimming of extraneous words. It's easy to do; all you need is an eraser.

EXERCISES:

1. The following paragraph is made powerful by a careful selection of adjectives:

> The fearful majority needs to be opposed by an articulate and courageous minority, by people who live for others, and not the opinion of others, who believe that they can forge their energy and their intelligence into

> the shapes of their own destiny and their own fu-
> ture. . . . I admire the courage of such people whenever
> I have the good fortune to meet them, but I have
> particular regard for those among them who choose
> to write magazine articles. I count it as a victory to
> find writers who speak in plain words and who report
> what they have seen and heard and thought rather than
> what they have been told.[5]

Rank the sentences in the order of their impact on the reader.
(Let 1 = *most impact*.) Count the number of adjectives in each
sentence. Which sentence has the fewest adjectives, which the
most? Cross out any adjectives you think Lewis H. Lapham, its
author, could have done without. Then discuss the usefulness of
the ones that are left. Should any of the following adjectives have
been inserted to modify the applicable nouns: *vigorously* opposed,
noble people, *often misguided* opinion, *boundless* energy, *God-
given* intelligence? Why or why not? What about these adverbs:
opposed *forcefully*, believe *rightly*, admire *enormously*, *really*
good fortune?

2. The following is a rewrite of the student's example quoted
at the beginning of this section:

> When my four-year-old eased a cigarette from her
> mother's ever-present pack, hung it from her lip, and
> drawled, "Hey Dad, howya doin'?" she shoved me
> into the final skirmish in my long battle against smok-
> ing.

Compare it with the original. Has any important idea been left
out? Has any image been changed, and in what way? List the
verbs used in the rewrite, and compare them with the verbs in
the original. Compare the nouns in both versions.

3. Find a paper of at least 500 words that you wrote. Revise it,
making changes that will improve accuracy, preciseness, vividness, and conciseness. Pay special attention to your use of limiters.

NOTES: CHAPTER 3

1. "How to Launch Your Own Business for Under $1,000 and Make $25,000–$50,000 a year!" *Success Unlimited*, November, 1979, p. 11. (Typographical error corrected.)

2. Lillian Smith, *Killers of the Dream* (Garden City, Doubleday Anchor, 1963), p. 86.

3. Robert Louis Stevenson, "The Foreigner at Home," *College Book of English Literature*, James Edward Tobin, Victor M. Hamm, and William H. Hines, eds. (New York: American Book Company, 1949), p. 1009.

4. Harry Golden, *Only in America* (New York: World Publishing, 1958) p. 46.

5. Lewis H. Lapham, "house ad" for *Harper's*, May, 1980, p. 9.

CHAPTER 4
BUILD STRONG IDEAS

Writers seldom write the
things they think. They simply
write the things they think
other folks think they think.
Elbert Hubbard

Traditional grammars and composition texts generally discuss nouns in one unit (telling you to pick the most concrete ones you can find) and verbs in another (advising in favor of the active, not the passive), as if each part of speech must be considered separately. But that isn't how people write, except in some composition classes. We write in terms of ideas. We don't pick out a noun and then add a verb to it; we play mental games with an idea until a sensible combination of words results.

Consider this simple thought, which may be expressed with a noun and a verb:

1. The fox ran.

The good writer rejects it as incomplete. After further thought, he changes the sentence to reflect more precisely the complex action that he really wants to express:

2. The running fox vanished.

In doing so, he retains the concept of running, but instead of expressing it with a verb as in sentence 1, he says it with an adjective. Now watch what happens to *run* in sentence 3, a stronger way of expressing the thought:

    3. Like a bullet, the fox flew into his den.

To be strong, ideas needn't be stated in their baldest terms. It is often more forceful to add concrete words as in sentence 2 or to substitute concrete examples as in sentence 3.

    Sentence 2 is precise, and sentence 3 is vivid; accuracy, precision, conciseness, and vividness are one set of criteria at your disposal as your mind sorts out and makes written sense of what you have to say. Another set, overlapping the first, is the vast spectrum between *abstract* and *concrete*.

    Far too many composition text authors advise beginning writers simply to strive for the concrete. They duck the fact that the real world's demands sometimes make it inadvisable for writers to choose the most concrete terms. To fill the gap, and to avoid turning out confused or incomplete writers, we will examine the panorama of degrees of concreteness offered by our rich language, and suggest some guidelines for usage. For word families that show ideas, it is helpful to think in terms of concrete vs. abstract; for word families that show things, the continuum is more clearly from the general to the specific. For example, *organism* is a general word and *ape* a specific one when you consider the two words together; *resolve* is an abstract word and *toughness* a relatively concrete one. For ease of discussion, we will use the two sets of terms interchangeably.

4.1 THE CONTINUUM BETWEEN CONCRETE AND ABSTRACT, AND BETWEEN SPECIFIC AND GENERAL.

To review some high school terminology, you may have learned that nouns come in two varieties: concrete and abstract, and that proper nouns (*Chattanooga, John Brown, the president*) are always concrete, whereas common nouns can be either concrete—naming physical, visible, tangible objects such as *dog, town, water*—or abstract—naming ideas that can't be seen, touched, smelled, tasted, or heard. All this is true. But it avoids all the exceptions to the rule.

Some nouns are easy to group into concrete and abstract. Try marking *abstract* or *concrete* after the nouns in this list:

milk
burp
thought
dream
toast
need
smell
smoke
anguish

Now, go over the list a second time, sorting out the words as *verbs*. Notice that every word on the list is both noun and verb, and retains close to the same meaning regardless of its part of speech.

Not all words lead two lives. We chose ours with this double purpose in mind, to show that concreteness and abstractness are not qualities peculiar to nouns. We also selected words that are clearly either abstract or concrete. Other words are not so easy to qualify. *Dog* is concrete, but *animal* is listed in some grammars as abstract; *lullaby* is considered concrete, but *music* abstract. The problem here is that *concrete* and *abstract* are themselves abstractions: they are words for ideas, and a writer's ideas cannot be made completely clear, whether as noun, verb, or adjective, unless he presents *concrete examples*. The way we've really built our entire language is not according to arbitrary lines between nouns, verbs, adjectives, and such, or between concrete and abstract, but in a continuum. At one end, words relate mostly to concrete things; at the other end, mostly to abstract ideas. In between the end-points the words generally are concrete to a degree or abstract to a degree.

To create a concrete example for this abstract idea, let's relate the concept of word continuums to a more familiar, and therefore more concrete, continuum: the animal kingdom. As it is graphically organized in biology textbooks, its terms begin with the most general (abstract) and proceed to the most specific (concrete). Here is the progression from *organisms* to *apes* and *man*:

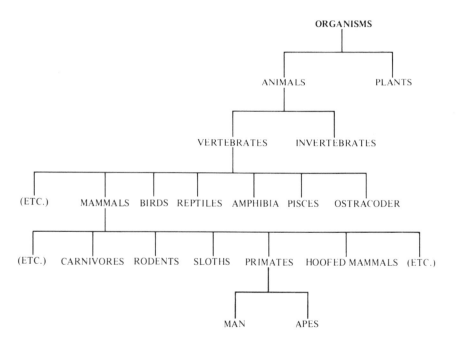

For many word families in our language, we could draw a similar kind of diagram, moving from the most general or abstract to the most specific or concrete. Using entries listed in *Roget's Thesaurus* for the word *resolve*, here's a modest diagram:

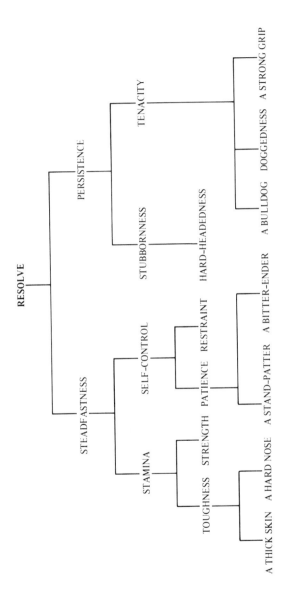

Let's look more closely at the levels of meaning exposed in the word diagram. At the uppermost level is *resolve*, an entirely abstract word meaning *fixed purpose*. On the second level are *steadfastness* and *persistence*; each reveals a little more about the fixed purpose: it's either active resolve (persistence) or passive resolve (steadfastness). Already, we're getting more concrete.

The third level adds more to the *resolve* idea: *stamina* and *self-control* suggest subtle distinctions between strength of body and strength of spirit; *stubbornness* and *tenacity* delineate slightly different shades of *persistence*. By the time our chart reaches its bottom line, the once abstract, general idea is so precisely defined that it narrows down to the most specific meaning possible for each kind of *resolve*. Almost every specific entry is concrete enough to call up a sensory image in readers: *thick skin, hard nose, bitter-ender, stand-patter, hardheadedness, a bulldog, doggedness, a strong grip.*

These concrete words are certainly the most vivid in the *resolve* family, and are the ones to choose from if your goal is vividness. But they are not always the most accurate, nor are they appropriate in all kinds of writing. For example, if you don't know whether a person's steadfastness is a result of the more specific *stamina* or *self-control*, you had better choose a word no more specific than *steadfastness*. And if you are writing a formal document—for example, a will—you had better not write, "With the hardheartedness of my forefathers, I hereby decree . . ." even though your resolve may be as specific as that.

Once you understand the concrete-to-abstract continuum in our language, you will learn to choose your words from the correct part of the hierarchy to do what you want them to, and your writing will become rich with meaning and fluid with variety. If you purposely want to encompass the broadest nuances in meaning, you'll choose from near the abstract end of the continuum. If you want to build concrete images for your readers, so that your specific ideas are completely understood, you'll select from the concrete end.

In discussing the spectrum of subtleties possible in the word family *resolve*, we diagrammed the progression in the noun form of the word. We could have equally well diagrammed the verb *resolve*, the adjective *resolute*, or the adverb *resolutely*. In fact, some of the words contained in the noun's diagram cannot, as a rule, be used smoothly in their noun's clothing: for example, we don't usually say, "He is a hard nose," but, "He is hard-nosed." When you're looking for the best way to express your ideas, it is important to sort through all the ways of saying the *idea*, not the *noun* or the *verb*.

Here are two examples of fine writing. One relies on very concrete nouns, the other generally on abstract verbs. Both selections make their points perfectly well, because one point requires vividness and would be weakened with words that are less concrete, whereas the other point *is* abstract and could not be made accurately with words that are more concrete. (Of course, once that abstract point is made, the writer goes on to give examples that make the meaning clear.)

> Arabs are everywhere in London these days. The Bedouin burnoose is seen almost as often as the British bowler and brollie in the crowds thronging Regent Street and Piccadilly. Half the ladies shopping at Harrod's seem to be wearing either a black mask or a veil. At London's gaming tables, the clickety-clack of Arab worry beads is almost as loud as the clatter of the roulette wheel's bouncing ball or the rattle of dice. The British Tourist Authority happily predicts that 400,000 Arabs will land on British soil during 1977, each spending well over twice what a typical American tourist brings into British coffers. It has been the most successful Arab invasion of Europe since the days of Suleiman the Magnificent.[1]
>
> Arturo F. Gonzales, Jr.

> Picking up stakes can, at the right moment, energize your life. Moving, like travel, broadens. It can en-

hance a career. It also has a way of solving problems, if only by getting rid of them. If you're mired down in your present circumstances, a change of scene can put you onto firm, fresh ground.[2]

Leonard Gross

The point of Gonzalez's paragraph is, "A lot of Arabs go to England nowadays." Notice how much information is shared, with specifics piled on specifics. Not just Bedouins' clothes are seen, but a specific type of clothing. Arabs don't *go* to *Britain,* but *land* concretely on *British soil.* Concreteness and vividness often go hand in hand.

In a few places Gonzales chooses more general words: *"well over twice,"* for example. Perhaps he does it for variety. More than likely, his research data do not support more specific words.

The point of Gross's paragraph is, "Moving renews and broadens people, helps careers, leaves problems behind, helps people start again." It is a general point, and specifics would narrow the meaning to less than Gross wants to say. Still, there are some vivid words to keep the reader's interest: *stakes; mired down; firm, fresh ground.* It is unlikely that either Gonzalez or Gross, at their typewriters, thought, "Hm, should I use lots of nouns or pay more attention to my verbs?" Instead, they concentrated on finding the words that most effectively did the jobs they needed done.

EXERCISES:

1. Rewrite Arturo Gonzalez's paragraph changing his concrete words into words that are as abstract as possible. You should change at least fifteen words including these: *Arabs, Harrod's, veil, clickety-clack, 400,000, 1977.* (You may have to rewrite more than just a word at a time.)

2. Rewrite Leonard Gross's paragraph changing his general words into words that are as specific as possible. You should change at least ten word groups including these: *picking up stakes,*

right moment, broadens, enhance, present circumstances, change of scene. (You may have to add some facts of your own.)

3. Consider how your rewrite changed the vividness, accuracy, preciseness, and conciseness of Gonzalez's paragraph. Was it enjoyable to read after the changes? If you were reading a popular magazine for pleasure, which of the two paragraphs—Gonzalez's or yours—would best meet your expectations? If you were the vice-president of a company considering investment in London businesses that might appeal to Arabs, which paragraph would best meet your expectations?

4. Consider how your rewrite changed the vividness, accuracy, precision, and conciseness of Leonard Gross's paragraph. Was it as enjoyable to read after the changes? If you were reading a popular magazine for pleasure, which of the two paragraphs— Gross's or yours—would best meet your expectations? If you were the owner of a real estate firm that specializes in finding homes for long-distance movers, which paragraph would best meet your expectations? If you were a sociology professor doing background research on the impact moving makes on American families, would your paragraph or Leonard Gross's best meet your expectations?

4.2 FIGURES OF SPEECH: THEY STRENGTHEN IMAGES AND TURN ABSTRACT INTO CONCRETE.

The category of words and phrases called *figures of speech* is a large catch-all into which grammarians have thrown all the tricks of language that help explain difficult ideas or call attention to important ones. Theodore M. Bernstein, in *The Careful Writer*, lists twenty-nine different kinds of figures of speech, from *allegory* to *zeugma*, and says his catalogue is by no means complete. John Nist, in *Speaking into Writing*, comments that more than two hundred different kinds have been counted in Shakespeare's works.

Learning the names of two hundred figures, or even twenty-nine, is not going to make you a better writer. Instead, here we'll concentrate on teaching you some of the ways you can play tricks with words and use these tricks to call attention to certain ideas or to help explain others. We'll mention some of their fancy names in passing. As you read for pleasure, notice how these devices—and others—are used by good writers and misused by poor ones. Soon you'll discover for yourself some of the two hundred figures Shakespeare stumbled on.

One large group of figures of speech explains an idea in terms of a concrete image. It is useful if you need to explain an idea the reader doesn't know, especially an abstraction. Just substitute your image—preferably a very concrete one—that the reader is familiar with. Like all good writing, the image should be expressed with words that are accurate, precise, concise, and vivid. In order for a substitution to work, you must make a connection for the reader between the idea and the image, unless the connection is obvious.

The figure of speech that substitutes an image for an idea has been chopped up into many subcategories. For writers, it's easier to learn just three divisions: comparison, simple substitution, and comparison with substitution.

Comparison is the easiest figure for the beginning writer to work with. She need simply ask herself, "What can I liken the idea to that the readers would know?" The comparison is usually signaled by the word *like* or *as*, though other words are sometimes used. Most comparisons come under the heading *simile*, which you probably studied in earlier years.

Here is a simple comparison, the kind we take for granted. It's by John Mack Carter.

He looked more like the Lone Ranger than a doctor.[3]

And here is an abstraction—shifting job opportunities—likened by Joseph S. Coyle to something very concrete:

> Like a saucer tipping south, the U.S. economy is spilling vast numbers of new job opportunities into the cities of the Sunbelt and draining them away from the established industrial centers up north.[4]

The following anonymous comparison is straightforward:

> He stepped into the city like an adolescent into his first love affair—with a huge heart and an immense curiosity.[5]

But a comparison need not be just a phrase. It can extend through several sentences, in which case it becomes an *analogy*. Here's one Margaret Mead thought up to explain her statement that "nobody knows how to be married today."

> It's getting like the New York subway. There are no maps in the station; you have to get on a train to discover you're on the wrong one. You have to make a mistake before you do the right thing.[6]

Was Ms. Mead correct in assuming that even non-New Yorkers would understand the comparison?

The following comparisons, the first by Sandman and Paden and the second by Lewis Lapham, use neither *like* nor *as*:

> They fixed the reactor the way a mechanic fixes a car—they tinkered.[7]

> No wonder the bookstores resemble circuses and fairs.[8]

Notice how, in almost every example above, the author finds a concrete object or action that can be visualized by the specific readers he's writing for—the Lone Ranger, a tipping saucer, fountains, a car—to substitute for an abstract or unfamiliar idea or thing—an unknown doctor, a characteristic of the economy, clear writers, a reactor. A few bold writers compare abstractions and unknowns to less tangible things—religion, adolescents in love. When these intangibles are commonplace, they can usually be counted on to call forth clear, appropriate images in readers' minds. But if you choose an intangible, you may find yourself wanting to play safe—like the author of the adolescent-in-love image, by taking the time—and words—to explain the intangible example in concrete terms. Then you risk several of the problems with figures of speech that we discuss later in this chapter: the feeling of having reached too far for your substitution, and the diversion of the reader's attention off the track of the primary thought, the one you've been trying to explain.

Simple substitution is harder than comparison for the writer to write, but more fun for the reader to read. To write it, after asking yourself, "What can I liken it to that the reader would know?" you must go a step further and delete the *like, as, just as, the way, as if, in a way that,* or other guidepost that leads the reader along. By permitting her to discover for herself that a comparison is being made, you entice her to take a direct role in creating your paper. When you've substituted a concrete image for an abstraction—especially a concrete image the reader hasn't ever looked at before as something that could stand for the abstraction—and the reader suddenly sees the connection and understands your idea in a new way, the result is often startling and dramatic.

There are many ways to use simple substitution. The *metaphor* is a favorite device of writers, including textbook writers. It is popularly divided into several groups. Because they are convenient designations for learning to use substitution, we'll review them here, but with the warning that the parameters of these categories are imprecise. It is difficult sometimes to know when an implied metaphor has passed into the common language and become an idiomatic metaphor, and when an idiomatic metaphor has been used so often that it is dead. The best way to learn to use these valuable devices for making the abstract concrete, the unfamiliar familiar, and the dull lively, is to watch for them when reading and to evaluate their effectiveness.

1. The formal metaphor

A formal metaphor expresses in words both the original idea and the one that's substituted for it. The original is often an abstraction, and the substitution a concrete image. It's ordinarily expressed in "this is that" terms, and then just a fine line separates it from a *comparison*. Here are examples by George Christoph Lichtenberg and Richard Seltzer.

> A book is a mirror: if an ass peers into it, you can't expect an apostle to look out.[9]

> The pancreas was swollen, necrotic—a dead fish that had gotten tossed in, and now lay spoiling across the upper abdomen.[10]

The *Reader's Digest* often collects catchy metaphors in its section, "Toward More Picturesque Speech." The following have a common theme: Autumn is . . .

> . . . leaves hang-gliding in the wind.

> . . . pumpkins bellying up to the warm sum.

> . . . summer cottages closing their eyes for winter.

> . . . crab apples clinging to a branch, afraid to let go.[11]

2. The implied metaphor

The implied metaphor is informal: instead of announcing its existence, it substitutes one thing for another without mention of the first. Often the first idea is an abstraction and the second a concrete image, or the first thing unfamiliar and the second familiar to the readers. The chief value of the implied metaphor to a writer is its ability to make the writing concise without sacrificing vividness.

The good writer reaches this kind of metaphor by degree. In casting about for an effective way to picture immortality, his thinking might take the following path. First he begins with a simile:

> Men seek immortality like babes suckling at a dry breast hoping it will give milk.

After some reflection, he may change it to a metaphor for greater drama:

> Men are babes suckling at the dry breast of immortality
> hoping it will give milk.

But it still needs an entire sentence, and he prefers, if possible, to continue the thought in the same sentence. Convinced that his readers have sufficient understanding of the meaning of a dry breast, he rewrites the line as an implied metaphor, which requires only a short phrase:

> The dry breast of immortality . . .

and goes on:

> disappoints all but the most tenacious of us.

Because of the mental steps taken to get there, and the mental steps the readers need to take to decipher it, the implied metaphor is one of the most sophisticated figures of speech in the writer's bag of word tricks. Writers love to devise it, and readers love to read it. There are many scattered throughout our writing in this book. These were written by Tamar Lewin, David W. Ewing, and Norman E. Isaacson:

> In response, the pro-draft chorus has been growing steadily louder.[12]

> The Administration gets high marks for a good try.[13]

> There probably has never been a prize competition devoid of controversy. . . . Firecrackers large and small have always popped around the Pulitzer prizes. . . .[14]

3. The idiomatic metaphor

If an author creates a really superb metaphor, he can be sure others will borrow it. Borrowed often enough, it becomes part of the common language and, like other idioms, has a meaning apart from the meaning of the individual words. For example, a *hired gun* hires out to a *big gun*—although someone learning English as a second language might wonder why the big gun needs a hired gun. Here are some more idiomatic metaphors:

Name your poison.
spaced out
deep-sixed
Give me five.
grease the wheels
knock the wind out of his sails

You face two problems when you try to use an idiomatic metaphor. First, you must be certain that your readers' understanding of the phrase is close to your own. Otherwise the substitution will muddy, not clarify, what you have to say. Second, idiomatic metaphors are broadcast so far so quickly, in this TV age, that they become overused and dated in no time. In fact, most idiomatic metaphors are on a steady descent into the world of **dead metaphors**, commonly called *clichés*. When they've reached that point, they're no longer dramatic or even explicit enough to serve good writers.

Here, from the pages of current magazines, are a few idiomatic metaphors that some people feel are already dead:

He's going through an emotional wringer.

Solar heating is moving out of the horse-and-buggy stage.

That town is a prize catch for the land-hungry oil company.

4. The resurrected dead metaphor

Some dead metaphors are just too grand to bury. With a kick in the ribs, you can get those tired horses going again—as we just did when we combined two clichés, *kick in the ribs* and *tired horse*. This figure of speech is closer to the pun than to formal and implied metaphors. It usually makes readers smile, so use it when you're poking fun or making satiric comment. Shun it when you're serious about an idea and don't want to detract from it with your cleverness.

Thoreau must have sat alongside Walden Pond deliberately

trying to revive dead metaphors. Here are some examples he
penned:

> It is not necessary that a man should earn his living
> by the sweat of his brow unless he sweats easier than
> I do.[15]

> Besides, clothes introduced sewing, a kind of work
> which you may call endless; a woman's dress, at least,
> is never done.[16]

> With consummate skill he has set his trap with a hair
> spring to catch comfort and independence, and then
> as he turned away, got his own leg into it.[17]

> Sometimes we are inclined to class those who are once-
> and-a-half-witted with the half-witted, because we ap-
> preciate only a third part of their wit.[18]

There are many kinds of simple substitution in addition to the
metaphor. For example, if you use either a comparison or a
substitution that refers to "a literary character or situation or to
a proverb or topical saying," says Theodore Bernstein, you have
created an *allusion*. The *Lone Ranger* comparison a few pages
back is an allusion; so is this one by Jack Richardson:

> Assuming he is no well-known Micawber, his appli-
> cation is most likely approved, and he finds himself
> welcomed into the happy, fluid world of credit buy-
> ing.[19]

Metonymy, synecdoche, and *personification* are also substitutions. They substitute, in order, the attribute of one for the attribute of another, the part for the whole, and a person for a
thing. Fine writers learn to use substitutions not only singly but
in tandem. Here, for example, is a combination of a metaphor
and a double synecdoche used by Jimmy Breslin:

> *Soon the rumor would be in robes.*[20]

First Breslin set up the simile: *Soon the rumor would be as if a law*; then he moved to the metaphor: *soon it would be law*; and finally he substituted a *judge* for the law and *in robes* for the judge. That's the work of a master. If you can learn to think that intricately about substitutions, you won't have to account to anybody for the names of the processes you use in your writing. Just doing it will be awesome enough.

Comparison with substitution: In some cases, comparison or simple substitution is retained for several sentences. This usually is true either when the idea you're trying to explain is so complex or unfamiliar that you have to choose a substitute that itself needs explanation, or when the comparison or substitution is so apt that it can be extended longer to provide even greater accuracy, precision, or vividness. The big problem is knowing when to stop, which is when conciseness has been sacrificed and no benefit to the reader substituted for it.

We have decided to call this device comparison with substitution because usually there is a full statement of the two ideas or things being compared, as well as a substitution of one for the other. We have found the device listed among none of the Greek terms for figures of speech, but it is used frequently by good writers. Here is an example by John Simon:

> Yet the real horror in these remarks lies in the supine willingness to compromise with sloth, ignorance, and anti-intellectualism. If a man threatens to beat me to a pulp, I don't offer, by way of compromise, to let him beat me black-and-blue; rather, I defend myself with might and main. Then, if he still trounces me, too bad; but at least I put up a good defense, and the rest was inevitable. One does not intentionally compromise with any sort of evil; what happens in most cases is that a compromise takes place of itself.[21]

Simon was trying to show "supine compromise"—compromise taken lying down. He decided to compare this intellectual compromise with the compromise that takes place "of itself" in a fist fight *after* someone refuses to take something lying down. He needs several sentences to make the point of his example, so to get the reader back on track he reiterates his first point: "One does not intentionally compromise with any sort of evil; what happens in most cases is that a compromise takes place of itself." There is implied substitution of the concrete for the abstract, and then the abstract is substituted back again.

If you get into a long comparison with substitution like this one, it is always a good idea to resubstitute when you're done.

Here's how Jimmy Breslin used comparison with substitution:

> In politics, however, there are game rules which must be observed. You cannot play baseball unless you go onto the field and play baseball. And one cannot play politics unless one understands the nuances of rumor. A political rumor, if repeated often enough and spread widely enough many times, is converted to fact. . . . You see, along the line the rumor would reach the mayor, and the mayor, a player himself, would hear the rumor, repeat it and then begin to believe it as fact.[22]

And finally, here's an example of how we used it in one of our articles to explain a difficult concept:

> It's dark. Somewhere deep inside your body a T-cell is on patrol. . . . Suddenly, the T-cell tenses because its stubby tentacles brush against a strangely shaped cell. It doesn't belong there. It's a runaway cell that, left to its selfish devices, would become a tumor crowding nearby cells and robbing them of nourishment. Instantly, the T-cell patrol sends out an alarm, a special bit of protein excreted only in emergencies. That alerts the body's soldiers, the killer-cells, and their not-so-smart but hard-working helpers, the macrophage cells. Yet, even before help arrives, the T-cell attacks, attaching itself to the tumor cell. . . . Ten minutes later, the barrier is breached, the tumor cell

disintegrates, and the triumphant cells slowly move away.[23]

Our substitution was suggested to us by the fact that *killer-cell* is actually the scientific term for the type of cell we were describing.

There is another kind of figure of speech that is used not to help the reader understand your ideas better, but simply to play with the language, providing amusement for the writer and— if he is lucky—the reader as well. This group includes *onomato-poeia, alliteration,* and the like. Since none of these figures is important for good writing, we'll leave them to the books that explain how to be a critic, not a writer.

Effective use of figures of speech demands great care. But your troubles are rewarded by great impact. Your attempts will be successful if you keep in mind the following warnings:

1. Don't mix your metaphors (or other figures of speech). If you use one concrete image to explain something abstract, don't confuse by working another substitution into the same set of phrases or sentences.

> The hope for immortality is a babe suckling at a dry breast. But on rare occasions, comets have fallen to earth.

That is a mixed metaphor. The reader has to switch from one image (breasts) to another (comets), and it gets in the way of communication. Here is the information presented without mixing the metaphor:

> The hope for immortality is a babe suckling at a dry breast. But on rare occasions, even dry breasts have been known to give milk.

If your image is strong enough, it will linger in readers' minds for at least a paragraph, so it's a good rule never to mix metaphoric images within the same paragraph. Often, further separation is desired, but this is something your experience will teach you.

2. Don't reach too far for figures of speech. Writers sometimes get caught up in the challenge of metaphors and end up straining to make them work. If you have to try too hard, your reader will sense the strain, and your figure of speech will fall flat:

> There was the smell of fear and imminent failure in the form of freshly mimeographed sheets that demanded the impossible.

This student was trying to make test-taking anxiety concrete, and remembered the smell of freshly mimeographed papers. She reached—and tripped. The sentence neither compares nor substitutes. If she'd substituted *odor* for *form*, she would have been clearer—but still have had no substitution, because *mimeographed sheets* cannot be made into a concrete image for *fear* or *failure* no matter how long a reach you have.

Here's another student's comparison:

> The red markers squeaked across the pages like dry windshield wipers decrying my fallibility.

This begins with a nice simile, but the comparison won't stretch to cover *decrying* or *fallibility* because readers don't link those attributes to markers or wipers.

3. Be wary of clichéd metaphors. If you find them creeping into your writing, kick them into life by turning them around. Here are two more examples of rejuvenated clichés:

> Denise swam like a fish out of water: she flopped, wheezed, and frantically wiggled her tail.

> Sheldon made a name for himself, only it wasn't a name I'd like to be called.

4. Don't overuse figures of speech. Beginning writers who've learned to use them often find them so much fun that they carry them to extremes. Call on them if they're the most precise and vivid way to share information and ideas, or if you need to give

the reader a shock or a smile. Nothing should get in the way of communication, not even your cleverness.

5. Don't let your figure of speech throw you far from your original idea. Once you've supplied your concrete image, get back to the business at hand.

EXERCISES:
Rewrite each of the following. Use figures of speech to make the ideas more concrete.

1. There are many anomalies about the ordinary kitchen refrigerator. One is that it requires several heaters. The automatic defrosting mechanism is essentially a heater coupled to a timer. There's another heater that keeps the freezer compartment door from freezing shut. Another heater keeps moisture from forming near the refrigerating compartment door. Often, other heaters keep the channels that carry melted ice away from the defrosting coil from freezing up.

2. Tumors come in two major types, malignant and benign. However, even experienced pathologists all too often have trouble distinguishing one from the other because there are some tumors with intermediate kinds of properties as well. This is because many profound changes take place in the transition period between being a normal cell and being a malignant or benign cell. Many times these changes take place all at once, but often they take place sequentially.

3. When you buy your first home, you will have to learn the meaning of many strange terms such as mortgage, land contract, building loan, earnest money, escrow account, closing fees, and title insurance. Short definitions of these terms are seldom adequate. You will have to know how each term applies to your own circumstances.

4. There are many myths about coffee and what its caffeine does to us. In fact, there are so many that it is hard even for scientists

to sort out fact from fiction. Also, while many people worry about the 100 to 150 mg. of caffeine in their coffee, they sip tea, which contains a like amount of caffeine, or a cola drink, which contains 35 to 55 mg. of the stimulant.

Write one or two sentences that revitalize each of the following clichés:

5. No news is good news.

6. There's no fool like an old fool.

7. It's never too late to learn.

8. like a dog chasing its tail

4.3 USE THE SIMPLEST FORM OF EACH WORD.

To understand an idea or process, the reader must visualize the *doer* before he finds out what the doer *does* and to whom it is *done*. That's why good writers put their words in a cause-and-effect sequence—subject, verb, object—unless they want the reader to stop and notice something special. They signal the doer and the one it's done to with nouns; they signal what is done with verbs. The signals make for quick, easy reading.

Unfortunately, many writers—and not just students—are under the misapprehension that there's something babyish about quick, easy reading. They deliberately turn around the placement of their subjects and verbs and change their verbs into nouns, on the assumption that it's a sophisticated way of writing. In the next chapter we'll show you how to add sophistication without sacrificing strength and clarity. Inversion and nominalization usually muddy up sentences and sap their strength. Here's an example of how a simple statement can be shoved along the road to ruin:

1. Simple sentence: Eagles like to catch fish.

2. Nominalization: Eagles enjoy the catching of fish.

3. Inversion: The catching of fish is enjoyed by eagles.

4. Inversion and nominalization: The catching of fish provides enjoyment for eagles.

If the example above seems exaggerated, it is only because we've separated the steps that lead to these nonsensically neutered sentences. Language like this spews daily from the halls of academia and from desks in bureaucracies. The best way to avoid it in your writing is to stick to the most straightforward sentence construction and the simplest form of each word unless you see a good reason for doing otherwise.

There are three clues that will help you cut the clutter and keep concise:

1. Study the position of your subject. If your sentence has a subject, and the subject is more important than the object, you owe it to your readers to put that subject in front of the verb that tells what the subject does. A writer who inverts his sentences asks a great deal of the reader: he insists that she mentally file away the action that's done, and often the object that's acted on, before he gets around to revealing who or what is doing the acting. Although the information obscured by inverted sentences has to be filed in readers' memory banks for only split seconds, multiply that by a couple of dozen sentences on each typed page and by eight pages in a report, and the effect is exhaustion. Worse, the writer risks the chance that the reader who can't follow his inversions will completely misunderstand him.

Picture the following sentences:

5a. The ball was tossed to the right of the plate down along the base line by the pitcher.

6a. Families, governments, and societies are undermined by existentialism.

7a. Buying the wine was his responsibility.

Notice how much quicker your mind grasps the following translations:

> 5b. The pitcher tossed the ball to the right of the plate down along the base line.

> 6b. Existentialism undermines families, governments, and societies.

> 7b. He had to buy the wine.

2. Look hard at all past-tense verbs that are preceded by a form of be or get. These are passive verb forms, and nearly all inverted sentences use them. Grammar books call them passive because they *are* passive; they are not strong words. Equally important, they often signal indirect, illogical progressions. Where they do, replace them with active verbs, which not only put cause and effect in their proper order but are forthright, succinct, and less open to misinterpretation.

In the first two examples of inverted sentences (5a, 6a), the passive verbs are *was* toss*ed* and *are* undermin*ed*. Notice that inverted sentence 7a eliminates the active verb entirely, substituting the intransitive verb *was*. If you can't find the action in a sentence that should have action, you've probably inverted your sentence.

Here are some more inverted sentences with passive verbs:

> 8a. By this consolidation, duplication of functions was eliminated.

> 8b. Translation: This consolidation eliminated duplication of functions.

> 9a. The car is getting fixed by the mechanic.

> 9b. Translation: The mechanic is fixing the car.

The passive voice does have a place in good writing. It is often the best approach when the subject is unknown or of less importance than the object of the sentence:

10. In 1850, no trace of the glacier was found.

11. Human passions cannot be easily pacified.

12. Fish was being fried everywhere.

As we've pointed out, inversion slows the reader down, and you may want to do just that. Putting the subject at the end can emphasize it, and you may want to do that as well. Notice how inversion strengthens the image and places the emphasis where the writer wants it:

13a. *Simple:* The barrel of a gun cannot shoot forth democracy.

13b. *Inverted:* Democracy cannot be shot out of the barrel of a gun.

3. Check the nouns that end in -ing, -tion, -al, -ity, -ment, -ance, -ness, and other suffixes. They all come from verbs. Make sure they're needed as nouns.

Poor writers, often afraid to write forcefully, turn their strong verbs into static nouns and substitute verbs that have no force at all. The result is insipid, needlessly wordy writing. Here are some examples of needless noun-making:

There is a division of labor between the president and his staff.
Translation: The president and his staff divide the work.

There are those who feel that the deciding of a controversial issue such as the drafting of college-age students is nowhere better done than in the political arena.
Translation: Some feel that a political **debate and vote** should decide the controversy over whether to draft college-age students.

The measurement and assessment of children's performances will have to be maintained.

Translation: Children's performances will have to be measured and assessed.

We'll bet that each bad example above resulted from ducking a writing problem. The first writer probably didn't know which was correct: *the president and his staff divide* or *the president divides with his staff.* So he found a way around it. The second writer probably didn't have enough facts to make the subject of his statement precise, so he chose an abstraction, *arena*, and hung it at the end in the hope that people wouldn't notice. (Actually, the end of the sentence is the part people notice most.) He also didn't want to come right out and make a specific statement about drafting college-age students, so he stuck in a general statement and a *such as.* The third writer didn't want to name the subject, but in dodging it she lost her verbs.

Very often, writers who are guilty of using too many passive verbs are also guilty of excess nominalization. Even a government agency that recognizes the value of clear writing sometimes lets inversions and nominalizations sneak by:

Not only was the 1976 new house market dominated by previous homeowners, it was also typified by affluent families—households in the top quarter income bracket, having annual incomes of $20,000 or more. NAHB's national survey indicated that in the 1975–76 period 60 percent of the new houses were bought by affluent families, with the annual median income being $21,600 and two or more incomes being common.[24]

Translation: Previous homeowners, especially households with incomes of at least $20,000, which put them in the upper quarter income bracket, dominated the 1976 new house market. NAHB's national survey showed that in 1975 and 1976, affluent families, many with two or more incomes and a median income of $21,600, bought 60 percent of the new houses.

In rewriting the agency's paragraph, we uncovered two pieces of fuzzy information. Did you catch them? Does *in the 1975–76 period* mean all of those two years, or are they referring to a fiscal year period? And in those *affluent families*, many of which have *two or more incomes*, is that median income of *$21,600* for the family as a whole or for each of their two or more salaries individually?

EXERCISES:

Rewrite the next three sentences three times each. In the first rewrite, nominalize the verb. In the second, also invert the subject and verb. In the third, complicate the sentence further by adding meaningless words.

1. The red fox caught a bluejay.

2. In September, John spent $3,400 for a used car.

3. Alchemists in the Dark Ages boiled and bubbled snake eyes and lizard teeth hoping to create gold.

Three of the next four sentences contain the passive voice. a) Tell what clues show which is active and which are passive. b) Rewrite the passive sentences with active verbs so that all the words are in the simplest form.

4. No information was found in the files of the CIA, FBI, State Department, or Department of Defense to lead us to the conclusion that there had been any improprieties committed by these agencies.

5. Even considering the unseasonably cold temperatures, the experimental cars performed no better than cars without the test carburetors.

6. Laboratory rats given massive doses of Vitamin K were found to be cured of impotence, asthma, acne, and athlete's foot.

7. The goals and objectives of the cost-containment committee were assigned to department heads for implementation.

4.4 HOW HE/SHE
INTRUDE(S) WHEN I/WE
WRITE FOR YOU
(THE READER).

Wordy, convoluted sentences are often the result of trying to depersonalize our prose, or of trying to avoid the entrenched sexism of the English language. Disembodied prose is a common disease even among otherwise careful writers.

Something is missing from the following three paragraphs. See if you can spot it.

> 1. How can one predict for the next decade in parent education? With the devastating conditions in the world today, one would hesitate to make predictions of any kind.[25]

> 2. As a matter of fact, if one could get a bird's-eye view of the whole country, all the activities which have been described would appear as only small bits of influence here and there. . . . [26]

> 3. It is important that those having experience—administrators of existing units—be consulted and that an open mind and flexible stance be maintained. There is still much myth and bias associated with the mentally ill, and it is the myth and bias that must be overcome to set up a successful psychiatric unit in a general hospital.[27]

The authors of the above paragraphs carefully avoided all traces of human authorship, probably because in some teacher's classroom they were taught that modest writers erase their personalities by using *one* for *I* or *we* or even *you*. This rule of formal writing dates back to an era when high necklines and long skirts hid all traces of a lady's skin, and a decent man covered his chest even on the beach. Readers don't expect Victorianism in print these days. They don't like wishy-washy prose that purports to have leaped onto paper unassisted by human minds and hands.

Compare the following rewrite to paragraph 1 above:

> How can I predict for the next decade in parent education? With the devastating conditions in the world today, I would hesitate to make predictions of any kind.

Notice the livelier, more assertive tone that's achieved just by substituting *I*.

Not only is it good writing to admit authorship of your ideas, but it is good writing to admit that you hope to be read, and that you want to be friends with the reader. The personal pronouns *you* and *we* should be used wherever needed. Look how that would have cleaned up paragraph 3:

> It is important that you consult with experienced administrators of existing units, and that you keep an open mind and maintain a flexible stance. We still have to overcome much myth and bias about the mentally ill, in order to set up a successful psychiatric unit in a general hospital.

It is possible to end up with stilted writing by inserting too many personal pronouns. For example, instead of writing *in order to set up* we could have chosen *so that we can set up*. As in all good writing, your best guide is your ear. Just write the way an educated person speaks to a new acquaintance, and you can't go wrong.

Many research and trade journals have relaxed into the personal writing style that fits today's reader. Here's an example by C. Colburn Hardy:

> The basic rules remain simple: Take a tax loss only if the benefit amounts to 20% or more; if you're planning a rollover (as with municipal bonds) do your calculations first, and check with your broker and tax advisor before going ahead.[28]

When writers attempt to sidestep sexist words, they often substitute words that are unmanageably clumsy. In bringing sexual equality to society, you don't have to subjugate the English language. Sexist nouns are usually easy to avoid. Careful thought often unearths nonsexist alternatives. It's possible to signify gracefully that not all *letter carriers* are *mailmen*, and that *U.S. Representative* Elizabeth Holtzman needn't be called a *congressman* any more than *U.S. Representative* Robert Kastenmeier has to be called a *congressperson*.

When you're troubled by a word that carries sexist connotation, don't automatically substitute *person* for *man*, or the effect will more than likely be clumsy, attention-getting, and distracting. Words like *henchperson* make people smile no matter how serious the context. A good way to avoid mutant words is to consult your thesaurus. There you'll find nonsexist synonyms like *gilly, goon, lackey, flunky, stooge,* and *sycophant*.

The personal pronoun *he* is difficult to avoid. Our language doesn't yet offer a good nonsexist alternative. Some students try the *s/he* or *he/she* ploy:

> If a doctor wants to succeed, s/he has to put up with irregular hours.

> A teacher has to make sure he/she does not pass subtle sexism on to his/her students.

Generally, once writers learn to appreciate the uninterrupted flow that signifies good writing, they reject these coinages for the clumsy nonwords they are. Some scholarly journals solve the problem by pointing out, parenthetically or in a footnote, that although the personal pronoun *he* is used, it's meant to include the *she*s of the world. We prefer random selection. We use *he* sometimes and *she* other times, as comfortable with our solution as the journals are with theirs. Choose a device you feel comfortable with—choose anything but those distracting slash-words.

EXERCISES:

Rewrite the following paragraphs, by injecting an author's presence, so that the sentences are direct and forceful:

1. When one speaks of New York, the mind's eye sees bright lights, milling throngs, and garbage everywhere. However, once one has been to that great city, other memories take their place. What is remembered most is the sound of taxicabs, beeping their horns as one races to cross Broadway. One is accosted by speed and noise at every turn.

2. Alaska is a land of plenty. The vast amount of resources available will in all likelihood serve as a magnet for years to come to draw the interest of a wide variety of parties. Interest in various social and economic problems, such as the regional relocation of industries, employment opportunity issues, and environmental and health related issues, is not likely to diminish in future years. Given this interest, and the vast amount of resources, increasing vigilance as to Alaska's direction will be maintained on the part of the interested parties. One is tempted to ask what the future will bring in terms of controlling legislation.

3. To improve profitability during 1980, efforts have been directed on the part of this corporation toward the attraction of those classes of business that have been historically most profit-making. In addition, concentration has been effected in the area of attracting business in geographic environs which present the greatest profit opportunities. In addition, steps have been continued to be taken to achieve a better balance between liability and holdings. The corporate profits have therefore been maintained at a level commensurate with the previous year.

For each word or expression on the following list, find a synonym that incorporates neither *man* nor *boy*. Select no more than two *person* words. Use your thesaurus as needed:

4. con man_____

5. fireman_____

6. hangman_____

7. chessman_____

8. "Man, oh man!"_____

9. cowboy_____

10. batboy_____

11. water boy_____

12. man about town_____

13. watchman_____

14. mankind_____

15. manly_____

16. A man's home is his castle._____

NOTES: CHAPTER 4

1. Arturo F. Gonzalez, Jr., "London's Got the Sheiks," *Signature*, February, 1977, p. 26.

2. Leonard Gross, "How to Pick Your Ideal City," *New West*, December 5, 1977, p. 38.

3. John Mack Carter, "Editor's Notebook," *Good Housekeeping*, August, 1978, p. 4.

4. Joseph S. Coyle, "Job Meccas for the '80s," *Money*, May, 1978, p. 41.

5. "Brassai: Secret Paris of the 1930's," *Camera*, March, 1979, p. 60.

6. Carol Kahn, "An Interview with Margaret Mead," *Family Health*, October, 1978, p. 48.

7. Peter M. Sandman and Mary Paden, "At Three Mile Island," *Columbia Journalism Review*, July–August, 1979, p. 47.

8. Lewis H. Lapham, "Guests of the Management," *Harper's*, July, 1979, p. 7.

9. W. H. Auden and Louis Kronenberger, *The Faber Book of Aphorisms* (London: Faber & Faber, 1962), p. 288.

10. Richard Seltzer, "Rooms Without Windows," *Harper's*, August, 1979, p. 15. (Typographical error corrected.)

11. "Toward More Picturesque Speech," *Reader's Digest*, October, 1979, p. 182.

12. Tamar Lewin, "Again?" *TWA Ambassador*, June 1979, p. 63.

13. David W. Ewing, "Canning Directions," *Harper's*, August, 1979, p. 16.

14. Norman E. Isaacson, "Pulitzers: A Staunch Defender Calls for Change," *Columbia Journalism Review*, July–August, 1979, p. 16.

15. Brooks Atkinson (ed.), *Walden and Other Writings of Henry David Thoreau* (New York: Modern Library, 1950), p. 63.

16. Ibid., p. 20.

17. Ibid., p. 29.

18. Ibid., p. 289.

19. Jack Richardson, "Life On the Card," *Harper's*, July 1979, p. 24.

20. Jimmy Breslin, "The USA *vs.* John T. Moran," *New Times*, December 28, 1973, p. 32.

21. John Simon, "Stop Compromise Now!" *Esquire*, November, 1979, p. 129.

22. Jimmy Breslin, *New Times*, December 28, 1973, p. 32.

23. Franklynn Peterson and Judi R. Kesselman, "Your Immunity to Cancer," *Science Digest*, May 1978, pp. 48–49.

24. Controller General of U.S., *Why Are New House Prices So High . . . ?* May 11, 1978, p. 9.

25. Sidonie Matsner Gruenberg, "Parent Education," *The Annals of the American Academy of Political and Social Science*, November, 1940, p. 87.

26. Lydia J. Roberts, "Status of Nutrition Work with Children," *ibid.*, p. 119.

27. Robert M. Jones, "Teamwork, Planning Keys to Success," *Hospitals*, July 16, 1979, p. 252.

28. C. Colburn Hardy, "Tax Loss Strategies That Can Pay Off," *Physician's Management*, December, 1978, p. 17.

CHAPTER 5
SENTENCE STRUCTURE
HAS MEANING TOO

*It takes less time to learn how
to write nobly than how to
write lightly and straightforwardly.*
Friedrich Nietzsche

To communicate with readers, you must organize your ideas into quickly recognizable units. As we have seen, sentences are those units. We have also seen that it is possible to communicate effectively to readers using only strong, simple words in strong, simple sentences. If you've ever watched a three-year-old make her needs known, you'll agree that there are few simple ideas that can't be communicated that way.

Why, then, doesn't our language confine itself to these easy-to-make, easy-to-follow patterns of simple subject + simple verb + simple object? Because *life* isn't simple. Simple sentences are adequate for simple ideas. Long chains of simple sentences express a small degree of complexity, and children use them that way. But these sentence chains don't relate the ideas to one another. To report with the realism and sophistication that adult readers demand, you must show complex ideas and explain quickly and concisely how they relate to one another. For this, you must use other kinds of sentences.

This chapter does not offer a complete discussion of sentence structure. In the first place, there are entire books devoted to that subject alone, and we think even *they* don't cover the topic definitively. More important, you don't need a detailed understanding of sentence structure in order to write well. Your instincts ought to be your guide as you grapple with the problems of communicating your ideas and their relationships. What follows is a brush-up course for your instincts.

5.1 WHAT SENTENCE STRUCTURE SAYS TO READERS.

The wealth of information that can be passed from writer to reader just by adroit use of sentence structure is rarely discussed by grammar teachers. There are many ways to build a sentence, and writers should become adept at using all the ways for three basic reasons:

1. We help keep readers interested when we vary the structure from one sentence to another.

2. We share our assessment of the relationship of our ideas through the way we organize them into sentences.

3. We call readers' attention to particular ideas, without having to add extra words, when we choose one or another kind of structure as a shorthand.

We achieve all three purposes simultaneously, as a rule, when we make a deliberate effort to communicate effectively. Look, for example, at the rich variety of sentences in this small passage by Lewis Thomas:

> More likely, language is simply alive, like an organism. We tell each other this, in fact, when we speak of living languages, and I think we mean something more than an abstract metaphor. We mean alive. Words are the cells of language, moving the great body, on legs.[1]

Read this excerpt aloud, and see if anything jumps out at you. Thomas used several kinds of complicated sentence structures to express his ideas and their relationships. But to single out one idea from all the others, and at the same time to admit that he personally regarded this one idea most highly, he deliberately injected a three-word sentence to say it. Unconsciously, if not consciously, he was aware of all three reasons for varying sentence structure.

To show what happens when we don't vary the structure of our sentences, we've rewritten a paragraph from Dee Brown's *Bury My Heart at Wounded Knee*:

> There were white men from the United States. They talked much of peace. They rarely practiced peace. There were other white men from Mexico. The white men from Mexico had conquered the Indians there. Both groups were marching to war. The war with Mexico ended in 1847. The United States took possession of vast territory. The territory stretched from Texas to California.

The above paragraph certainly doesn't want for information. But there's no doubt that it's dull writing. Look what happens when a good writer varies his sentence structure, adding signposts that not only join his ideas but tell how they relate to one another, and which ones he wants to emphasize. Here's how Brown wrote the same thoughts:

> The white men of the United States—who talked so much of peace but rarely seemed to practice it—were marching to war with the white men who had conquered the Indians of Mexico. When the war with Mexico ended in 1847, the United States took possession of a vast expanse of territory reaching from Texas to California.[2]

EXERCISES:

The following, from books for children, use almost nothing but the simplest sentence structure. With only the information contained in each passage, rewrite the sentences so that they sound like they were written for an adult.

1. The sled hit a bump.
   Bob and Ben fell from the sled.
   The little sled did not stop.
   It ran on and on.
   It ran into a red barn.
   The barn bent the little sled.
   And the sled dented the barn.
   Bob and Ben got wet.[3]

2. Every day we see and hear a great deal of advertising. The words and pictures on our box of breakfast cereal are advertising. Our carton of milk usually has advertising on it. The commercial we hear on radio and both see and hear on television is also advertising. So are most of the circulars our mailman brings.

   Newspapers are full of advertising. Some advertisements are tiny want ads. Others fill several pages. Sometimes what seems to be a comic strip may turn out to be advertising. Magazines, too, carry advertisements.[4]

5.2 FANCY TRICKS WITH SIMPLE SENTENCES.

We explained in the last chapter that the most direct way to say something is with subject + verb + object. But now we've added another thought: that the good writer may have a more urgent goal in mind than directness. In that case, even a simple sentence can be restructured. The choice of structure depends on the goal. Some common goals are to question, to deny, to shift attention, and to insist.

To question:

Question words such as *why, where, who, what, when,* and *how,* signal readers that information is being requested:

> When was the book stolen?

But writers can also draft questioning sentences by turning around the subject and the verb (or part of the verb phrase):

> Was the book stolen?

Skilled writers like Harry Golden set readers thinking with *rhetorical* questions, ones that they feel have no easy answers or need no quick response:

> How can you tie knots in a necktie that costs fifteen dollars? I am saving them for a special purpose.[5]

To deny:

Our denial tools are the negative words, words like *no, not,* and *never.* Used assertively, they don't add much complexity to the sentence's meaning:

> I didn't believe it.

But added to rhetorical questions, simple negatives tend to involve readers more strongly in the writer's train of thought:

> Isn't that what he said the last time he ran for office?

> Why not use the same string-cutter principle for lawn-mowing?[6]

To shift attention:

In the last chapter, we warned that poor writers overuse passive verbs. However, applied in moderation, the passive voice is valuable in two instances: to call attention to the subject of your sentence, and to remove an unimportant subject altogether.

The passive voice slows down readers, and when they're slowed down they pay more attention to subtle shifts in emphasis.

Most of the time the object is last, and that's what the reader remembers:

Paul stole the book.

But a shift to passive focuses attention on the subject:

The book was stolen by Paul.

And removing the subject, after changing the verb to its passive form, focuses attention on the action:

The book was stolen.

A child has to stamp her feet to emphasize her words. A careless writer has to underline passages that require emphasis. A skilled writer seldom underlines for emphasis, because he has learned to use sentence structure to make his readers notice the important words.

To insist:

If you think your readers may doubt your statement, you can structure your sentence to show that you insist you're right. One way is to precede your verb with a form of *to do*:

Marie Curie did perform the experiment.

Many writers try to get the same insistence into their writing with the verb *to be*:

Existentialism is answering today's needs.

Unfortunately this can also be read as simply showing continuing action; avoid this usage if you want to show strong insistence.

In formal writing it is possible to achieve control over where your sentence's emphasis lies by inserting one or two pronouns, sometimes in combination with inversion, sometimes in combination with a form of *to be*:

It **was** Paul **who** stole the book.

It **is** existentialism **that** answers today's needs.

The **one who** stole the book was Paul.

The philosophy **that** answers today's needs **is** existentialism.

Writers in too big a hurry seldom pause to put their thoughts into one of these naturally emphatic forms. Instead they reach for the ! keys on their typewriters.

Paul stole the book!

Does the writer want you to be surprised that it was Paul, or that he stole, or that what he stole was a book? Exclamation points are usually that ambiguous.

5.3 COORDINATE SENTENCES.

What traditional grammars call *compound sentences* we've elected to call coordinate sentences. Like the coordinates of a mathematical graph, they are *related* units *of equal importance*, and the writer joins them in a sentence the way the related and equally important coordinates of a graph are joined to form a point.

For the writer, the coordinate sentence is a shortcut: its sentence structure signals to readers the fact that the ideas are of about equal importance and in some way related. The word *and* is the most common signal for coordination, as shown in this example by Isaac Asimov:

It is not easy to study the enzyme molecule directly. There are too few of them and too many other molecules mixed with them.[7]

When a child first discovers that she'll get more attention from her listeners if she varies her sentences, she is usually too young to judge which ideas are the most important, or which ideas relate directly to each other. Consequently, her first experiments with coordinate sentences look like this:

> I went to the candy store and I saw Johnny and he gave me a penny and I spent it and I bought candy and it tasted good.

With some maturity, she recognizes that the five ideas don't fit gracefully into that one sentence. There is too much information all at once; the reader needs to be fed data in bits and pieces to be able to digest it thoroughly. Here is one way she might rewrite the above sentence:

> I went to the candy store so I saw Johnny. He gave me a penny but I spent it. I bought candy; it tasted good.

Here is another way:

> I went to the candy store, saw Johnny, and he gave me a penny. I spent it so I could buy candy, and it tasted good.

Notice that the two rewrites establish different relationships between the ideas. The writer shows the reader the relationship between cordinate ideas in two ways: in the *context* in which the sentence is used, and in the author's choice of *conjunctions* to link the coordinate ideas.

Let's look at three of the most common uses of coordination: (a) to express a simple, balanced relationship; (b) to express sequence; and (c) to express comparison.

5.4 SIMPLE COORDINATION: TO EXPRESS A BALANCED RELATIONSHIP.

The simplest coordination of two (or more) ideas in one sentence merely expresses the fact that the ideas are related and of equal importance. Balanced coordination is signaled by the *semicolon*, or by using a word such as one of the following: *and, but, for, or, yet, so, nor.* The two rewrites in the preceding section are examples of simple coordination. So is the previously excerpted sentence by Asimov:

> There are two few of them and too many other molecules mixed with them.

That sentence is made up of two complete and separate thoughts:

> There are two few of them.
> There are too many other molecules mixed with them.

To create one sentence, he added the two thoughts together, skillfully and almost without thought:

> There are too few of them and (equally important) there are too many other molecules mixed with them.

He eliminated *there are* because it had become redundant. And by coordinating the sentences, he added something to them—the fact that he considered both facts *equally important.*

When choosing the coordinate sentence, the writer has to be sure that he wants readers to infer the balanced interdependent relationship signaled by that structure. Here are two sentences, each of which stands grammatically on its own:

> We are a nation that worships the frontier tradition.
> Our heroes are those who champion justice through violent retaliation against injustice.

Now read the way the Reverend Dr. Martin Luther King, Jr., combined those sentences:

> We are a nation that worships the frontier tradition, and our heroes are those who champion justice through violent retaliation against injustice.[8]

Dr. King was striving to make a strong point as strongly as possible. He wanted readers to understand that he definitely linked together these two thoughts in his mind and gave each of them approximately the same weight. He made his point with the simple insertion of the one word *and* to coordinate the two messages.

Even in coordinate sentences, you should usually put your topic near the very beginning and your most important or most surprising information near the very end of the final coordinate element. That's how King organized his thoughts, and how Asimov did, too, in his coordinate sentence about molecules. Look back at both sentences to see if, upon first reading, you instinctively recognized each author's primary concern.

Old grammars taught students always to separate with commas the two or more elements in coordinate sentences. That rule is being relaxed now, especially if *and* or *or* is the coordinate flag word and the meaning is clear without commas. Some writers now omit commas before *but* as well. Our two guidelines for commas are: (a) Is the meaning clear without the comma? (b) Do I want to slow down the reader's eye with a comma, or let it speed quickly into the next part of the coordinate sentence?

5.5 COORDINATION IN SEQUENCE.

The previous section demonstrated that sentences can be joined to show balanced relationships. Another way of joining two or more equal sentences adds another element to the relationship, that of sequence. The flag words that signal sequential coordination include *however, therefore, moreover, nevertheless, consequently*, and *furthermore*. The grammar texts that call this kind of sentence organization *conjunction* refer to these words as *conjunctive adverbs*.

Sequential coordination is useful to show a time change or a logical progression in the ideas you are joining. Here is an example in which Noam Chomsky joins two ideas in one sentence with the flag word *moreover*:

In mentioning such possibilities, we must take note of the widespread view that modern investigators have not only conclusively refuted the principles of traditional universal grammar but have, moreover, shown that the search for such principles was ill-conceived from the start.[9]

Many writers avoid formal sequential coordination in which a comma generally ends the first clause and a coordinating flag word begins the second. They prefer to end the first thought with a period or semicolon, but still include a coordinating flag word in the next sentence to show its relationship to the first. Kaj Johansen used that construction in this example:

> For example, there has never been a documented coronary death of a person who has completed a marathon race; further, heart-attack victims in exercise rehabilitation programs in Honolulu and Toronto have a vastly lower incidence of repeated coronaries.[10]

If we make separate sentences of two clauses that can be coordinated into one, the flag words that show sequential coordination needn't begin the second thought, but can be moved to emphasize its different parts:

> Though Seattle seems more humane . . .
> Seattle, though, seems more humane . . .
> Seattle seems more humane, though . . .

Therefore, for writers, they are doubly useful tools, as Raymond Mungo's example here shows:

> Any city has its derelict and poverty-stricken population. Seattle, though, seems more humane toward it than many other places.[11]

5.6 COORDINATION
BY COMPARISON.

One other way to join two separate but equal sentences is by comparing them: using -er than or as . . . as. You may never have regarded this format as coordination because, when you employ it, the second sentence includes so many parts that become re-

dundant—and are therefore left out in combining the two ideas—
it rarely resembles a complete sentence in its combined form:

> As the wind came down shrieking from the sea, the
> mists fled before it across the barrens, but the snow
> clouds were thicker and whiter than the mists had
> been.[12]

To put together the last part of the above sentence, Rachel Carson
did combine two separate and equal thoughts:

The mists had been thick and white.

The snow clouds were more thick and white.

But it's unlikely that she was thinking, at the time, "I'm writing
a coordinating sentence."

When you can combine coordination within coordination
and tack on subordination, all without thinking—the way Ms.
Carson did—nobody will bother to ask you for the names of your
devices.

EXERCISES:

1. Rewrite the following so that each exercise is a single, smooth
sentence. Use coordination.

> a. Mr. Jackson went downtown. When he was down-
> town, Mr. Jackson left his car at the municipal parking
> lot. From the parking lot, Mr. Jackson walked to
> Woolworth's. He bought a package of gum there.
> After that, Mr. Jackson walked back to his car. Then
> he drove home.
> b. The professor listed twenty-seven reasons for the
> eventual decline of democracy. After that he listed
> eighteen reasons why anarchy would follow the decline
> of democracy. He concluded with a warning that, if
> he is right, the world will come to an end by 1997.
> c. Harriet received passing grades in her freshman
> year. Ezra did even better than Harriet in his freshman
> year. As a freshman, John got higher marks than any-
> body else.

2. Using information about some hobby or pastime you understand, write a short paragraph that incorporates all three kinds of coordinated sentences discussed in Sections 5.4, 5.5, and 5.6.

3. In a book or magazine, find a sentence that includes at least two kinds of coordination.

4. Using information you already know, write your own sentence in which you include one coordinated statement within other coordinated elements.

5.7 SUBORDINATE IDEAS.

What we call the *subordinate sentence*, many grammars call the *complex sentence*. We'd like you to ignore that term for now, because these sentences are complex only in the sense that they do several things at once. Many grammars spend more space explaining what they look like from an outsider's perspective than writers (on the inside) really need to know. Subordinate sentences aren't at all complex to use.

The subordinate sentence relates and interprets several major and minor ideas simultaneously. It takes many pieces of information, expresses them as clauses instead of as complete sentences, and assembles them into one sentence rich with information and interpretation. Most adults speak easily and naturally in subordinate sentences most of the time. When you are thoroughly informed about the topic of your writing, you, too, will automatically choose them to express your own rich knowledge.

Perhaps we can illustrate how commonplace subordinate sentences are in our language by listing some of the more popular connectors that flag this sentence structure. They are words that show:

1. **relationship**
    who, what, which, that . . .
2. **reason**
    because, since, for, so that, why, in order that . . .

3. condition

if, unless, even though, whether, as, as if, although . . .

4. time

when, then, while, till, after, as long as, before . . .

5. place

where, wherever, whereon . . .

Every subordinate sentence is built on the backbone of an idea that can stand alone. It is called the *independent* clause. All the other information, like ribs or leg bones, attaches by way of *dependent* clauses, sometimes known as *subordinate clauses*. Transformational grammars refer to the process of depositing information into subordinate clauses as *embedding*, and it's an apt term for the way our minds stick in these extra ideas.

Ernest Hemingway begins and ends the following sentence with subordinate clauses (notice his use of commas):

> If you are lucky enough to have lived in Paris as a young man, then wherever you go for the rest of your life, it stays with you, for Paris is a moveable feast.[13]

Did you spot the main clause in the sentence? It is *it stays with you.*

Do not let the grammatical terms *independent* and *subordinate* mislead you. The independent clause does not have to go at the beginning; it can go anywhere in the sentence, as the preceding excerpt shows. And a subordinate clause is only *grammatically* subordinate. Writers often put into their independent clauses the information that is most familiar to readers; then, into their subordinate clauses they fit the less familiar, new, shocking, or most vital facts. Thus subordinate clauses may not *limit* the statement in the main clause, but expand it instead.

Here's how Jean Burden expanded the old-familiar with a subordinate clause:

> Many years ago a black and white cat named Gypsy achieved a certain notoriety because he could tell time.[14]

Ms. Burden put her independent clause at the beginning of the sentence not because that's where it belonged, but because it permitted her to save her shocker for the punch line. The previous sentence by Hemingway was also constructed quite deliberately to save the strongest image—*a moveable feast*—for the end.

The following example by Rachel Carson contains several subordinate clauses:

> The summer before, when the pollock had been a yearling, the launce had appeared to him the most fearful fish in the sea as they followed and harried the pollock fry, singling out their victims and falling upon them with the ferocity of a pike.[15]

Whether they expand the meaning or limit it, subordinate clauses do *modify* certain aspects of the main clause. Readers should never have to guess which of your ideas is being modified by which subordinate clause. It is wise to play safe and keep the clauses as close as possible to the words they modify, unless you are certain that there is no doubt about your meaning.

As with other kinds of sentences, your writing here is more easily read if you let readers know the topic of your sentence near its beginning, even if a dependent clause comes first. Notice that Hemingway put *Paris* in his first dependent clause, and that Carson put *the launce* up as close to the beginning as she could (even though the first dependent clause modifies *to him*, not *the launce*). Some fledgling writers forget that even a lengthy subordinate sentence needs *one* cohesive topic, and that all the components of the sentence must be in some way related. The purpose of sentence structure, after all, is not only to share bits of information, but also to show how the bits relate to each other. If they are not related, they belong in separate sentences. If you do see a relationship among them, the right subordinating flag word will quickly and smoothly share that relationship with readers.

There is no limit, short of your imagination and your grasp of correct grammar, to how many subordinate clauses you can work into a single sentence. In fact, you can subordinate one clause to another clause that is already subordinate to the independent clause, as Ron Rosenbaum does here:

> I never found out for whom or what the reception was,
> nor why Roffman was invited, although he does seem
> to have a number of Yugoslav clients, including a guy
> who wants to market a line of Balkan frozen foods.[16]

But, like Rosenbaum, like Hemingway, like Carson and Burden, save your most dramatic revelations—whether independent, subordinate, or coordinate—for the end. It'll keep readers intrigued enough to keep reading on.

The only punctuation needed to separate clauses in subordinate sentences is the comma, and that should be used as sparingly as possible. You do not need a comma in addition to a subordinating flag word if your sentence's meaning is clear without one. We've found that the easiest way to test whether a comma is necessary is to let your ear be your guide. Read the sentence in question aloud or silently, and notice whether you deliberately pause in front of a subordinating flag word. If you do, you should have a comma there.

Most of our previous examples needed commas. But here's one by Hemingway that has two subordinate clauses and no commas. In place of one comma, he puts the more formal *then*. (If he had put commas before *because* and *then*, the sentence's meaning would be slightly different.)

> If a writer omits something because he does not know
> it then there is a hole in the story.[17]

EXERCISES:

1. In books or magazines, locate five sentences that use subordination. Write them down. In each, underline the independent clause. Circle each subordinating flag. If there is also a coordinate element in any of your selected sentences, identify it by drawing a square around the coordinating flag word.

2. Write a sentence that uses at least two subordinating elements and two coordinating elements.

5.8 SENTENCE FRAGMENTS.

The sentence fragment is incorrect only if it confuses the reader. If your meaning is perfectly clear, a fragment has a lot of power. Like a dissonant chord used amongst a series of perfect triads, it jars the inner ear. So it should be used only infrequently and for the specific purpose of making the reader sit up and take notice, as Saul Bellow does here:

> And so we are told by critics that the novel is dead. These people can't know what the imagination is or what its powers are. I wish I could believe in their good-natured objectivity. But I can't. I should like to disregard them, but that is a little difficult because they have a great deal of power. Not real power, perhaps, but power of a sort. And they can be very distracting.[18]

5.9 RUN-ON SENTENCES.

In earlier grades you've been taught *never* to use run-on sentences. That's a good rule for a beginning writer. However, as you become more adept at employing sentence variety to improve your writing, there will be rare times when the only way to make your point is with a skillful run-on.

The reason a run-on is almost never effective is that the reader loses track of your ideas unless you put in the punctuation guideposts that tell him which are the important thoughts and which the minor ones. However, sometimes the very thing the writer wants is to make the reader chase him, breathless, down an endless tunnel of information:

And then they would all set about cutting them into strips and putting them out to dry, it took days, and then grinding them up into powder and packing them into gelatin capsules or boiling it down to a gum and putting it in the capsules or just making a horrible goddamned broth that was so foul, so unbelievably vile, you had to chill it numb to try to kill the taste and fast for a day so you wouldn't have anything on your stomach, just to keep eight ounces of it down. But then—*soar*.[19]

Notice how Tom Wolfe effectively juxtaposed a run-on and a fragment to make his readers not just picture, but actually feel the rush and the punch. Observe how he placed commas to free the reader to collect the special information he felt was important in the sentence.

As Wolfe and Bellow show in these excerpted nonfiction passages, all the rules that teachers hand would-be writers are rules meant to be broken as long as communication continues beyond the break. Instead of thinking of them as rules, consider them guidelines handed down from writers experienced in the craft of influencing readers' minds, to writers just learning the craft.

NOTES: CHAPTER 5

1. Lewis Thomas, *The Lives of a Cell* (New York: Bantam, 1975), p. 158.

2. Dee Brown, *Bury My Heart at Wounded Knee* (New York: Bantam, 1972), p. 8.

3. Glenn McCracken and Charles C. Walcutt, *Lippincott's Basic Reading* (Philadelphia: Lippincott, 1963), p. 36.

4. Bertha Morris Parker, *The Golden Book Encyclopedia* (New York: Golden Press, 1969), vol. I, p. 8.

5. Harry Golden, *Only in America* (New York: World Publishing, 1958), p. 159.

6. E. F. Lindsley, "'79 Mowers," *Popular Science*, May, 1979, p. 79.

7. Isaac Asimov, *The Chemicals of Life* (New York: Signet, 1954), p. 34.

8. Martin Luther King, Jr., *Why We Can't Wait* (New York: Signet, 1964), p. 37.

9. Noam Chomsky, *Language and Mind*, enlarged edition (New York: Harcourt Brace Jovanovich, 1972), p. 157.

10. Kaj Johansen, "Running on a Health Ticket," *Playboy*, November, 1976, p. 249.

11. Raymond Mungo, "Blissed-Out in Seattle," *Mother Jones*, November, 1978, p. 32.

12. Rachel Carson, *Under the Sea Wind* (New York: Signet Science Library, 1955), p. 29.

13. Ernest Hemingway, *A Moveable Feast* (New York: Scribner's, 1964), title page.

14. Jean Burden, "Cats and ESP," *Woman's Day*, February, 1977, p. 2.

15. Rachel Carson, *Under the Sea Wind*, p. 74.

16. Ron Rosenbaum, "Richard Roffman and His Unknown Famous People," *New York*, December 10, 1979, p. 102.

17. John Bartlett, *Bartlett's Familiar Quotations* (Boston: Little, Brown, 1968), p. 1045.

18. Saul Bellow, "Distractions of a Fiction Writer," *New World Writing, Number 12* (New York: Mentor, 1957), p. 233.

19. Tom Wolfe, *The Electric Kool-Aid Acid Test* (New York: Farrar, Straus, and Giroux, 1968), p. 48.

CHAPTER 6
CREATIVE PUNCTUATION

*A fluent writer always seems
more talented than he is.*
Joseph Joubert

Punctuation in writing does the same job your voice levels and pauses do in speaking: it signals inflections as well as pauses in thought. If you say your sentences in your head when you write, you should get your punctuation correct nearly all the time. For guidance—or reassurance—here is a list of the major punctuation marks and how they compare to spoken equivalents. Although the period and the question mark are rarely misused, let's begin with them for comparison.

6.1 PUNCTUATING BY EAR.

● Period
The voice pitch and volume fall, then stop on a conclusive note to signal that a complete thought or series of related ideas has ended.

- Question mark

The voice pitch and volume rise, then stop as long as for a period.

- Comma

The voice pauses without its pitch or volume falling noticeably, to signal that one idea segment within a sentence has ended and another one is beginning. The key determiner of when a comma is required is clarity. If your meaning is unquestionably clear without the pause—or comma—then the comma probably is not required; an uninterrupted flow of ideas makes reading faster. But clarity must never be sacrificed to speed.

Listen to your voice as you say the following sentence:

> At any rate almost immediately the bottom fell out of
> both her world and his.[1]

In the above example, many writers would have inserted a comma after *at any rate*, but Leonard Woolf chose not to. He speeded up the flow of his sentence without sacrificing clarity. In the example below he saw a need for commas to avoid confusion, during quick reading, about whether the voice was to pause after *cheques, warrants,* or *arrest:*

> He had been swindling people up and down the country
> with dishonoured cheques, and warrants for his arrest
> were issued in Kandy, Nuwara Eliya, and Colombo.[2]

The previous chapter more thoroughly discussed comma usage in coordinate and subordinate sentence structures. Refer to it if you have problems with those specific uses.

- Colon

The voice stops abruptly, but with emphasis that shows that an elaboration of the just-completed idea will follow immediately. Listen to how your voice signals *colon* in the following sentences, the first by Manuel J. Smith and the second by Alice Lake:

> In most cases, the coworker is not malignant in intent
> but just someone who wants something you have and

really doesn't give a damn how you feel: a conflict where most learners have no difficulty in refusing to give reasons to justify or explain their behavior to the other person.[3]

They appear relatively unconcerned about it, recalling a famous showgirl's remark: "I have everything now that I had 20 years ago except it's all lower."[4]

● Dashes

The voice pauses at the first dash, emphasizes slightly the material set between dashes, and resumes its former tone after the second dash, showing that another thought is interrupting the sentence's normal flow of thoughts. When the emphasized material ends the sentence, only the first dash is required; a period ends the emphasized portion and the entire sentence with one stroke. As with all other forms of emphasis, when it's overused the dash loses its impact.

Beginning writers often confuse dashes, commas, and parentheses. Actually, years ago dashes were little used, and parentheses were preferred to commas (that's why those small elaborations or asides writers put between commas are still referred to in many grammars as parenthetical phrases). Our modern system is a refinement in reader-signals. Set between dashes, the interrupting idea is flagged by the author as important. Set between commas, it is shown to be neither more nor less important than its neighbors. The parentheses (see below) are for unimportant asides.

Another mistake novices make is to use the dash where a colon is the better choice. Keep in mind that the dash signals an emphasized aside, whereas a colon signals a to-the-point elaboration.

Listen to your voice as you say the following sentences by Willard Uphaus and James Nathan Miller:

I sat on the metal cot—there was no chair—and stared around my cell by the light of a single electric bulb high on the back wall.[5]

Along Montana's Rocky Mountain spine, the picture-book part of the state is now enjoying its biggest boom since mining days—and it has some people worried.[6]

Some writers use a great many dashes in their writing. This usually signals to the reader either that the writer has not organized his thoughts into logical units, or that he has not taken the time to decide what should or should not be emphasized. If lots of dashes creep into your writing, it's a signal to stop and decide whether all the asides are really important and, if so, whether they ought to be elaborated on separately.

In order to avoid confusion between *hyphens*, which join compound words, and *dashes*, which separate ideas, writers must use the physical style that readers have come to expect. Type a hyphen by hitting the - key only once, and do not space before or after it. Type a dash by first hitting the space key, then the - key twice (--) and the space key once more. In writing by hand, make your hyphen short and keep the joined words very close together; make your dash a longer mark, with space at both sides of it.

● Parentheses
The voice pauses, then de-emphasizes the information set between parentheses. This punctuation device is supposed to clarify a thought without shifting the reader's attention to the clarification. It isn't as effective as most of our punctuation marks because it slows down the eye, often creating the emphasis it's trying to avoid. That's why it's a good idea to resist using parentheses unless they're absolutely needed. Listen to how your voice shows where the parentheses fall in these examples by Robert and Peggy Stinson and by Manuel J. Smith:

He was admitted to the Pediatric Hospital Center (PHC) weighing 600 grams (1 lb. 5 oz.) on December 24, was placed on a respirator . . .[7]

Arnold found out in this interaction that the much heralded obstinacy of repair mechanics and garage managers is a myth (probably artificially cultured and promoted by the nonassertiveness of many of their customers).[8]

● Underline

The voice emphasizes the word or words underlined. Careful writers pick words and sentence constructions that emphasize naturally, and use underlining only as a last resort. Careless writers make it a crutch, attempting with it to impart drama to a particular point that otherwise falls flat.

> Careful writers pick words and sentences that naturally emphasize. Underlining is used only as a last resort by careful writers.

> Translation: Careful writers pick words and sentence constructions that emphasize naturally, and use underlining only as a last resort.

The underline rarely appears in print; when the typesetter sees it, he substitutes italics.

● Exclamation point

The exclamation point attempts to instill drama in an entire sentence. But like a Broadway show, if the production itself isn't dramatic no amount of flashing marquee lights can convince showgoers that it is. In English (unlike Spanish) the exclamation point appears only after your verbal play is done. If the sentence is dramatic, the reminder is redundant. Save exclamation points for true exclamations—the short bursts of sentence fragments that share strong feelings with readers, as in this example by John Vinocur:

> "Peace!" he cried. "Only peace!"
> And the great throng answered him with thousands repeating the word: "Peace!"[9]

● Quotation marks

Voice inflections, pauses, and the subtle mimicry that, in speaking, signal that you have duplicated somebody else's words, are conveyed on paper with quotation marks. That's why the *he said* and *she said* of speaking can often be omitted in writing. (In Chapter 10 we'll suggest guidelines for using other people's words in your papers.)

Sometimes quotation marks are used by writers to disown words: to show the reader that the writer knows they're slang, or are used unconventionally, or express ideas with which the writer doesn't agree. Readers faced with this use of quotes seldom know why the word or phrase is being disowned, and the attention-getting device generally ends up looking sophomoric. (Some people have taken to using quotation signs in speaking: they hold up their fingers in mimicry of two quotation marks to show disavowal. It falls as flat in speech as it usually does in writing.) A careful writer takes the space to show not just her disdain, but the reason for it. If the reason is unimportant, she doesn't make an issue of the difference in opinion. In the following two examples the author uses quotation marks that we consider superfluous:

> The eternal stillness outside my door formed a barrier protecting my soul. I could "hear myself think."

> The city is so "small" that we see the same faces, the same friends, day in and day out.

In the first example, the author is signaling to the reader that he knows *hear myself think* is a cliché. Why do you think he feels that obligation? In the second example, he is signaling that he doesn't really mean *small* in the usual sense of the word. What he may have meant to write—and should have taken the time to write—is this:

> City dwellers move so habitually in the same circles that we see the same faces, the same friends, day in and day out.

6.2 OTHER PUNCTUATION MARKS.

There are several forms of punctuation that occur in writing but don't have counterparts in oral communication. The following three add sophistication to the expression of ideas, and are therefore worth including in the writer's repertoire. It is important to keep in mind that punctuation is a convenience to the reader, not the writer (who usually knows already how his sentences should be read). Like all the rules of grammar, rules of punctuation can be broken if there is a better way to convey your message accurately, precisely, and concisely.

● Semicolon

The semicolon is usually used as a weakened period. It joins two sentences, each of which is grammatically complete. But it signals that the ideas are so closely aligned that, for maximum clarity, the two sentences ought to be read as one, as in this example by Richard Langer:

> I have experimented with some mitecides, in desperation over a particular mango tree I simply could not bear to dispose of; however, I have found them ineffective in the long run.[10]

On occasion, writers use the semicolon as a supercomma. In a string of coordinated thoughts, commas ordinarily separate the individual thoughts. But if one or more of the thoughts itself has to contain a comma for clear meaning, the reader may become confused about what's coordinate and what's subordinate. In such cases, most writers employ semicolons to signal the wider separations between thoughts. Here is an example by Ronald Schiller:

> They most frequently strike in three areas: where ocean plates are thrusting under land plates, as is happening

along the coasts of Alaska and Central and South America, and the island arcs of Japan, Indonesia and the Caribbean; where the plates are grinding past each other, as in California and Turkey; and where continents are running into each other, as in China, Iran, and the countries of the Balkans and eastern Mediterranean, which are slowly crumpling under the pressure exerted by northward-moving India, Arabia and Africa, respectively.[11]

- Ellipsis

A series of three dots signals to readers that you've left out some words. At the end of a sentence, where a period is required, a fourth dot should be added. Some writers use ellipses at the ends of sentences as shorthand for *and so forth*, but that practice is still frowned on by most grammars on our reference shelf. Willard Uphaus uses the ellipsis correctly here:

Lest anyone who reads this think I might exaggerate, let me quote here from a later opinion expressed by Justice of the Supreme Court Brennan. "This investigation . . . on its surface has an overwhelming appearance of a simple, wide-ranging exposure campaign. . . ."[12]

- Brackets

When you want to quote another author's exact words, but don't want to be bound by just those words, brackets provide an effective escape from the quandary. If, for instance, all you need to quote is one sentence, but the sentence is unclear out of context, you can provide the missing information within brackets:

"It [his bungalow] was in a side street, smothered in trees, hot, stuffy, full of mosquitoes and geckos—not a breath of air ever found its way in."[13]

In the above excerpt, we quoted Leonard Woolf's words exactly, adding our own clarification in brackets. In informal writing, authors often omit the word that requires explanation:

"[His bungalow] was in a side street . . ."

We prefer to avoid brackets wherever possible:

His bungalow "was in a side street, smothered . . ."

Brackets are used to insert corrections as well as amplification, as in this fictitious example:

"It was in a side street [actually its front entrance was on the main street], smothered . . ."

To show only that there's an error in the quoted passage, write *sic*, either in brackets or parentheses, in the proper place:

"From our start, our group of writers lay [sic] claim to perfect grammar," said the president.

The use of [sic] implies tongue-clucking disapproval and is used, these days, more to polemicize than to show a love for accuracy. Inserted carelessly or to excess, it may reflect unfavorably on you. It's usually wise to paraphrase quotations that contain wrong information. Then, depending on your purpose, you can either correct the misinformation fully and smoothly, or omit it altogether.

To offer parenthetical information within a sentence that's already set inside parentheses, the bracket doubles as a subparenthesis. Most typewriters do not have bracket keys, but you can make a bracket by typing a slash (/) and two underlines.

EXERCISES:

1. In books or magazines, locate and copy at least two examples of every form of punctuation discussed in this chapter.

2. From the set of sentences found for Exercise 1, choose two that can be improved with either a different form of punctuation or a different sentence structure, and rewrite them.

3. From the same set of sentences, choose two that show excellent use of punctuation, and explain why they do.

4. Find a paper of at least 250 words in length that you wrote for this class or another one, and improve it by paying particular attention to your choices in punctuation, rewriting if necessary. As much as possible, retain the words you used in the original paper.

NOTES: CHAPTER 6

1. Leonard Woolf, *Growing* (New York: Harcourt Brace and World, 1961), p. 131.

2. Ibid., p. 131.

3. Manuel J. Smith, *When I Say No, I Feel Guilty* (New York: Dial Press, 1975), p. 215.

4. Alice Lake, "The Myths of Menopause," *Reader's Digest*, October, 1979, p. 147.

5. Willard Uphaus, *Commitment* (New York: McGraw-Hill, 1963), p. 188.

6. James Nathan Miller, "Cowboys, Copper Kings and Coal: A Montana Montage," *Reader's Digest*, October, 1979, p. 177.

7. Robert and Peggy Stinson, "On the Death of a Baby," *Atlantic*, July, 1979, p. 64.

8. Manuel J. Smith, p. 144.

9. John Vinocur in *The New York Times*, quoted in "Nine Days that Shook the World: The Pope's Return to Poland," *Reader's Digest*, October, 1979, p. 139.

10. Richard Langer, "Plants Around the House," *House and Garden*, September, 1978, p. 32.

11. Ronald Schiller, "Where Will the Next Earthquake Strike," *Reader's Digest*, October, 1979, p. 120.

12. Willard Uphaus, p. 154.

13. Leonard Woolf, p. 64.

CHECKLIST FOR UNIT II: TECHNIQUES FOR IMPROVING SENTENCES

Because sentences are the building blocks of good writing, this unit has devoted more space to them than do most composition books. By now the text, examples, and exercises should have begun to change your reading habits so that you're reading more critically—your own writing as well as that of others. To help you along, the following checklist summarizes all the techniques you've learned so far. Refer to it often.

1. Can you read the paper?
   a. Is it legible?
   b. Are the words spelled correctly?
   c. Is punctuation in line with what you've become accustomed to reading?

2. Can you understand it easily?
   a. Do the words make sense?
   b. If there are some words average readers might not understand, can they figure them out from the context?
   c. Do the sentences make sense?
   d. Do the ideas make sense?

3. Are the right words chosen?
   a. Are they accurate?
   b. Are they precise?
   c. Are they concise?
   d. Are they vivid?

4. Are words chosen from the best level of concreteness or abstraction?
    a. Are there too many abstractions?
    b. When abstract words are used, are they really the best choice, or are more concrete words needed?
    c. Are there any jargon words?
    d. Are there too many clichés or dead metaphors?
    e. Do figures of speech reach too far?

5. Are verbs vivid?
    a. Are active verbs used whenever possible?
    b. Is the passive voice employed only when it's the preferred choice, or is the writer sometimes careless about its use?

6. Is wordiness a problem?
    a. Are words in their simplest form?
    b. Are excess words omitted?
    c. Are there needless redundancies?
    d. Are obvious ideas amplified too fully?
    e. Are some words left out that could have been inserted for clarity?

7. Is every qualifier necessary?
    a. Are there too many adjectives?
    b. Are there too many adverbs?
    c. Are there too many phrases and clauses that needlessly limit or qualify major elements of the sentences?
    d. Could you rearrange or revise some sentences to get rid of excess qualifiers?

8. Are sentences varied in length and construction?
    a. Are short sentences mixed with long ones for dramatic effect?
    b. Do sentences flow smoothly from one to another?

9. Are coordinate sentences used for ideas that are about equal in importance and related to each other?

    a. Are they used only for equal, related ideas?

    b. Are they used for all equal, related ideas?

    c. Can readers see quickly why the ideas are related?

    d. Is the internal order of the ideas arranged logically?

10.   Are subordinate sentences used for ideas that depend on other ideas?

    a. Are they used only for ideas that belong together?

    b. Can readers see quickly why the ideas are related?

    c. Are clauses that rely on each other kept together, and clauses that don't directly relate kept apart?

    d. Is any sentence hard to read because it has too many ideas or clauses?

    e. Does any sentence seem simplistic because there is too little information given?

11.   Are words and ideas positioned carefully so that emphasis falls on the most important ones?

    a. Is the sentence's topic near the beginning?

    b. Is the most important or most dramatic idea near the sentence's end?

    c. Can you improve on placement?

12.   Are the main noun and verb phrase in each sentence in agreement?

    a. Do they agree in subject? In tense? In voice? In viewpoint? In number?

    b. Is there agreement where it's needed even if the noun and verb are widely separated by phrases or clauses?

13.   Is the pace of the sentences comfortable?

    a. Do they seem too slow-moving? Can lengthy sentences be trimmed or taken apart to remedy the problem?

    b. Is the pace so fast as to leave readers breathless? Can choppy sentences be combined to remedy the problem?

14. Is the chosen punctuation the best one possible?
   a. Do commas separate clauses that must be separated for clarity?
   b. Are commas inserted that aren't required for clarity?
   c. Are parenthetical ideas put between commas?
   d. If dashes or parentheses are used, are they necessary?
   e. Are exclamation points and disowning quotation marks overused?

EXERCISES:

1. In Illustration II / 1 we have reproduced a portion of the first draft of a student's paper on discrimination. With your pen, revise the paper using the checklist as a guide. Do not change the order in which sentences occur, shift paragraphs around, or alter the author's meaning. Do improve sentence structure and organization; choose more accurate, precise, vivid, and concise words in line with the purpose of the paper; and replace words that are too abstract with more concrete ones. Where the author's original meaning is obscured by ambiguity, choose your own interpretation for this exercise.

2. In Appendix A we have reproduced our annotated revisions of the paper used in Exercise 1. Compare your revisions to ours, but remember that when it comes to writing there are many different ways to say the same thing correctly. After you've studied our revisions, see if you can improve them.

3. Bring to class a photocopy of a nonfiction paper of about 1,000 words that you wrote for either this course or another one. Be sure the paper is double-spaced and neat, even if it's handwritten, so there's room to edit. Exchange papers with a classmate and, using the do's and don'ts given in Exercise 1, revise the paper and return it. Be prepared to defend all your changes.

   (Note: We are purposely rejecting the practice of teacher-corrected papers. Having taught many writing courses, we've observed firsthand how much more is learned about writing improvement through correcting someone else's writing than through having someone else correct your writing. Approach your task not as criticism, but as objective observation of the writing craft. The more vigorously you dig in and examine another person's technique, and show her how to perfect it, the more quickly you will improve your own writing skills.)

4. On the original of the paper you brought to class for Exercise 3, and again following the list of dos and don'ts from Exercise 1, revise your own paper before seeing your classmate's revision of it. Compare your revisions with his. Rewrite the paper, incorporating your choices for the best of both sets of revisions.

5. Now you're ready to write your own good sentences. On a nonfiction topic, write about a 1,000-word *first draft*. Do not worry unduly about words and sentences; strive to get your ideas down on paper as simply as possible. Do double-space as you write.

As soon as you feel a bit remote from the paper, take it up again and edit it (following the same do's and don'ts of Exercise 1) as thoroughly as you practiced in earlier exercises. Copy your corrected paper, marking it *Second Draft*. Bring both versions of the paper to class either to turn in or to exchange with a classmate.

ILLUSTRATION II/1

What are illegal grounds for discrimination? The grounds will differ with the law, but most laws are based on the Civil Rights Act of 1964, prohibiting discrimination on the basis of race, color, sex, religion, creed or national origin. Other laws cover areas such as age, handicap, sexual preference and even student status. Discrimination can occur in many ways. The following are some of the ways an employee can be adversely affected by employment discrimination: failure of the employer to hire you, failure to promote, discharge, denial of health or medical benefits, sexual harassment, verbal harassment (for example, racial slurs), and retaliation for filing a discrimination complaint.

In the often long and drawn out interim period after you file a complaint and some action is taken, you may forget the details of your complaint, dates, witnesses, etc. A helpful aid to remembering is to immediately start your own file of the incident. Have a list of any important dates involved in the charge. This will help refresh your memory. Documents are also important. Any letters received from your employer, along with progress reports or evaluations of your work, a copy of your employment contract, and letters of correspondence or medical reports from your doctor (if disability or sickness is an issue in your complaint).

You may think that this is a lot more time, work and effort than you bargained for, and well it may be, but if you hope to have the discriminatory act rectified you'll find a way to persist. What is in it for you? You've heard about the huge settlements that large companies have made for discriminating against a group of employees. Such settlements may run in the millions. But what you may not realize is that these mammoth settlements didn't go to one individual or a small group of individuals. Six-figure settlements usually result from class-action suits and the money is sometimes divided up between thousands of class members.

In the majority of cases, the only remedy sought is an individual one. As an individual, you can recover several types of damages. You can recover money in the form of back pay, or personal damages, attorney's fees (usually only recoverable under federal law). Nonmonetary relief can be granted in reinstatement, a promised interview for a job or promotion, or an admission of guilt by the employer. Once again different laws allow for different remedies, and you should check to see whether the remedy you want is available under the law you file under. Having a clear idea of what you want and finding out how such a remedy is available to you will save you frustration and disappointment.

Perhaps one of the most important things to remember when filing a complaint with a government agency is to be patient. Both the EEOC and state-level equal rights agencies suffer from a tremendous backlog of cases to be resolved. This is not because bureaucrats working for equal rights agencies are more inept than those working in other agencies, but is rather the result of constraints beyond the agencies' control. These agencies were given broad mandates to end or eliminate discriminatory practices in society and aid victims of discrimination by providing remedies. Every agency decision is open to question and attack in the courts.

UNIT III

PAPERS: HOW TO MAKE THEM SERVE YOUR PURPOSE

CHAPTER 7
DECIDE WHAT YOU'RE
WRITING ABOUT

*Everything that is written merely to
please the author is worthless.*
Blaise Pascal

Writing a good paper is like dancing: the more you do it, the easier it is to do. Like dancing, it is a collection of steps that, once learned and made habitual, turn awkward effort into graceful performance.

The steps that result in good writing extend way beyond just setting words on paper. They should begin the moment you decide to write something—or a project is assigned to you—and should lead you through the processes of topic organization; research; choice of nonfiction techniques; organization, with transitions, into paragraphs; editing and polishing the first draft; continuing even up to the moment you submit your completed paper. We will discuss each of these processes and the working habits that simplify them, in approximately the order in which writers face them.

Other composition books typically discuss paragraphs as collections of sentences, and papers as collections of paragraphs. But the paragraph is no more than a device, within a paper's organization, for presenting information to readers in easily digested entities. So we've put the paragraph where it belongs, among the writer's other tools that organize information for readers.

There are many terms for the end product of our writing: paper, theme, essay, review, article, report, thesis, assignment, critique. For now we've chosen arbitrarily to include them all in one term, paper, because even for the terms that mean just one special kind of paper, there is essentially just one structure when it comes to the writing. Only the content or purpose varies from one type of paper to another, as we'll point out as we go along.

7.1 KEEP THE PURPOSE OF YOUR WRITING IN MIND.

The big mistake so many writers make as they start work on writing projects, is forgetting to define the exact purpose for writing. Without a sharply focused purpose in mind, they wander off the subject, or include more information about it than the purpose requires, or neglect to cover all its important aspects. To guard against this is easy if you make sure that you know the purpose, or object, in writing—as well as the subject, or topic, of your paper—before you even begin to research. The theme of a paper is not fully stated unless it includes both the subject and the purpose.

Most students know before they reach college that a paper must be about one—and only one—subject. On the surface this seems an easy requirement to fulfill. Everyone knows that you don't include skiing in a paper about the post office, or the sunrise in a paper about the sunset.

However, can you include a discussion of tar content in a paper on cigarette smoking? Or a discussion of running in a paper on jogging shoes? Or data on current postal rates in a paper on the post office? Or information about gold in a paper on double-digit inflation? Or frostbite hazards in a paper on skiing? To judge whether these topics belong, you need to decide on the paper's purpose. Is the first example's purpose to *persuade* against cigarette smoking? Or is it to *report* the history of cigarette smoking? A discussion of tar content probably belongs in the first paper but not in the second.

Let's review the four major purposes of factual writing which, you'll remember from Chapter 2, are also the four ways in which the factual writer offers intellectual benefit to the reader:

1. To *offer directions* on how to do something

2. To *report* whom something happened to, what happened, why it happened, when it happened, where it happened, and how much of it happened

3. To *explain* an idea

4. To *persuade* on behalf of a viewpoint assumed to be at odds with the reader's

Readers generally expect one major purpose in any paper they read (although they are not surprised if they also detect secondary purposes). By focusing on a clear purpose, as well as a sharp topic, you will be helping yourself and your readers stay on the subject.

It is certainly possible to incorporate two or more of these purposes into a single paper. Sophisticated writing often does. Until you reach such a level of sophistication, you and your readers may be better served if you concentrate your energies on meeting one major purpose at a time.

7.2 START WITH A WORKING TITLE.

One of the surest ways to define both your topic and your purpose at the beginning is to choose an appropriate working title. We use the term *working* title because it's the title you ought to stick with while you're working on the paper. After you've written your final draft, you may want to change the title so it says less but is catchier.

Your working title will help keep you on the subject if you make it do three things:

1. It must show the boundaries of the subject.

2. It must tell nothing that is off the subject.

3. It must incorporate the main purpose of your paper.

Let's restate some of the topics mentioned in Section 7.1 as working titles, each of which includes the entire theme, both subject and purpose:

1. The Benefits of Jogging Shoes (implies persuasion)

2. How the Federal Government Divested Itself of the Post Office (reports events)

3. How to Ski (gives directions)

4. The Meaning of Double-Digit Inflation (explains an idea)

Having fully stated these themes, we can now answer the questions we asked earlier:

1. *Will you discuss running in a paper on "The Benefits of Jogging Shoes"?* Yes, you'll have to show how jogging shoes help you run better.

2. *Will you discuss current postal rates in a paper on "How the Federal Government Divested Itself of the Post Office"?* No, it doesn't fit into the expressed purpose.

3. *Will you discuss frostbite in a paper on "How to Ski"?* Probably not. It doesn't belong unless your treatment is broad enough to include not only the mechanics of how to keep both feet under you while you're skiing, but also what to wear when skiing, how to keep from getting hurt, and similar ancillary information. And if that's the case, then you should consider rewording the working title.

4. *Will you discuss gold in a paper on "The Meaning of Double-Digit Inflation"?* If the changing price of gold affects inflation, then *yes*, you will have to include it. But if inflation affects the price of gold, then *no*, you will not include it because your topic is limited to an explanation of double-digit inflation itself, not the impact it has on other facets of the economy. In order to work this other information into your paper, you could change the working title to "The Meaning of Double-Digit Inflation and How it Affects the Rest of the Economy." But then you would be obliged to discuss how double-digit inflation affects not only gold prices but unemployment, foreign trade, taxes, investment capital, and almost everything having to do with the economy. If you are not prepared to research and write such a far-reaching paper, you'd better carefully limit your working title at the outset.

The complete statement of your theme, your working title, is for most purposes also the best final title for your paper. If you learn to state your theme fully so it includes both topic and object, it will be easy to keep extraneous topics from creeping in. Equally valuable, you will make efficient use of your research time, compiling enough information to fully amplify your theme without getting sidetracked by irrelevant facts and figures.

EXERCISES:

1. Read the paper in Illustration 7/1 at the end of this chapter. The student who wrote it had not yet learned the value of laying out his exact topic and purpose in advance and sticking to both of them. Identify at least three possible themes the author had in mind.

2. Using the list of four purposes of writing given earlier in this chapter, find at least two purposes that seemed to guide the author as he wrote the paper. What are they?

3. Explain what the author's shift from one purpose to another did to your understanding and appreciation of his paper.

7.3 HOW TO
GIVE DIRECTIONS.

Leaf through any dozen magazines and you'll soon notice that the most popular type of article by far is the one that gives the reader directions. That's because editors know that readers enjoy learning how to do something, whether it's something as tangible as how to paint a house, or as intangible as how to cope with stress. Editors use this kind of article so universally they've nicknamed it the *how-to*. But its usefulness extends well beyond popular magazines, to lab manuals, medical seminar papers, investment guides, and so forth.

A paper that gives directions divides easily and sensibly into paragraphs, each paragraph concerned with one stage of the process that is being described. In the paper's first paragraph (or several), the writer generally puts the entire subject into perspective and tells the reader what she can expect to learn from the article. Often, before describing each specific step, the writer also generalizes about that step so the reader knows what lies ahead.

In writing about how to do something *tangible*, the best arrangement of steps in the process is naturally according to time sequence: first you do this, then you do that. Readers must usually follow these directions in the same order you present them in order to get the promised result.

When writing about *intangible* actions, the choice of which information to put first, second, or third is often less crucial. You should still strive for a logical progression for the instructions. Sometimes you can move from the most general actions toward the most specific ones, sometimes from the easiest to the hardest. Often, more interesting points have to be interspersed with less interesting ones to keep your reader moving along. The good writer always outlines her points before sitting down to write, carefully figuring out the most logical progression. Later in this unit we will discuss organization at greater length.

When giving directions, keep your language simple and straightforward so that it never gets in the way of the information you're imparting. If there is only one precise word for what you mean, it is more important to use that word—even if it causes dull repetition—than to choose an imprecise synonym.

One of the most straightforward ways to share information is by speaking right to the reader in the second person or imperative present tense: *next you connect this*, or *next connect this*. If you consider it shockingly familiar to converse directly with your readers, reread Section 4.4 in Chapter 4: "How He/She Intrudes when I/We Write for You (the Reader)."

Examples of everyday papers that give directions are the instruction pamphlets that come packed with everything from color TVs to assemble-them-yourself toys. A lot of us have learned through bitter experience how frustrated the reader becomes if the writer puts directions out of order, omits steps, or chooses imprecise words. If you've ever been frustrated that way, keep it in mind the next time you sit down to explain your computer program or lab procedure in writing.

Exactly like the how-to in purpose is the how-I-did-it, a paper that describes an action or procedure that the author went through. Often the information is written down so the reader can duplicate the process in her own lab, factory, or office. Research papers in scholarly journals are excellent examples of how-I-did-it (or how-we-did-it).

How-I-did-it papers are easy to organize. You simply tell what you did, in the order in which you did it, again keeping your language as precise and straightforward as possible.

Another sibling of the how-to-do-it paper is the *how-it-works*. It, too, requires that information be presented in a strictly logical progression, generally in time sequence: *The electrons flow into the field coil, magnetize it, and polarize the coil. The polarized coil moves toward the permanent magnet. . . .* One way of viewing the how-it-works paper is as if it were a how-to-do-it written from the perspective of the machine you're explaining.

EXERCISES:

1. Read the how-to article reprinted in Illustration 7/2 at end of this chapter. List the major points covered by the article. Decide *how* the authors probably organized the points: in time sequence, most general to most specific, hardest to easiest, easiest to hardest, most interesting interspersed among least interesting, or what.

2. Create working titles for direction-giving papers based on these topics:

   a. The coal industry and Kentucky's hills
   b. Leonardo da Vinci and the Mona Lisa
   c. The princess telephone
   d. Wood stoves
   e. My education

7.4 THE REPORT.

The report, a narration of who, what, why, when, where, and how or how much, is easy to write once you've learned your craft. Its aim is to inform the reader about an occurrence, or about several simultaneous or chronological occurrences. It reviews the event in consecutive order whenever possible, and uses the appropriate tense: simple past for an event that took place at some earlier time; present tense for an ongoing occurrence, as in a status report on flow of water over a dam; and future tense for a projected event.

The report reader's goal is usually to witness, vicariously, the reported occurrence, so your goal has to be to make it as vivid as possible. Include as much significant detail as is needed to make the reader see the total picture of what happened. On the other hand, guard against the temptation to include extraneous information, or you may confuse the reader and dilute the impact of your report.

One way to guard against unwanted details is to insert the

word *history* into your working title. For example, in a paper that you call, "A History of How the Federal Government Divested Itself of the Post Office," you will be more likely to leave out paragraphs about whether the divestiture was good or bad, and how it affected postal rates.

Beginning writers seem possessed of urges to offer opinions and pass judgments on material they include in their reports. But readers remain adamant about expecting reports to contain only objective reporting.

One of the surest ways to persuade is to hold your personal opinions and judgments close to your chest and to let your selection of objective facts, figures, and sensory observations do the persuading for you. If your data doesn't convince readers, your arguments probably won't either. And the instant you begin to emphasize your subjective evaluations, readers will question how objective you've been in reporting the rest of your data. In Chapter 11 we'll discuss how to present persuasive evidence effectively.

Among this century's most talked-about reports was the newspaper series on Watergate that persuaded a nation to unseat a president. If you study it you will see that Woodward and Bernstein prepared it with what appeared to be impeccable objectivity.

The report format is also widely used by other kinds of investigators: insurance adjusters, social workers, police officers, to name a few. Branch office managers report to head office executives, association executives report to members, and secretaries of organizations report on meetings. Corporations issue reports to stockholders explaining significant events in the corporate year, and the president reports every January on the state of the nation; however, many of us regard these two examples as exercises in unmitigated persuasion. You would do well to remember that merely typing *Report* at the top of your first page will not in itself convince readers that you have rendered an objective report.

One type of report does require your personal involvement

within its pages and paragraphs. If your goal is to inform readers about events that you have lived through, and if you are sure your readers want to know how they impressed you or affected you personally, then write what is known as a *personal experience* paper or *reminiscence*, and do it in the first person: *I did this* or *we did that*. Before you begin writing a personal experience paper, however, be certain your readers do want your own experiences, not impartial observation.

EXERCISES:

1. Read the report reproduced in Illustration 7/3 at end of this chapter. For each paragraph, write a one-line description of its major point.

2. From the points you singled out in Exercise 1, describe how the author organized his information.

3. Reread the report. This time look for (a) places where the author injected personal opinion or judgments, and (b) places where a less careful author might have injected personal opinion or judgments.

4. Create working titles for reports based on these topics:
    a.   The coal industry and Kentucky's hills
    b.   Leonardo da Vinci and the Mona Lisa
    c.   The princess telephone
    d.   Wood stoves
    e.   My education

7.5 HOW TO EXPLAIN IDEAS.

The first two major purposes of writing, giving directions and reporting, involved things that could be *seen:* people, places, objects, events, actions. *Explaining ideas* and *persuading* deal with abstractions. Not surprisingly, they are more difficult to write about successfully. However, writers have developed ways to explain ideas surely and effectively. Once learned, they enrich all writing no matter what the major purpose.

The paper that explains (often called a *theme* or *thesis*) usually starts by stating the entire idea as directly as possible. This can be done in the *lead*, the *topic sentence*, or in an early paragraph or several paragraphs. (Lead and topic sentence will be explained in great detail in the next chapter.) The more complex the idea, the more space you may require for establishing just what it is you intend to explain. But keep in mind that the reader does not, at this stage of the paper, have to understand the idea itself. That probably will not happen until the end of the paper. The reader simply has to understand what the idea is that will be discussed throughout the paper.

Read illustrations 7/4 and 7/5 at the end of this chapter. Notice how the authors of two entirely different kinds of papers, both of which explain ideas, introduced their subjects early and simply. In the first, the opening sentence states the complete idea:

> . . . a group of writers and writers' agents, in conjunction with the law firm . . . have organized the First Amendment Defense Fund, for the single purpose of providing low-cost legal protection to writers against the special risks they run as writers.

In the second paper, the idea comes at the end of the opening paragraph:

> . . . hazards of the reborn skateboard craze.

The remainder of each paper amplifies the idea. Just as the panel of controls on a hi-fi amplifier permits us to raise or lower the sound level, control its flow through the speakers, filter out noises, and alter the balance in pitch, we have a panel of five devices that help us amplify ideas:

- reword the idea
- offer examples of it
- add specific details to it

- support it with evidence from authorities
- evaluate it from different perspectives.

Rarely will you employ all five devices in the same paper. Just as rarely will you be able to use only one. Your choice will depend on how abstract the idea seems to be to you and to your audience of readers, how you've researched to amplify the idea, and how ambitious a writer you are. Let's look at each device in turn.

Reword the idea.

Your readers are not a homogeneous audience. They have different educations, different social and economic backgrounds, different firsthand experiences and acquired knowledge that they bring with them to your paper. Often, simply expressing the basic idea in various ways clarifies it dramatically. In the defense fund article, the author restated the idea in paragraph 5 using nearly the same words as in his opening sentence:

> The purpose of the First Amendment Defense Fund is to protect writers by making lawyers available at low cost.

The skateboard hazards article's author reworded her idea completely in paragraph 4:

> . . . it is a popular neighborhood pastime—and a very dangerous one.

and again in paragraph 9:

> Enhancing or not, a wipe-out can be a serious matter.

The English language is alive with synonyms and figures of speech that let writers restate ideas in almost endless ways. You can *define* some of the individual words in your basic idea, especially the toughest and most abstract words; you can *metaphorically liken* the idea or words within the idea to more commonplace words; you can substitute concrete terms for abstract ones according to guidelines we established in Section 4.1.

Often the words you choose in restating your idea are less precise than the original ones, but in this case it is acceptable to sacrifice precision to achieve vividness. Readers struggling to understand a difficult concept will appreciate your efforts to make the job easier. A simplified restatement of the "hazards of the reborn skateboard craze" comes at the end of paragraph 5, in a quotation:

> "When they think they've mastered the boards, that's when they start taking chances and really hurt themselves."

Did the imprecision annoy you as you read the quotation in context?

Offer examples of the idea.
One of the most effective ways to make an abstract idea seem concrete for readers is to offer specific, concrete examples. This is a favorite tool of magazine writers, and the skateboard hazards article is full of anecdotes that make the dangers come alive for readers. The author of the legal defense fund paper also employed this technique at the end of his paragraph 3 and all of paragraph 4. If you cannot locate real situations that serve as examples, hypothetical ones will have to do.

The use of examples is so important to all kinds of writing, that we devote a major part of Chapter 10 to the subject.

Add specific details to the basic idea.
The legal fund paper's author didn't simply talk in general terms about the fund and its purpose; wisely, he gave as many concrete specifics as he could find about the abstract idea. Paragraph 8, for instance, offers four very specific details, and the next three paragraphs continue with more details. Reread the entire paper right now, and watch how paragraph 8 starts to dissipate the earlier feeling of fuzziness about just what the fund is to do.

There are other ways to offer details to readers. You can discuss the idea's history or background, the causes that led to its creation, its effects—any information that illuminates part of the idea, not just its entirety.

Support the idea with evidence from authorities.

Academic readers demand to see evidence in the papers they read. Nonacademics generally expect to find ideas supported by evidence unless the paper's author is a recognized authority. Not only does evidence help support an idea, but it makes the idea, or parts of it, more concrete. Keep this in mind as you work on your papers. (Section 10.3 on quotation will expand this concept for you.) The skateboard article is laced with evidence from authorities: doctors, police officers, and even a skateboard sales clerk. Notice that the pieces of evidence do much more than merely support the author's premise that skateboards are hazardous:

● The doctor, in paragraph 4, offers insight into how extensive the hazards are numerically, the types of injuries caused by the hazards, and whether the problem is growing in scope.

● The Long Island policeman, in paragraph 6, provides strong proof that the hazard exists in a real locality, and then offers dramatic examples of the hazard as part of his evidence.

● The sales clerk cited in paragraph 8 is authoritative enough to bolster the author's argument that the hazardous fad is widespread, and his evidence contributes even more drama and credibility to the overall idea.

● The medical journal quoted in paragraph 9, aside from presenting one more piece of supportive evidence, offers readers more concrete insight into the abstract idea of skateboard hazards.

The defense fund paper begins presenting evidence by paragraph 2. Unlike the skateboard author, who drew on outside experts, its writer searched his own files for evidence that would explain why the threat of lawsuits can inhibit writers. Like the skateboard paper's author, he used his evidence to broaden readers' understanding of the basic, abstract idea.

Evaluate the idea from different perspectives.

Sometimes your explanation of an idea is still not made concrete or clear enough even after you do your best with the other methods. Then, it often helps to examine the idea from several vantage points. The following are the most common methods of doing this:

● You can compare the idea to other concepts that are already familiar to your readers. The legal fund paper's author might have compared the concept to doctors' malpractice insurance funds, contrasting the relative costs, coverages, benefits, restrictions, and similar aspects.

● You can separate the basic idea into several parts and then thoroughly analyze each of the simpler units. In the legal fund paper, for example, the author could have explored in depth the value of libel coverage, invasion of privacy coverage, and coverage for two hours of free consultation.

● You can evaluate the merits of the idea: Will it work? What are the problems if it's accepted? Has anything like it ever worked? Is it too simpleminded as presented? Will the public shy away from such a radical plan? In short, what are the pros and cons and how do you defend the pros and respond to the cons? The evaluation of the idea will carry greater weight if any part of it can be attributed to outside experts.

Neither of our examples includes evaluation of the idea's merits. The defense fund paper was written for journalists who didn't have to be sold on the pros and didn't want to hear about the cons. The author of the skateboard hazards example found no authoritative evidence that skateboarding wasn't hazardous, and decided her case was strong enough without mentioning that fact. But if a discussion of the merits is needed to strengthen your paper, include it. And if you can quote authorities who bolster your case, make it an important part of your paper.

Many beginners carefully avoid presenting evidence that countermands a paper's basic premise. If you fall into that trap you may, instead of strengthening your paper, destroy its credibility. Readers today are sophisticated enough to know that very few arguments are so one-sided that an author can't find evidence that disagrees with her major contentions. If readers know that you're sidestepping counterevidence, they'll be leery of accepting all your assertions. On the other hand, if you can present counterevidence and ably refute it, you will broaden the readers' perspective on your paper's ideas. An example of counterevidence that was presented and then turned to the author's advantage, is found in paragraph 13 of the legal fund paper.

In writing academic papers, if your research has uncovered no evidence contrary to the paper's basic idea, it's wise to say so.

EXERCISES:

1. Create working titles for papers that explain ideas based on these topics:
   a. The coal industry and Kentucky's hills
   b. Leonardo da Vinci and the Mona Lisa
   c. The princess telephone
   d. Wood stoves
   e. My education

2. Study the paper in Illustration 7/4 (at end of this chapter). For each paragraph, decide if the author
   a. reworded the basic idea,
   b. offered examples of the idea,
   c. supported the idea with evidence,
   d. evaluated the idea from a different perspective,
   e. added details to the basic idea.
On a separate sheet of paper, list the paragraph number followed by the letter of your choice. If you choose more than one letter for a paragraph, explain.

3. Study the paper in Illustration 7/5. Repeat the instructions in Exercise 2.

7.6 PERSUADING.

The three purposes of writing we have discussed assume that your reader begins with a willingness to accept what you have to say. Persuasion is like explanation in that you're writing about ideas, but here it's assumed that you've got to woo the reader to your point of view. You need

- a clear statement of your point of view in your working title,

- a strong opener to overcome the reader's disinclination to read what she may not believe or accept,

- enough facts to support your contention,

- sound reasons that link the facts with your contention.

Therefore, in addition to defining your subject and your object, you must also know what your point of view is. It's a good idea to include it in your working title.

Based on the topics discussed in Section 7.2, here are some working titles for persuasive articles:

- How Jogging Shoes Can Help you Run

- The Costly Error of Federal Divestiture of the Post Office

- How Skiing Separates the Men from the Boys

- Double-Digit Inflation: Specter of a Cold War Economy

In defining the exact purpose of your persuasive article and choosing its working title, refrain from taking a defensive attitude. As in the boxing ring, you score no points for defense, only for offense. If you approach the topic defensively, you run the risk of making otherwise neutral readers defensive as well.

Persuasion, sometimes called argument, may use any of the techniques for amplification discussed in Section 7.5. The most important technique, however, is support: offering authoritative evidence, then offering and refuting counterevidence for the opposing point of view. In other types of papers, it isn't always necessary to consider the opposition, but in persuasion you must deal with the other side of the issue or the reader will rightly accuse you of biased writing and refuse to take you seriously.

Even though the underlying purpose of your persuasive paper is to convert readers to your point of view, unless you know for a fact that they want to read your opinions you should not insert them. Opinions are like red capes, and waving them only invites attack. Instead, select words carefully, present evidence forcefully, and make a low-keyed appeal to the readers' emotions; combined, they will lead readers subtly to your point of view. (Section 10.2 and Chapter 11 will expand on specific techniques useful in writing persuasive papers.)

In Illustration 7/6, we reproduce a persuasive article that, in only 1,500 words, explains the degree to which textbooks were racially biased in 1967, how they became that way, and what concerned people did about the problem. Coauthor Peterson, who wrote it, had strong feelings on the subject but he produced evidence, not opinions, to influence readers.

Personal opinion paper

The personal opinion paper, sometimes called an essay or critique, is closely related to the persuasive paper. The difference is, it makes no bones about the writer's bias. In fact, its emotional content is often stronger than its intellectual weight. Writing personal opinion papers is fun. But the fact is, unless you're a recognized expert on the subject, your personal opinion is of little interest to readers.

For example, if playwright John Osborne were to write about Neil Simon's plays, his opinion would interest lots of readers. On the other hand, if he were to offer his opinion of various stocks for investment, most readers would yawn and stop reading unless he convinced them at the outset that he'd made a killing on Wall Street.

Until you become a recognized expert, it's a good idea to avoid the personal opinion paper for anything but a letter to the editor, and to stick with its much stronger cousin, persuasion.

EXERCISES:

1. Create working titles for papers that persuade based on these topics:
    a. The coal industry and Kentucky's hills
    b. Leonardo da Vinci and the Mona Lisa
    c. The princess telephone
    d. Wood stoves
    e. My education

2. Create working titles for personal opinion papers based on the five topics in Exercise 1.

3. Compare the titles created in Exercises 1 and 2. Explain how each working title in Exercise 1 shows that the paper's purpose is to persuade, not to vent your opinion.

4. For the "Flunk, Dick and Jane!" article reproduced as Illustration 7/6, assess the following, paragraph by paragraph:
    a. What supportive evidence does the author offer?
    b. What counterevidence does he refute?
    c. What personal opinions does he express openly?
    d. From the evidence he has chosen, list his opinions on the subject. Show what led to your conclusions.

7.7 BE MODEST
IN YOUR GOALS.

The biggest mistake inexperienced writers make, in choosing topics, is to bite off more than they can chew. You cannot cover all aspects of any subject in a thousand words—or even five thousand. To write a meaningful history, topography, geology, and sociology of Mount Olympus requires a book, not a paper.

To select the correct main theme, the trick is to narrow the subject to its smallest possible circumference, and then to squeeze in as much detail as possible. We were able to carry through five exercise topics from section to section of this chapter, and make of them any kind of paper we wanted, because as originally stated they were all-embracing. For example, from the topic *The coal industry and Kentucky's hills* we can create at least four different working titles simply by considering the four different writing purposes:

- How to mine coal in the hills of Kentucky (how-to)

- How the coal industry located coal deposits in Kentucky's hills (report)

- The impact of coal mining on Kentucky's hills (explaining ideas)

- How the coal industry ruined the hills of Kentucky (persuasion)

Even though each of these working titles considerably narrows the basic theme, it may still be too sweeping to produce a meaningful paper. There is no hard and fast rule that will keep you from chomping on more topic than your paper can digest, but there are three questions we use as guidelines:

How much amplification will the readers expect?
The only statements a careful writer can safely make without amplification are those that readers can be expected to understand and accept from the outset. When in doubt, offer more information than you think they require, never less. Unless your tone of writing talks down to your readers, they almost never hold it against you if you tell them something they already know. But if you leave out information they need, they may decide your writing is too difficult to follow, and stop reading.

Look closely at the following paragraph by Isaac Asimov. Try to decide what minimum education level of readership this former medical school professor of biochemistry had in mind:

> If we were to study the human body very closely, we would find it to contain a number of different chemical substances. In the first place, we would find water; a great deal of it. About three-fifths of the body is water. Quite ordinary water too; the kind you can find in any reservoir.[1]

The selection is from *The Chemicals of Life*, a book aimed at the widest possible readership. Do you think that, with this audience in mind, Asimov was correct in spending time on such widely known details as that the body contains mostly water? Does his vivid image make up for telling you the obvious? Does his paragraph seem sophomoric to you? (Our dictionary defines *sophomoric* as "conceited and overconfident of knowledge but poorly informed and immature.") What would your reaction be if you encountered the same paragraph in *The American Journal of Biochemistry?*

How much space do you have?

The space available to most writers is limited. Book publishers, scholarly journal editors, and most teachers all put formal limits on the number of pages writers can submit. The length of business reports, too, is limited—by practicality, because reading takes time as well as substantial energy, and in the business world time is money. Long reports are read less attentively than short ones, and go unread more often. A short report that has been carefully thought out, drafted, and honed can tell as much as a long, loosely written one.

Never sacrifice depth of coverage; if length is limited, narrow the breadth of coverage instead. If your main purpose is threatened, either because the paper is getting too long or its thrust is being weakened by other purposes, sacrifice any or all of your secondary purposes and concentrate on one main goal.

But if you're like the vast majority of students, your problem isn't too much but too little. Most neophytes attack subjects so superficially as to barely dent their surfaces. So we hope you will file away our last warning for now and concentrate on writing more and more details about more and more specific subjects until you reach the point in your endeavors when you finally have more to say than space permits.

In later chapters, we'll go into greater detail about the various techniques and tools we've touched on in this overview.

EXERCISES:

1. Decide whether the goal for each of the following topics should be to write a *paper* or to write a *book*. Take into account the amount of amplification readers will expect, the breadth or narrowness of the topic as stated, and the purpose of the given working title. (For this exercise consider thirty typewritten pages, or about 7,500 words, to be the maximum length for a paper.)
   a.   Napoleon's Career as a General
   b.   How to Buy a Piano
   c.   How Cancer Kills Cells
   d.   Autos Should be Abolished
   e.   Television Isn't a Waste of Time

2. For each of the five working titles in Exercise 1, create a new title that turns the book into a paper or the paper into a book.

3. Illustration 7/1 reproduces a 1,000-word paper that attempts too many goals at once. Using information at hand or obtainable with about one hour of research, correct it by doing the following:
   a.   Choose one purpose and one goal; retitle the paper in line with your chosen purpose and/or goal; copy the paper eliminating all material that's extraneous to the new working title's purpose.
   b.   Rewrite the paper, adding whatever is needed to fill all the original author's goals. Aim for a 1,000- to 1,500-word paper.

NOTES: CHAPTER 7

1. Isaac Asimov, *The Chemicals of Life* (New York: New American Library, Signet Edition, 1954), p. 13.

ILLUSTRATION 7/1

The Forest Signal Patrol

The avid hunter, the very few highly experienced nature study people, and those who have been born and raised in the forest know that walking into the forest without disturbing its composure is practically impossible. Such an experience can be likened to walking into a village populated by fifty different kinds of people, each speaking a different language, yet understanding each other's.

It is a society of living creatures ranging from chickadees to hawks, from mice to badgers, from the fox to the mountain lion, from the deer to the bear; each with his own language and each knowing the fears of each other, and the dangers affecting each other. It is a harsh world of survival, with many creatures feeding on the mistakes of other creatures. Even the lovely deer feeds on the succulent, life-sustaining foliage of young trees and they die as a result.

The gossips and chatterboxes of the forest could be called its ground and air signal patrol. The chatterbox that takes first honors is the common red squirrel. The minute something moves that he doesn't like or understand, he starts to scold loudly while moving slowly toward the object of his concern. This is transmitted to the keen ears and telescopic eyes of the crow, who curiously circles above to pinpoint the danger and spread the alarm from the air.

If you sit in a spot you like in the forest, and listen without movement or a sound, you will be scolded fiercely by the birds when you first sit, and until you are observed to be doing no more. Gradually their conversation will change to the noises of searching for food, singing songs, and chattering among themselves and at interfering animals.

This normal gossip is the sounding-board of safety for the larger animals—the wolf, the fox, the deer, and the bear, who alert their senses of smell only as the sound changes. With such marvelous aids for safety, the sense of sight becomes relatively unimportant. The bear is considerably near-sighted, and the deer is color-blind.

One of the most gracious little ladies of the forest is the female deer. To observe this, one must first visualize her size. She is barely four feet tall and possibly ten inches wide. Her feet, attached to toothpick legs, are about two inches long. Her dainty steps along the pathway in her territory are as charming as those of a princess strolling in her garden. Each is surrounded with flowers and shrubs that suit her taste.

If you wish to follow this dainty little creature's path to her living room, I suggest you take a compass and when starting into the forest, note the direction in which you are walking as you enter. Her meandering, narrow pathway may extend for several miles, and very shortly you will lose all sense of direction.

Her garden path will be comfortable for her size. It may proceed through a ravine or along the edge of a ridge. It may meander down to fresh clean water and then, well concealed, proceed to a hilltop. There you may see signs of rest spots where she has a clear view of her beautiful surroundings.

At first glance, her pathway will appear to be a tangled mess, until you stoop to her height and visualize her size. Then you'll realize that the overgrown path is only a comfortable walkway for that gracious lady.

Food for several deer must grow along these pathways. Each year nature presents our little lady with one or two babies to feed and teach how to live. Should proper vegetation fail to grow in adequate quantities, or should the winter's snow become so deep that food is not accessible, the food in her garden may be too scarce for her family. They may starve.

We, a more intelligent animal species, feel an obligation to help. She cannot talk and tell us what she likes to eat or where she likes to eat it. She will not migrate great distances and leave the home garden she knows. Should we leave her alone to grow weak from lack of food and become prey for the wild dogs, coyotes, and other carnivorous animals and birds? Should we pass laws that merely retard the harvesting of excess herd, creating greater starvation? Or should we treat them as semidomestic animals raised for food? We call our domestic food supply *beef, mutton, pork,* and *lamb.* Are *venison, deerskin jackets* and *gloves* such bad words?

We'd call in the humane society in a hurry if a farmer raised more animals than he could feed and let them starve, drop dead in the pasture to be eaten by wild dogs and carnivorous birds.

Our state Department of Natural Resources has a thorough knowledge of wildlife habitat management. Isn't it about time we let them manage the herd? We could then look forward to having our gracious little lady around and in good health for many years to come.

ILLUSTRATION 7/2

---

12 Ways To Get More Out of Studying*

Effective studying is the one element guaranteed to produce good grades in school. But it's ironic that the one thing almost never taught in school is how to study effectively.

For example, an important part of studying is note-taking, yet few students receive any instruction in this skill. At best you are told simply, "You had better take notes," but not given any advice on what to record or how to use the material as a learning tool.

Fortunately reliable data on how to study do exist. It has been demonstrated scientifically that one method of note-taking is better than others and that there are routes to more effective reviewing, memorizing and textbook reading as well. Following are twelve proven steps you can take to improve your study habits. We guarantee that if you *really* use them, your grades will go up.

1. Use behavior modification on yourself. It works. Remember Pavlov's dogs, salivating every time they heard a bell ring? Just as association worked with them, it also can work with you. If you attempt, as nearly as possible, to study the same subject at the same time in the same place each day, you will find after a very short while that when you get to that time and place you're automatically in the subject groove. Train your brain to think French on a time-place cue, and it will no longer take you ten minutes a day to get in the French mood. Not only will you save the time and emotional energy you once needed to psych yourself up to French or whatever else, but the experts say you'll also remember more of what you're studying!

2. Don't spend more than an hour at a time on one subject. In fact if you're doing straight memorization, don't spend more than twenty to thirty minutes. First, when you're under an imposed time restriction, you use the time more efficiently. (Have you noticed how much studying you manage to cram into the day before the big exam? That's why it's called *cramming.)*

Second, psychologists say that you learn best in short takes. (Also remember that two or three hours of study without noise or other distractions is more effective than ten hours trying to work amid bedlam.) In fact, studies have shown that as much is learned in four one-hour sessions distributed over four days as in one marathon six-hour session. That's because between study times, while you're sleeping or eating or reading a novel, your mind subconsciously works on absorbing what you've learned. So it counts as study time too.

Keep in mind that when you're memorizing, whether it's math formulas or a foreign language or names and dates, you're doing much more real learning more quickly than when you're reading a social studies text or an English essay.

3. Keep alert by taking frequent rest breaks. The specialists say you'll get your most effective studying done if you take a ten-minute break between subjects. (Again, it's akin to behavior modification. Pavlov's dogs were taught to respond on cue by being rewarded with tidbits. The break is your reward.) Dr. Walter Pauk, director of the Reading and Study Center at Cornell University, suggests you take that short break whenever you feel you need one, so you don't fritter your time away in clock-watching and anticipating your break.

Another technique for keeping your mind from wandering while studying is to begin with your most boring subject—or your hardest one—and work toward the easiest and / or the one you like best.

4. Study similar subjects at separate times. Brain waves are like radio waves: if there isn't enough space between inputs, you get interference. The more similar the kinds of learning taking place, the more interference. So separate your study periods for courses with similar subject matter. Follow your hour of German with an hour of chemistry or history, not with Spanish.

5. Avoid studying during your sleepy times. Psychologists have found that everyone has a certain time of day when he or she gets sleepy. Don't try to study during that time. (But don't go to sleep either. It hardly ever refreshes.) Instead, schedule some physical activity for that period, such as recreation or instrument practice. If you have a pile of schoolwork, use that time to sort your notes or clear up your desk and get your books together or study with a friend.

6. Study at the most productive time for your course. If it's a lecture course, do your studying soon *after* class; if it's a course in which students are called on to recite or answer questions, study *before* class. After the lectures you can review, revise and organize your notes. Before the recitation classes you can spend your time memorizing, brushing up on your facts and preparing questions about the previous recitation. Question-posing is a good technique for helping the material sink in and for pinpointing areas in which you need more work.

7. Learn the note-taking system the experts recommend. Quite a bit of research has been done on note-taking, and one system has emerged as the best.

Use 8½-by-11-inch loose-leaf paper and write on *just one side*. (This may seem wasteful, but it's one time when economizing is secondary.) Put a topic heading on each page. Then take the time to rule your page as follows:

A. If the course is one in which lecture and text are closely related, use the 2-3-3-2 technique: Make columns of two inches down the left-hand side for recall clues, three inches in the middle for lecture notes and three inches on the right side for text notes, and leave a two-inch space across the bottom of the page for your own observations and conclusions.

B. If it's a course where the lectures and the reading are not closely related, use separate pages for class notes and reading notes, following the 2-5-1 technique; two inches at left for clues, five in the middle for notes, and an inch at the right for observations. (After a while you won't need to draw actual lines.)

In the center section or sections belong your regular notes, taken in the form you've evolved during your years of schooling. Probably you have also evolved your own shorthand system, such as using a *g* for all *-ing* endings, an ampersand *(&)* for *and,* and abbreviations for many words (e.g., *govt.* for *government* and *evaptn.* for *evaporation).*

The clue column is the key to higher marks. As soon as possible after you've written your notes, take the time to read them over—not studying them, just reading them. Check now, while it's all still fresh, to see whether you've left out anything important or put down anything incorrectly, and make your changes. Then, in that left-hand column, set down clue words to the topics in your notes. These clue words should not repeat information but should designate or label the kind of information that's in your notes. They're the kind of clues you would put on crib sheets. For example, to remember the information contained so far in this section on note-taking, you need just the following clues: 8½-by-11 loose-leaf, one side; 2-3-3-2; 2-5-1. As you can see, they're simply memory cues to use later on in your actual studying.

Dr. Robert A. Palmatier, assistant professor of reading education at the University of Georgia, suggests that you study for tests in the following manner: Take out your loose-leaf pages and shift them around so the order makes the most sense for studying. Take the first page and cover up the notes portion, leaving just the clues visible. See if you can recall the notes that go with the clues, and as you get a page right, set it aside. If you're going to be taking a short-answer test, shuffle your note pages so they're out of order. (That's why it's important to use just one side of the paper.) "This approach provides for learning without the support of logical sequence," Dr. Palmatier says, "thus closely approximating the actual pattern in which the information must be recalled." If you're going to be taking an essay test, you can safely predict that "those areas on which the most notes are taken will most often be the areas on which essay questions will be based."

The beauty of the clue word note-taking method is that it

provides a painless way to do the one thing proved to be most conducive to remembering what you've learned—actively thinking about your notes and making logical sense of them in your mind. If instead you just keep going over your recorded notes, not only will you get bored, but you'll be trying to memorize in the worst way possible.

8. Memorize actively, not passively. Researchers have found that the worst way to memorize—the way that takes the most time and results in the least retention—is to simply read something over and over again. If that's the way you memorize, forget it. Instead use as many of your senses as possible. Try to visualize in concrete terms, to get a picture in your head. In addition to sight use sound: Say the words out loud and listen to yourself saying them. Use association: Relate the fact to be learned to something personally significant or find a logical tie-in. For example, when memorizing dates, relate them to important events whose dates you already know. Use mnemonics: For example, the phrase "Every good boy does fine" is used for remembering the names of the musical notes on the lines of the treble clef. Use acronyms, like OK4R, which is the key to remembering the steps in the reading method outlined in point 9, below.

9. Take more time for your reading. It really takes less time in the long run! And read with a purpose. Instead of just starting at the beginning and reading through to the end, you'll really do the assignment a lot faster and remember a lot more if you first take the time to follow the OK4R method devised by Dr. Walter Pauk.

O. Overview: Read the title, the introductory and summarizing paragraphs and all the headings included in the reading material. Then you'll have a general idea of what topics will be discussed.

K. Key ideas: Go back and skim the text for the key ideas (usually found in the first sentence of each paragraph). Also read the italics and bold type, bulleted sections, itemizations, pictures, and tables.

R1. Read your assignment from beginning to end. You'll be able to do it quickly, because you already know where the author is going and what he's trying to prove.

R2. Recall: Put aside the text and say or write, in a few key words or sentences, the major points of what you've read. It has been proven that most forgetting takes place immediately after initial learning. Dr. Pauk says that *one minute spent in immediate recall nearly doubles retention of that piece of data!*

R3. Reflect: The previous step helps to fix the material in your mind. To really keep it there forever, relate it to other knowledge: Find relationships and significance for what you've read.

R4. Review: This step doesn't take place right away. It should be done for the next short quiz, and then again for later tests throughout the term. Several reviews will make that knowledge indelibly yours.

10. Devise a color and sign system for marking your personal books. Dr. Palmatier suggests red for main ideas, blue for dates and numbers, yellow for supporting facts. Circles, boxes, stars, and checks in the margins can also be utilized to make reviewing easy.

11. Clue your lecture notes too. Underline, star, or otherwise mark the ideas that your teacher says are important, thoughts that he says you'll be coming back to later, items that he says are common mistakes. Watch for the words—such as *therefore* and *in essence*—that tell you he's summarizing. Always record his examples. In fact, in such subjects as math your notes should consist mainly of the teacher's examples.

Pay closest attention in your note-taking to the last few minutes of class time. Often a teacher gets sidetracked and runs out of time. He may jam up to a half-hour's content into the last five or ten minutes of his lecture. Get down that packed few minutes' worth. If necessary, stay on after the bell to get it all down.

12. Beware the underlined textbook. Of course, if the book doesn't belong to you, you won't be underlining at all. But if you underline, do it sparingly. The best underlining is not as productive as the worst note-taking.

Over-underlining is a common fault of students; only the key words in a paragraph should be underlined. It should never be done in ink (something you think is important at the time may not seem so in retrospect), and it should be done only after you've finished the OK part of your OK4R reading.

If you're buying your books secondhand, *never* buy one that has already been underlined. You would tend to rely on it—and you have no idea whether the hand that held the pencil got an *A* or an *F* in the course!

Research has proven that it's not how much time you study that counts but how well. In fact, in at least one survey students who studied more than thirty-five hours a week came out with poorer grades than those who studied less. Use your study time wisely, and you too will come out ahead.

For more information on studying, consult the following books: *How To Study in College*, second edition, by Walter Pauk (Houghton Mifflin) and *How To Study*, second edition, by Clifford T. Morgan and James Deese (McGraw-Hill). Both available in paperback.

*Judi R. Kesselman, "12 Ways to Get More Out of Studying," *Seventeen,* September, 1976, pp. 140-41, 176-77.

ILLUSTRATION 7/3

Good-bye ICG!

Those rumbling Illinois Central Gulf (ICG) freight trains, with their friendly crews waving to our neighborhood children, will likely end nearly 100 years of service to the rural communities of south central Wisconsin sometime this year. In November the Interstate Commerce Commission finally granted the railroad permission to discontinue its unprofitable service on the line which runs through our neighborhood on its way from Madison to Freeport, Illinois. The state has appealed the decision, but reversal seems unlikely, according to Roberta Leidner, Dane County supervisor and chairperson of the South Central Wisconsin Rail Transit Commission.

This passing of an era leaves Westside neighborhoods from the Nakoma Plaza Shopping Center at the Beltline to Park Street overpass with a unique corridor of land varying from 75 to 200 feet in width. This corridor presents a rare opportunity for the city, since no city could afford to assemble such a path from its center to its outskirts, nor could Madison afford to reassemble this corridor once it is broken up. As early as a few months from now our city government may have to make a decision whether the city wants to preserve the corridor.

The ICG tracks run in almost a straight shot from the Beltline to within a few blocks of the university and Downtown, and parallel the busy Verona Road–Seminole Highway–Nakoma Road–Monroe Street artery. With already heavy traffic and continued development in North Fitchburg and Verona, these streets are likely to become overburdened, and the corridor is a natural for some alternative form of transportation.

However, it also has great potential for recreation, as much of its length is scenic and it touches the Odana and Glenway golf courses, the city cemetery, Camp Randall, and passes within a few blocks of the UW Arboretum and Vilas Park. With the planned redevelopment of the West Washington Railyard, it could be connected with Law Park on Lake Monona and John Nolen Drive. With prairie and woodland plantings along the way, it could serve as a commuter and recreational bikepath (with very few street crossings, it is a safe and direct path to the university and downtown), a cross-country ski trail, and hiking path which could take some pressure off the Arboretum. Play areas could be located in wider stretches where a neighborhood needs more playground space. A "par course" (with carefully planned exercise stations) could be included for physical fitness buffs.

For much of its length, the corridor has no street access and is too narrow for residential development or a freeway, so neither much additional housing nor a highway is a likely alternative.

There may be other uses, but the city to date has not done a careful study of possible uses of the corridor. The corridor appears on the city's official map as a "transportation corridor."

Otherwise only a brief 1976 memo to then Mayor Soglin from the City Planning Department addresses the issue of the corridor. It lists four possible uses for this land: (1) mass transit, (2) bikeway, (3) linear park, and (4) land banking (this last is not really a use at all, but a hedge which says we don't know yet what we want to use this for, but we think we will need it. It's a good investment that keeps our options open). No priorities were set.

In August the Dane County Regional Planning Commission will complete its Alternative Transit Technology Study which, among other things, should shed some light on which if any form of mass transit is feasible for the ICG corridor.

At the moment it appears the corridor will probably continue to be used for a time as a rail line. Dane and Green Counties have been promised a grant through a new state program to continue rail service on the line. The counties plan to buy and rehabilitate the tracks and the state takes title to the land (a 20–80% split in costs). A local or "short line" railroad company is prepared to lease the line from the government, expecting that with a better sales and service effort, it can turn a profit. Volume would, of course, have to increase, but it is expected that increased shipping would show mostly in longer trains, not in a significantly increased number of trains.

The deal has not been struck yet, and may fall through on specifics yet to be negotiated. This would probably force the city to consider whether it has a future interest in the corridor in the very near future. Estimated price for the portion of the ICG corridor within the city is $1.6 million. Even if the project goes ahead, the rail company can default on its contract at any time. No doubt it would if it couldn't make a profit, so there is no guarantee this short line plan will preserve the corridor without city action at some point.

The corridor may be freed for city use even with an operating, profitable rail line. The ICG tracks pass close to a Northwestern line just west of Madison, and there are virtually no Madison customers served by the ICG line. An interchange there would get the short line company's trains to the rail yard, and it could be built for under $1 million (with state and federal help a possibility). The city would probably have to buy the ICG corridor within the city limits from the state for this option to materialize.

The city must decide within the next few months whether it is more advantageous to purchase the land now without knowing quite what to do with it, or to wait and buy it from the state (assuming the short line project gets underway) when its use could be clearly laid out. If the short line project dies aborning, the city would probably have to make the decision whether it has a future interest in the corridor now or see its dissolution. Estimated price: $1.6 million.

Illustration7/4

The First Amendment Defense Fund

¶1   During the past few months, a group of writers and writers' agents, in conjunction with the law firm of Clark Wulf Levine & Peratis, have organized the First Amendment Defense Fund, for the single purpose of providing low-cost legal protection to writers against the special risks they run as writers. The risks to be covered by the fund include suits for libel and invasion of privacy; the compelled production of notes, tapes, records, and other work-product; government interference with news collection; and civil actions to suppress publication on national security or obscenity grounds. The fund will provide only the service of lawyers. It is not a general insurance program and will *not* pay costs of judgments that might be levied against members.

¶2   The idea for the fund grew out of the knowledge that lawsuits and the threat of lawsuits inhibit the full freedom of writers to write as they please. Though the risk of losing libel suits and invasion of privacy suits has been marginal because of favorable Supreme Court doctrine (a condition that may change owing to some recent unfavorable decisions in the First Amendment area), the cost of employing lawyers to defend such lawsuits is an enormous burden. The standard provision in publishing contracts making authors responsible for payment of all or a large part of their publishers' legal expenses and judgments, adds to the burden.

¶3   Though most writers are never sued for libel, and though most writers are not subpoenaed to produce their notes at trial, what they write is often affected by their fear of lawsuits, and results in self-censorship. The generally conservative attitude of publishers' lawyers who read for libel also affects the final version of a book or article. When authors do not have easy access to lawyers who will represent their point of view rather than their publishers', they are at a great disadvantage. Most publishers' contracts require submission of an "acceptable manuscript" before any money due the writer or any publication will be delivered. If

the writer refuses to make the changes demanded, then the manuscript is not acceptable, further payment is stopped and advances may be demanded back.

¶4   All of this grievously undermines writers' freedom of speech.
However careful, thorough, and precise they are, when there is
no one to defend them, writers are less likely to write freely. Libel
suits—win or lose—are an easy way for those, especially for those
with money to burn, who don't want certain things said to discourage writers from saying them.

¶5   The purpose of the First Amendment Defense Fund is to
protect writers by making lawyers available at low cost.

¶6   The fund involves creation of a pool of money from annual
prepayment of dues. The legal services will be provided by the
firm of Clark Wulf Levine & Peratis, whose members have the
experience and commitment to First Amendment rights that will
make the program possible. The firm is willing to provide their
services to the fund at the rate of $50 an hour for partners' time,
which is one-half to one-quarter of what other lawyers of comparable experience and standing would and do charge for the
same services.

¶7   The cost of membership at the outset will be 1% of an ap-
plicant's estimated gross income from writing for which protection
is sought, but not less than $150 or more than $500.

BENEFITS OF MEMBERSHIP

¶8   Membership in the First Amendment Defense Fund entitles
members to representation in the following categories of legal
proceedings:

1. When named as a defendant in a lawsuit for libel, slander or
invasion of privacy

2. When named as defendant in a civil suit brought by an agency
of federal, state, or local government to enjoin, suppress, or otherwise penalize publication of the member's work on the ground
that it is said to threaten the national security, to be obscene, or
otherwise to be in violation of a law that, in the judgment of the
First Amendment Defense Fund's board of directors, impairs the
vitality of the First Amendment

3. When the subject of a subpoena or other legal process to compel testimony about, or production of, notes, interviews, drafts, research materials, or any work product in criminal or civil cases

4. When the victim of government interference with the news collection process, such as when a court closes a proceeding to the press

¶9   Members will be entitled to 200 hours of legal services at no cost, and additional legal services for the same proceeding at a fee of $25 an hour. If sued twice in the same membership year, members will be entitled to free legal services for whatever time is left over from the 200 hours allocated to the first suit, then to an additional 200 hours at $25 an hour, and another 200 hours at $50 an hour. Costs and expenses of litigation are borne by the fund when members are entitled to free legal services. Otherwise, the members pay these costs.

¶10   The fund will provide no-cost legal services to members if adversaries appeal. The fund's board of directors will have the authority to decide whether to support appeals by members, should their cases be lost at trial.

¶11   Members will also be entitled to two hours of consultation with fund attorneys at no cost on any question relating to publishing, writing contracts, or questions within the fund's purposes, and to twenty additional hours of consultation at $50 an hour.

¶12   The fund has several limitations that are not to be overlooked. *First*, if the fund has to absorb the impact of numerous suits in its first two or three years and is unable to build up a reserve, full benefits to members may have to be suspended because funds have been exhausted. However, if benefits are suspended or exhausted, members will continue to be entitled to legal services from the fund's attorneys at a $50 an hour fee to the firm. *Second*, the fund will provide only legal services. It will not insure members against payment of judgments levied by courts. *Third*, if fund attorneys must travel outside New York City, the basic fee will be $75 an hour.

¶13   Whether the fund will work depends largely on the number of writers who join. Given the low cost of membership, and the decision that the fund will not begin to function until it has accrued a pool of $50,000, at least 200 writers will have to join at the outset. Perhaps some writers and others concerned about the First Amendment will want to make a special contribution because they support the idea behind the fund's creation; perhaps some foundations will provide seed money to assist the fund in its early years. But unless hundreds of writers join because they believe the principles of the fund are both right and vital, and the protections afforded are real and valuable, it will not succeed.

¶14   If the fund succeeds and reserves are created, within a few years it can offer even more substantial protection with lower dues until finally writers can be assured their First Amendment rights will not fail for lack of assistance of counsel.

¶15   The fund is in the process of formation. If you want to join, write to:

> First Amendment Defense Fund
> Eighth Floor
> 113 University Place
> New York, New York 10003

ILLUSTRATION 7/5

The Skateboard Menace*

¶1   Business is booming for orthopedists all over the country this year. Broken wrists, splintered elbows and smashed ankles are just three common hazards of the reborn skateboard craze.

¶2   Skateboarding became a short-lived fad about ten years ago, when out-of-season surfers attached roller-skate wheels to their surfboards and took to the hilly roads. As other young people took up the sport, manufacturers began to offer mass-produced skateboards. But as quickly as the fad blossomed, its popularity faded.

¶3   Two years ago, a California enthusiast tried something new: He screwed a set of new polyurethane wheels to an old board, achieving a faster, smoother, quieter ride. Almost instantly, a whole new generation of skateboarders emerged, and this time close to 150 manufacturers undertook to meet their needs. Today, skateboarding is a multimillion dollar business. In June, twenty-six top skateboarders met in New York to vie for $7,000 in prizes at the first World Masters Invitational competition, and in September the first open World Invitational meet will take place in California—with a $50,000 purse! At least one magazine for skateboarders or "hot dcggers" is being published, the first skateboard movies are making the rounds, and a TV series is in preparation. *Newsweek* magazine estimates that between six and ten million Americans are now on the boards.

¶4   But for most of these fans, generally boys in their teens and preteens, skateboarding is neither business nor semipro sport; it is a popular neighborhood pastime—and a very dangerous one. As Dr. Geoffrey Coll, orthopedic resident at Long Island Jewish-Hillside Medical Center in New York, says, "The year before last we saw no skateboard injuries in emergency orthopedics. Last year I remember only one or two. This year the numbers are significant: Out of twenty bad strains, sprains, and broken bones in a typical weekend, I'd estimate that 20 percent are from skateboard accidents. And," he pointed out, "I only see the more serious injuries. Minor scrapes and bruises are treated by the interns in our general emergency room."

¶5   Little accidents happen mostly to beginners, according to a Great Neck, New York, pediatrician. "The novices are cautious at first. They choose their roads carefully and avoid dangerous tricks. They fall on their fannies or scrape their hands and knees, but, in general, they get no more banged up than beginning bicyclists. When they think they've mastered the boards, that's when they start taking chances and really hurt themselves."

¶6   A Long Island policeman reports that people are complaining about teenagers trespassing upon neighbors' drained swimming pools to "ride" them. In this gravity-defying trick, picked up from a California skateboard movie, necessary momentum is gained to make the skateboard wheels cling to the curved upper sides of the pool, while the rider spins dizzily atop—or, more accurately, aside—his board. So many children perform "nose wheelies" and "tail wheelies" (tipping back or front) that some skateboards are now being manufactured with snubbed noses and flipped-up tails.

¶7   Tricks like these were not possible a decade ago, when skateboards were made of wood and wheels were steel or clay. Today's good-quality boards are flexible fiberglass, aluminum, or Lucite, and boast sophisticated "trucks," the mechanisms to which wheels are attached. The polyurethane wheels themselves provide the remarkable traction necessary for "riding" pools, and on a race track can carry their passengers as fast as 50 miles per hour.

¶8   Since mechanical advancements make it possible for almost any experienced skateboarder to do some fancy tricks, intense peer pressure ensures that youngsters will try. In fact, a cult glamorizing both risk and pain is rapidly developing around the sport. According to the code, if you haven't been badly hurt at least once, you haven't attempted a really difficult trick. "Wiping out is considered neat," explains Bill Colvard, a salesman in the Durham, North Carolina K-Mart sports department, where skateboards are the season's biggest-selling merchandise. "A kid who's experienced the pain of skateboarding is really big stuff. His image is definitely enhanced."

¶9   Enhancing or not, a wipe-out can be a serious matter. In New Haven, Connecticut, a young teen's braces cut right through his lip; a Chicago youth, swerving to avoid a dog, collided with a parked car and broke both kneecaps. In Haverstraw, New York, a high school junior struck a rut and wound up hospitalized for two days with a concussion. Severe scrapes and bruises are common enough to be referred to as "road rash," and so many youngsters have suffered arm injuries that, according to *The Physician and Sportsmedicine* magazine, doctors now call a shattering of the olecranon, "skateboard elbow." At least two fatalities have been recorded in California, and on a national level, skateboards caused a spectacular 27,522 injuries requiring hospital treatment in 1975—a record that promoted them from eighth to third place in accident frequency for all children's toys (except for bicycles, which are in an accident class by themselves). A recent three-month survey showed more skateboard casualties in some hospitals than in an earlier twelve-month period.

¶10   But kids aren't the only ones who wipe out. Young adults and senior citizens fall off skateboards, too. Parents are especially vulnerable. Says Dr. Coll, "It seems to be essentially an all-male sport, judging by the injuries we see. A significant number are fathers who've watched their sons do it, decided it looked easy—and found out differently very quickly." One who found out was Minnesota Congressman Tom Hagedorn. He broke his right ankle riding his son's skateboard and was hospitalized for almost two weeks.

¶11   A Wisconsin mother in her mid-thirties, having been virtually accident-free as a trophy-winning diver, college volleyball star, and expert skier, hit a large pebble on her first attempt at skateboarding and literally carried her foot to the hospital in three pieces. She was told how lucky she was: She'd be able to walk again.

¶12   It's one thing for a sensible parent to stay off skateboards after discovering that the game isn't worth the candle. It's quite another thing to keep one's children off when everyone else in the neighborhood is hot dogging. Fortunately, there are precautions that can help minimize the danger.

¶13   For a start, buy equipment carefully. Although no consumer service has tested skateboards, salesmen and manufacturers offer these comments:

● Choose polyurethane wheels for greatest surface grip and flexing. They should be well aligned, have rough surfaces and spin freely.

● Though boards come in different shapes and sizes, don't assume a little board is for little feet and a big board for big ones; the length and shape of a board vary according to the kinds of tricks it is designed to do. A wider board makes jumping easier—and also helps beginners balance better. Longer boards supply greater flexibility, traveling on rough surfaces and going around bends.

● Trucks are the most important components of all, so make sure they are cast iron rather than lighter-duty sheet metal, and are bolted right *through* the board, not merely *into* it. The larger the ball bearings, and the more there are, the smoother—and safer—the spin will be. Truck bolts, and lock nuts on the axles, should be lined with nylon insets to prevent them from working loose easily. Trucks should be readily adjustable; a loose truck helps the skateboarder take a tight turn without spilling. For even greater safety, look for a truck that allows for insertion of additional shocker pads.

- Don't economize too strictly. Skateboards can be outrageously expensive ($125.00 is not unheard of, and prices from $15.00 to $75.00 are common) but beware of your discount store's $7 bargain, which may be made of plastic that's so brittle it will break in the first hard fall, causing more injuries.
- If your youngsters are willing, outfit them in helmets, padded pants or knee pads, and impact jackets or elbow pads—costly, but cheaper than hospital bills. Urge your skateboard dealer to display such items not as safety precautions but as status symbols. (If the projected skateboard TV show features properly padded performers, children will probably start demanding this equipment!)

¶14   Once you've made a careful purchase, insist on careful maintenance.

- Wheels and shocker pads should be replaced as soon as they begin to show signs of wear. With regular use, this may be as often as every two or three months. Remember that asphalt is harder on polyurethane than concrete.
- Replace all bearings when the wheels start to sound noisy in a free spin. Bearings must be checked periodically to ensure that none have fallen out.
- Never oil wheels or bearings, since oil disintegrates plastic inserts and polyurethane. If dirt stiffens the bearings, try blowing them clean with an air hose. And if that doesn't work, buy a can of powdered graphite at a hardware store and squirt it into the wheels.
- Hold a family—or better still, a neighborhood—council about skateboard safety, and make sure the kids are there; they are most likely to obey rules they have helped formulate. Ask the youngsters to suggest safe streets (free of heavy traffic and unwary pedestrians) and/or low-risk hours for skateboarding. Select an area that can be reserved for the smallest riders and anyone practicing new stunts—no fast riding or racing allowed. Help organize a rotating hot-doggers' patrol to clear away accident-causing pebbles and sticks, and to report ruts to local authorities. Contact park departments, school and town officials, even congressmen, for assistance in setting aside local park areas for skateboarders. Remind the children that in a number of municipalities, including San Francisco, San Diego, Canton, Massachusetts, and Rye, New York, soaring accident rates and disregard

for safety precautions (which can endanger car drivers and strollers as well as skateboarders) have resulted in bans against skateboards.

¶15   And *don't* mention this consoling thought to anyone under twenty-one: If the fad lasts as long as it did the last time around, it'll be gone by this time next year!

*Judi R. Kesselman, "The Skateboard Menace," *Family Health,* August, 1976, pp. 34-5, 73.

ILLUSTRATION 7/6

Flunk, Dick and Jane!*

¶1   "The remedy for stupidity is education, education and more education. Ram it down [the Negro's] unwilling throat in massive doses, but stop lying to him that his casual paternity, thick dialect, prelogical thinking, and persistent truancy is 'equal'." That's what a Chicago teacher wrote recently about educating black children in his classes. You can imagine how much education children, black or white, will get from his lessons. At least there's the textbook, you say. But chances are the books your children use are just as bigoted as that teacher.

¶2   During grade school and high school your child will try to learn what's printed on 32,000 pages of textbooks. He'll use sixty or more books if he's in the average school. During classes about 75% of his time will be spent with textbooks, and for homework 90% of his time.

¶3   Imagine the image he will get of black slavery and the Civil War if he reads an eighth grade U.S. history book with the ironic title, *Our United States: A Bulwark of Freedom.* A fictionalized— very fictionalized—story about the Civil War and the Emancipation

Proclamation is included, to make easier the complicated lesson about abolition. The little tale opens when horses gallop up to the plantation owned by the Austin family, and Cicero, a young black slave, cries out, "Master Henry! The Yankees are coming."

¶4   The Austins and their house slaves carried out the few valuables they still possessed and some of their fine furniture. Around the corner the other slaves—women, children, old folks, and a few young men—were herded along by the squad of soldiers. The children were crying as they clung fearfully to their mothers. When the slaves caught sight of Mrs. Austin, they broke away from the soldiers, came to her, and crouched behind her as though asking her for protection.

¶5   (A young Union lieutenant then mounts his horse and reads the Emancipation Proclamation to the band of huddled slaves.)

¶6   When he had finished reading the presidential order, the lieutenant folded the paper and placed it inside his tunic. To his surprise the Austin slaves showed no joy over their freedom. They stood still, eying the soldiers suspiciously. Finally old Uncle Josephus stepped timidly forward.

¶7   "Please, sir," he said, cap in hand, "may we please go back to our work now?"

¶8   In 1962, Detroit's NAACP started to protest the use of a textbook so racist. One of its leaders even kept his son out of eighth grade history classes. By 1964 the publishers had revised the textbook, leaving out the Austin story and adding the material suggested by the Detroit protest group. The publisher unashamedly told them why: "If we win an adoption in Detroit, we don't care about Mississippi. *We sell more books in Detroit.*"

TEXTBOOKS THAT SELL

¶9   Making money. That's all that dictates whose picture is in a textbook, Frederick Douglas's or Jefferson Davis's; Adam Clayton Powell's or James Eastland's. The country's largest publisher of grade school textbooks will be proud to show you its reading books in which those two famous kids, Dick and Jane, go next door to play with Penny, Pam, and Mike, three black children. What the company won't tell you is that it still sells a "mint julep" edition in which Penny and Pam and Mike don't have a chance to play with Dick and Jane. Black kids don't exist in that reading series.

¶10 Some fourth graders in Chicago read about Benjamin Banneker, an early American astronomer who was the first man to build a clock in the New World. Banneker was black. But the Banneker story is not to be found in southern editions of the same reading book.

TEXAS LAW IS YOURS TOO

¶11 Before a textbook publisher puts a new book into print, every one of its salesmen reads it first and has a chance to recommend changes. Texas salesmen are especially important to the publication of a new textbook, because the state government of Texas buys the books for local schools. That makes Texas a $16,-000,000-a-year customer, the largest single buyer of textbooks in the country. It seems ironic, somehow, that before being reshipped to local schools, the textbooks are piled up in the Texas School Book Depository. That's where Lee Harvey Oswald allegedly took a shot at President Kennedy while sitting on a stack of "Think and Do" workbooks.

¶12 Under Texas state law, any publisher who submits a book for consideration must be willing to make *any* revisions requested by the screening committee. If the author refuses, not only will that company's textbook be tossed out, the publisher will be fined $2,500. So when Texas says change something, it gets changed.

¶13 It was Texas that decided that Langston Hughes, famous black poet, should not be included in schoolbooks.

¶14 "Only when all nations learn to work together in solving their problems can we be sure of lasting peace in the world." That simple statement in a fifth grade geography book rubbed somebody in Texas the wrong way, and children will never see it in print. One Texas citizen, angry with the UN, tried to have a song left out of music books—the spiritual "He's Got the Whole World In His Hands"!

THE INVISIBLE PEOPLE

¶15 With Supreme Court decisions and civil rights bills and protest groups showing up all over the country, unfavorable comments about blacks have been taken out of most schoolbooks. In fact, the black has been taken entirely out of the picture. New York City teaches fourth graders from *New York Past and Present*. The great big old melting pot story is told to eager ten-year-olds, and it includes just about everybody—even an eskimo. But no black-skinned Americans!

¶16   *New York Past and Present* was first published in 1956 and is still being used. After concerned black parents made things hot for the board of education, it had the same publisher prepare *The New York Story*, which deals almost entirely with minority groups. Can't you imagine the average white teacher using *that* book in her classes? Actually she is not expected to—it's window dressing to hold up at press conferences when angry black parents complain that black faces and black stories are invisible in textbooks.

¶17   A teacher in Scarsdale, New York, prepared a study of the thirteen U. S. history textbooks used in almost every junior and senior high school across the country. He found 1966 editions greatly improved over the 1950 books, but the black was still invisible on the pages of history between 1864's Reconstruction and 1954's Supreme Court school desegregation decision.

¶18   • Nobody mentions that blacks arrived with Spanish explorers and were, therefore, in the New World before English colonists.

¶19   • The abolition movement is painted Boston-white, omitting the important fact that blacks, both free and slaves, wanted their freedom and worked for it themselves.

¶20   • Slavery in school books is nothing but banjo playing and spiritual singing. It must not be educational to learn about chains and whips and broken families.

¶21   • Blacks never fought in any wars, according to history books. Except for Crispus Attucks, who was shot during the Boston Massacre and every school year since, textbooks overlook all the other black soldiers:

   • 168,000 black soldiers and 30,000 black sailors in the Union uniform during the Civil War, including 14 Negroes who won the Congressional Medal of Honor during the same conflict.
   • 200,000 World War I black soldiers.
   • 1,000,000 black soldiers who fought for freedom in World War II, including 6,000 officers.

BLACK POWER AND WHITE SCHOOLBOOKS

¶22   If Texas can decide what should be crossed out of schoolbooks, why shouldn't black parents be able to decide what should go in—pictures that look like them and their black heroes? They can. Newark's board of education, under pressure, made a try and succeeded. Detroit's board of education, under pressure, tried and succeeded. Any other group of parents can do the same if they convince textbook publishers they'll lose money if they don't come up with something better than the "mint julep" editions they've published so far.

¶23   As long as teachers rely on textbooks for what they teach, parents and boards of education must make the textbooks tell the whole story without stopping short of something Governor Faubus or Senator Willis would object to. So far, the report card on textbooks would have to read, "Oh, see Dick and Jane flunk. Flunk, Dick and Jane, flunk, flunk flunk!"

---

* Article was retitled and appeared in slightly different form as: Franklynn Peterson, "See the Textbook Publishers Flunk," *Ave Maria*, March 9, 1968, pp. 20–23.

CHAPTER 8
THE STRUCTURE OF
FACTUAL WRITING

To write well is to think well,
to feel well, and to render well;
it is to possess at once
intellect, soul, and taste.
Georges Louis Leclerc de Buffon

Think about the last personal letter you wrote. Did it have a central theme, or did you ask about health, describe the weather, report an experience, and explain an opinion all in the space of a page or two? Did you worry about losing your reader in your jumps from topic to topic, or did you assume that your ideas could leap the white space between sentences? Did you consciously attempt to keep your pal reading, or did you assume that friendship would make everything you had to say interesting?

Now, were you ever handed a personal letter written to a friend of yours by someone you didn't know very well? Were there references to places and people you didn't recognize, or attitudes that annoyed you for being opinionated? Were the jumps from thought to thought difficult to follow? Did the entire letter leave you less moved than it left your friend? Unless it was written with the care that is usually given to the writing of papers, we'll bet it did.

To the reading of personal letters from friends, we bring memories of shared experiences, incentive, and willingness to work at interpreting what is said. But when we read what a stranger has written, we expect it to be interesting as well as easy to follow. We look for a specific structure: a beginning, a middle, and an ending. We like to get our bearings before we plunge into unfamiliar waters, and we appreciate the writer's help in orienting us.

To satisfy the reader, a classic format for all papers has developed over the years. It helps writer and reader walk together on familiar ground. It includes all the structural elements the reader expects:

1. Lead (the introduction)
2. Topic sentence (the beginning)
3. Body (the middle)
4. Ending (the conclusion)

As writer Mort Weisinger used to like to tell beginning writers, "You invite the readers in, you tell 'em what you're going to tell 'em, you tell it to them, and then you tell 'em what you just said."

Like any writing rule, this one can be broken by a great writer. But until you're great, it'll make life easy for both you and your readers if you learn to use all four elements in structuring your papers.

8.1 THE LEAD.

Professional writers of fact call the beginning part of every article *the lead* because it leads the reader into the paper and makes her want to read more. Many composition textbooks call it the *introduction*, but we think *lead* more vividly describes the purpose you must keep in mind.

A good lead entices the reader in one or both of two ways:

1. It appeals to his intellectual curiosity.
2. It appeals to his emotions.

Some of your earlier textbooks may have suggested another kind of introduction, a paragraph in which you first make a broad generalization about your topic and then focus on the aspect that you plan to cover. That was a perfectly satisfactory way to begin a paper back when reading a report in a journal may have been the most exciting thing a person did with his day. There is nothing intrinsically wrong with writing school papers that way today, if your reader is obliged to read them no matter how dull their beginnings. It is an easy way out, and one that doesn't need any more explanation than we've already given.

But even scientists who want to keep up with new discoveries have little time to read nowadays amid the demands of work, radio, TV, and the golf course. Although research papers prepared by novice writers for scholarly journals often lack leads entirely, articles by the editors of those same journals—articles they want read—all have carefully thought-out leads. Here is an example of one such beginning from the *American Journal of Public Health*:

> During the past five years there has been close to a sevenfold increase in the number of Americans with dental insurance and more than a doubling of the money spent annually for dental care.[1]

It's a deliberate eye-catcher, not a generalization about the topic of the editorial, which is "controlling the cost of dental insurance."

Let's examine the two ways we can catch and hold the reader's attention.

Appeal to intellectual curiosity

Nothing appeals to curiosity more directly than a question that asks something readers have always wondered about. Next best is to ask something they've never wondered about, but ask in such a way that they suddenly wonder why they've never wondered about it. If you lead with a question, readers read on.

There's a catch, however. Your paper must answer the question to the reader's satisfaction or she will feel cheated, so don't choose a question lead unless you're prepared to answer it. Here are examples from widely read magazines:

> Are you the type that likes to spend time gazing at the clouds? Not just idly daydreaming but scientifically scrutinizing the clouds—distinguishing cirrus from stratus, stratus from cumulus, to deduce whether it'll rain this afternoon? If you're that kind of cloud-gazer, you're a candidate for a career in meteorology.[2]
>
> Dan Carlinsky

> Why is it so often true that the most intimate side of the relationship between a woman and a man is the one they talk about least? A tricky question, almost certainly with as many answers as there are marriages. But the fact remains that most couples, even when the marriage seems fine, can talk about everything—except their love life. Things can go along quite well this way for as long as both partners feel satisfied. But what if one or both of them want things to be different? How can they solve a problem they can't talk about?[3]
>
> Bonnie Remsberg

> "Where are your eyes? Your nose? Your toes?" In the little games we parents play with our young children we teach them about their bodies. . . .[4]
>
> Claire Safran

Another way to nudge the reader's curiosity is to make a statement that surprises him. He will read on to see if—and how—you can prove the shocking fact or idea. It needn't be a huge shocker—mild surprise will do. A description of something unusual, a hint at controversy, even a word or phrase that's unexpected, can

make the reader want to read more. Again, you'd better follow
through with proofs of your startling statement—but don't do it
immediately, or the reader, his curiosity satisfied, may decide
to stop right there.

Here are examples of shocking statements used as leads in
two articles in a medical journal. Both authors quote statements
made by somebody else; it's a favorite device of scholars and
researchers who want to show emotion without risking the charge
that they're emotionally biased themselves.

> "It was a nightmare," said Dr. Howard Baxter, talking
> about his experience when he sold his sprawling, two-
> acre, four-bedroom suburban Chicago home and
> moved into a luxury condominium closer to the city.[5]
>
> Ted Schwarz

> "When the Boston Globe recently headlined a gov-
> ernment report charging that doctors were making too
> much money, a lot of my patients started coming in
> with chips on their shoulders," a Massachusetts in-
> ternist says. "But," he adds, "I didn't mind so much
> this time around. The Globe had treated the medical
> profession unfairly before. For a while, it had some
> of my patients so worked up that they went out and
> joined a utopian kind of cheap community health
> group. But within a year they got fed up with the lousy
> medical care and they all came back to me . . ."[6]

A paradox—two statements that seem directly contradictory—is
also a curiosity builder that makes a fine lead. Look at this
paradox that begins an article by Alan D. Haas:

> If you had purchased it in 1972 for $50,000 you could
> have sold it currently for $235,000. What is it?
>
> A Picasso or other modern painting? A Russian
> sable fur, a rare diamond or postage stamp, a mansion
> in Beverly Hills, several gold bricks?
>
> No: none of these. . . .[7]

Does this lead by Marvin Grosswirth make you want to read on for a solution to his paradox?

> An osteopath is a fully recognized, fully licensed physician—but he is not an M.D.
> He has been trained in the art of manipulative therapy—but he is not a chiropractor.[8]

Many inexperienced writers think one kind of good intellectual lead is a sentence (or several) that justifies the need for the paper; for example: *Nothing has ever been written about the use of slave troops in the Civil War. That is why I have chosen to write about it.* But the reader doesn't really care why you chose the topic, only why she should read about it. So keep your reasons to yourself as you write your lead, or turn them into statements that entice the reader. Reworking the example above, we could begin: *Nothing has ever been written about the use of slave troops in the Civil War despite the fact that a careful study of their impact undermines the credibility of almost everything already in print about Civil War battles.*

To sum up, the major appeals to intellectual curiosity are the question, the surprise, and the paradox. Whether they're your own words, or quotations from others, they're effective leads.

Appeal to the emotions

An appeal to the emotions is stronger than an appeal to the intellect. Used well, it compels the reader to find out what you have to say. But if it's too dramatic, the reader may soon realize you've made too big a fuss and refuse to read further. With appeals to the emotion, it's better if you understate and let the reader's imagination do half the job.

We recently saw a classic example of dramatic overkill in a lead that began an article in a medical journal. It described a tense airplane scene, a near-mutiny by passengers at the end of a snowy runway in Boston. The author kept his fingernail-biting drama unwinding for 200 words. But then he socked us with his finale: American health care is like that tense airline mutiny.

We haven't read beyond the lead to this day.

Your leads can appeal to any of the emotions: fear, pride, anger, love, lust, comfort, amusement, pleasure, regret, relief, hope, guilt, vanity, and more. The stronger the emotion you choose, the more securely you hook the reader. But when appealing to the stronger emotions, it is especially important not to seem to be manipulating readers' reactions. The emotional tenor must be in line with the rest of your argument. An appeal to fear in an article that describes a life-and-death situation is probably appropriate. An appeal to fear in a paper that explains a new invention for peeling potatoes ends up sounding like satire.

For a statement of fact or a quotation to appeal to the emotions, it must have direct implications for the reader's well-being. Usually these implications are transmitted through emotional images. We'll show you some examples of what we mean.

● Piqued that local museums have started to charge steep admission fees, coauthor Kesselman-Turkel shares her anger with readers who, she assumes, can empathize with her:

> So the museums are doing poorly, are they? Well, I'm secretly glad to hear it. I've been doing poorly myself ever since they slammed their doors on me and my children several years ago.[9]

● Disgusted with his one-time weight problem, and delighted to have shed forty-seven pounds at long last, John Hirsh opens his report by appealing to the hunger pangs that millions of readers must have:

> I used to be a greaser. A food greaser. In a typical day I ate several quarter pounders with cheese, extra crispy fried chicken, deep dish pizza . . .[10]

● Flora Davis relies on her readers' empathy with her woman torn between love and exhaustion:

> Sarah has a job on Wall Street that's one long crisis from nine to five. By the end of the week she's worn out. Her husband is worried about her and wants Sarah

> to look for less demanding work. "He says I'm under too much pressure," she said, "and that stress can make you sick. But I love my job. I don't want to give it up."[11]

There are two special ways the writer can appeal to readers' emotions simply and directly. One is through flattery.

How do you flatter the reader? By addressing him directly, saying in effect, "I'm writing this for you." Here's a lead we wrote for a *Popular Science* article that does exactly that:

> If you, like most home-owners, dread the next time your house needs an exterior paint job, take heart! You won't have to repaint as often if you take advantage of the research data gathered by . . .[12]

Here's another, written by Vella C. Munn, that gets its strength from a combination of two techniques. She addresses (a) her question (b) directly to the reader:

> Ever been frustrated in your attempt to read to your toddler? One minute he's listening; the next he jumps up in the middle of the story and wanders off in search of something more interesting to do. You'd hoped to give him a glimpse of knowledge, to open the door to the wonderful world of books. What happens? He'd rather wrestle with the dog![13]

The other way to appeal directly to readers' emotions is with an anecdote, which is the nonfiction writer's name for a little story. Why does storytelling have such a compelling effect? Because everybody loves to hear a good tale.

If you begin with an anecdote, and it's interesting, that's one point in your favor. If it also relates to the reader—if she's been in the same situation or can imagine being there—your lead will be twice as strong. Flora Davis's lead about Sarah, the woman with a job on Wall Street, has that advantage because it was written for wives who work. The excerpted lead for a medical journal article on condominiums, about a doctor who has bought one, is a small anecdote.

Here's an anecdote that Lee Edson uses as the lead for his article about a burn injury:

> It was a snowy January morning in 1978. Having been up most of the night, Linda Short could barely keep her eyes open, but she would not give in to sleep as she watched over her eight-year-old daughter, Rena. The child was swathed in blankets in the emergency ward at Dorchester General Hospital in Maryland. The young resident doctor and local pediatrician who ex- amined Rena agreed that the little girl needed to be moved immediately to a larger facility—to Baltimore City Hospital. The doctors tried not to upset Linda (she had already been through an overwhelming or- deal), but they felt they had to be truthful. "Rena is badly burned," they told her. "If she lives two weeks, she may make it, but she'll be lucky to live two weeks."[14]

Anecdotal leads can start off history papers, too, as shown in the following example by coauthor Peterson:

> The space vehicle was just a nautical mile or two in the distance. All hearts on deck of the recovery ship paused for the duration of this momentous voyage. Breathing stopped as the small boats put out for the craft just returned from its trip around the moon. The Pacific Ocean itself seemed subdued and awestruck.
>
> And as one recovery boat drew near, all ears cocked to catch a sound of life. What momentous scientific lore would the three intrepid space travelers be dis- cussing at a moment such as this?
>
> "Queen! How is that for high?" a nasal voice broke the calm with its twang.
>
> It was followed by an even shriller response,

cloaked in a bit of an accent. "King! My brave, Mac! How is that for high?"

"Ace!" came still a third response. "Dear friends, how is that for high?"

High-Low-Jack! The three astronauts were so preoccupied with their game of high-low-jack they hadn't noticed the recovery vessels steaming toward them. A rousing game of cards was quite a fitting ending for a space voyage conjectured back in 1865 by none other than Jules Verne.[15]

To sum up, the three ways the writer appeals to the readers' emotions are through emotional images, flattery and story-telling. (In Chapter 10, we will discuss how to select and write anecdotes.)

How to find effective leads

The writers most courted by editors are the ones who consistently turn in compelling leads. Professionals and academics who need to produce papers to win recognition or advancement in their fields can count on being read if they, too, learn to write effective leads. Many people think it's a mystical art. Actually it's a skill anyone can learn.

To choose your own best beginning, examine the results of your research. Look for the most exciting anecdote, the most surprising fact, the most controversial quotation. See if you can find an opening that mixes two or more of the devices discussed earlier. The paragraph that combines both intellectual and emotional appeals, the anecdote that poses a paradox, the startling fact that draws instant reader identification, the quotation that asks a question—all are powerful leads and worth working to achieve.

What was the topic's question that *you* most wanted answered? That's usually the question uppermost in your readers' minds. Examine the material you've pinpointed for possible leads and ask yourself, "What made me sit up and take notice?" Make that your lead.

EXERCISES:

1. Use at least three different popular magazines to find a total of five different kinds of leads to articles. Copy them. Identify each type of lead according to terminology used in this chapter. (For each, cite the publication's name, date, and page numbers.)

2. Use at least three different scholarly journals to find a total of five different kinds of leads to papers. Copy them. Identify each type of lead according to terminology used in this chapter. (For each, cite the publication's name, date, and page numbers.)

3. Locate five examples of papers or articles that you believe have no leads or ineffective ones. (Do not take all five examples from the same publication title.) Photocopy the entire article for each example. Using only information contained within each article, write new leads for the five articles. (For each, cite the publication's name, date, and page numbers.)

4. Find three papers you wrote earlier. Reread them and decide whether you included effective leads. If you did, write a few lines for each that identify the type of lead and justify why it is effective. If you believe your original lead was ineffective, re-write it. Bring to class the original (or a photocopy) and the rewrite of all three papers.

8.2 THE TOPIC SENTENCE.

The topic sentence is a promise. It does for the readers what a good working title does for the writer: it tells her exactly what to expect in the paper. Why do we suggest that you repeat what the title may have already said? For two reasons:

1. Repeating it frees you (or an editor if you're writing for publication) to make your final title an eye-catching one.

2. Repeating it makes the job of reading as easy as possible so that the reader can concentrate on your ideas and your new information.

It is important to let readers know, right after you've caught their attention, the confines of what you're about to cover. Then they will expect nothing more and nothing different from what you're planning to deliver. If you deliver what you promise, the reader should end up contented. But if you fail to spell out that promise, the reader may imagine that something entirely different is coming, and wind up unhappy. The topic sentence gives the reader a mind-set, a frame of reference for everything that comes afterward.

A topic sentence may be less than a sentence, or even several sentences long. It may be smoothly sewn onto the end of the lead, or stand by itself, or begin the next paragraph, which starts the paper's body. It can be as old-fashioned as, "In this paper I will report the events leading up to . . ." or it can be disguised within a quotation, a question, or a statistic. Let's examine some topic sentences before discussing them further:

• In an article coauthor Peterson wrote for a group of Sunday-newspaper magazines, he uses the obvious, old-fashioned kind of topic sentence because his subject, as spelled out by the title, "The Nightmare of Nuclear Blackmail," has to be handled in an obvious, open, and direct manner. After his lead, he goes on:

> But around the globe, the haunting question remains: Will homemade or stolen nuclear devices become the terror weapons of the future?
>
> The possibility of this happening drew strong opinions from a panel of experts whose divergent views ranged from alarming to comforting.[16]

His words alert readers to exactly what the paper is about, and even how he has obtained his data.

• Earlier we looked at the beginning of Alan Haas's article about the bonanza in old cars. After hooking readers with his lead, Haas states what the body of his article is to be about:

> What was formerly a hobby, the collecting of Locomobiles, Cords, Bugattis, Isotta Fraschinis, for the

pleasure of owning, tinkering with, or simply admiring these splendid machines of the past, has, in the past decade, become a bonanza for knowledgeable car freaks.[17]

What do you think the article will discuss?

● After posing the paradoxical lead about doctors of osteopathy that we saw earlier, Marvin Grosswirth begins his article's body with a statistic that ties it to his topic sentence:

Approximately ten percent of all people who visit physicians' offices go to osteopaths, but many of them are unaware of any difference between a Doctor of Medicine (M.D.) and a Doctor of Osteopathy (D.O.). But there is one, and the osteopathic profession is determined to preserve it.[18]

What should you promise in your topic sentence? In Chapter 7 we discussed the two components of every paper's theme: its topic, or objective boundaries, and its purpose, or subjective goal. (Professional writers often call these two components the *focus* and the *slant*.) The topic is always part of the topic sentence. The purpose—whether you're going to report, give directions, explain, or persuade—is sometimes stated in the topic sentence using key words like *prove, report, show how to*. Often the purpose is implied by the way you write the topic sentence.

In the topic sentence which follows Bonnie Remsberg's previously excerpted lead about married couples, she spells out her purpose as well as her subject and, at the same time, begins sharing information with her readers:

To meet the needs of men and women who want their lovemaking to be the best it can be, a new breed of specialist has emerged—the sex therapist. Sex therapists, some of whom are psychologists, some psychiatrists, some gynecologists, are treating couples of all ages who have all kinds of sex problems. And they're doing so with great success.

What, the *Journal* wondered, are these experts

learning, not only about troubled marriages, but about flourishing ones as well? What, specifically, leads people to seek their help? And in what ways can the knowledge and expertise of reputable sex therapists benefit even the most contented couple? To find out, we initiated a cross-country search to talk to, and learn from, the leading practitioners of this new, important and growing field.[19]

At the end of her first topic paragraph, Remsberg reveals the subjective aspect of her topic, to report that sex therapists are doing a great job. She leaves no doubt about her approach to the material. In her next paragraph, she identifies the exact areas she intends to cover and ends with a statement about the research method she has employed.

Less lengthy, and less obvious, is Flora Davis's topic sentence. It comes immediately after her lead (quoted earlier in this chapter) and spells out her subject and her purpose:

Like so many people, Sarah wants it all: a life crammed to the brim with work, family, fun. And like others, she's concerned about stress. In recent years researchers have concluded that stress can contribute to various medical problems. . . .[20]

What is the subject of Davis's article? Stress, of course and, more specifically, stress caused by busy life-styles.

What subjective approach will she take? A report, as shown by "In recent years researchers have concluded . . ."

Look back and reread Lee Edson's anecdote. Edson's article is a scrupulously objective report of a life-and-death two-week drama. His anecdote's last line states the article's subject: "If she lives two weeks, she may make it, but she'll be lucky to live two weeks."[21]

Your first efforts at writing leads and topic sentences for your own papers are not likely to read as smoothly as the examples we've shown here. They're the work of pros. We suggest you begin by writing forthright topic sentences that state both topic and purpose straight out. If you have chosen your working titles well, you will have no trouble making them complete and accurate. (Don't forget: they can be as long as several sentences or as short as a phrase.) When you've mastered them, you can attempt to build more polished, less obvious ones: quotations, questions, facts you've discovered that encompass your entire theme.

As you read, watch how other writers create topic sentences. Remember their tricks and put them into your bag for future use.

EXERCISES:

Using your library's *Encyclopedia Americana* as your source of information, look up any five of the entries cited below and, for each subject, write from one to three paragraphs that begin a comprehensive paper. Choose a purpose that fits your intended paper, and include a working title, a lead, a topic sentence, and at least one sentence more:

1. Canada—The Acadian Refugees
2. Calculus
3. Gordon, Charles George (1833–1885)
4. Gyroscope
5. Halley, Edmund
6. Veneers and Veneering
7. Morgan, John Pierpont (1837–1913)
8. Morgan, John Pierpont (1867–1943)
9. Nature Worship
10. Prohibition

8.3 THE BODY.

The body is that long middle of the paper in which you put meat onto the skeleton of your topic sentence:

1. You divide your topic into sub-topics.

2. You report the details of an event, give complete directions for the reader to follow, or explain your chosen idea thoroughly.

3. If it's part of your purpose, you argue persuasively for your thesis.

How do you organize all the thoughts rattling around in your head so you can get them onto paper in an order the reader can follow? With an outline. If you learn to outline well, we promise that you'll cut in half the time it takes to write your first draft. (Remember, we believe it is nearly impossible to write any paper in only one draft.)

Before you begin to put words onto paper, it's important to get an unclouded perspective of how your first draft is to be organized. Your perspective may change once you've written the first draft. You may see relationships that weren't clear until you wrote down all of your ideas. You may discover that research data fit into different places, or lead to different conclusions, than you originally thought. But unless you begin with a clear plan, you'll end up with a hodgepodge of long notes instead of a first draft. The plan simply presents your details, directions, explanations, or persuasion in its most logical sequence so both you and your readers can grasp it with a minimum of effort.

Most professional writers prepare tentative outlines of sub-topics even before they begin to research. (That's why we've put our chapter on research *after* this one.) If they know the general areas into which their facts, figures, testimony, and anecdotes have to fall, it generally saves hours otherwise spent chasing down details that are tangential or superfluous to the thrusts of their papers. True, sometimes those tangents are fascinating, and you may decide to chase them anyway since half the fun of doing research is stumbling onto intriguing facts or ideas that lead to new avenues for future exploration. But don't let the tangents keep you from thoroughly researching your main circle of responsibility.

Very often the subject matter dictates the most logical sequence for writing it up. Reports of events beg for chronological organization. Descriptions of people, places, or things should be organized according to the order in which the eye might see them, generally moving from an overview to a description of each specific part in turn. These are forthright organizations, relatively simple to plan and execute. The only writers who get into trouble here are writers who aren't content to keep their writing simple. Remember, the object of writing is not to display your brilliance at making an intricate plan work in spite of its intricacy. The object of writing is to lead the reader down the easiest path to understanding.

The same holds true for papers that give directions. In fact, here it's imperative that you keep the order logical. The goal of your paper is to make it possible for the reader to achieve the promised result if he follows your instructions in the order you give them. A step-by-step progression is needed.

Most writers don't have trouble with step-by-step order. They slip up in leaving out steps. No matter how obvious any step seems to you, you must include every one. Readers follow you blindly, expecting that you have done all the thinking for them.

In papers that explain intangible actions or ideas, there is no built-in logical progression. Still, it remains your task as a writer to arrange your subtopics sensibly so the reader can follow your train of thought. You may have to impose logical order, such as by moving from easy to hard information, or grouping similar actions close together, or explaining a general subtopic and then specific examples. For instance, in a paper on how to influence local government, you may group all the actions involving letter writing and then all the actions involving personal contact. Within each of those groupings, you can then go from the easiest-to-do to the hardest-to-do, or from the least effective to the most effective.

You may even want to combine two different ways of organizing. But when you write your paper, be sure to use words that tell your reader the order you have chosen: "Easiest of all is . . . Not quite so easy is . . . But the hardest way of all is . . ." Usually these clue words fit into transitions between the subtopics. (We discuss transitions in Chapter 12.)

Whatever you do, once you've picked a pattern, stick to it. Writers sometimes confuse readers by reversing the pattern of their organization, for example going from the theoretical to the practical under one subtopic and from the practical to the theoretical under the next. Although variety in sentences and words can be a good thing, a lot of variety in organization pattern defeats the purpose of your organization.

You can also defeat your purpose by carelessly imposing the wrong kind of organization on your material. In a paper that persuades, you may choose to move from weaker to stronger arguments; but never move from stronger to weaker or you'll lose your credibility page by page. (You can, with good results, see-saw from strong to weak and back to strong, or scatter your weaker arguments among the stronger.)

Also keep in mind that not all subtopics demand equal emphasis in your paper. The more space you devote to a subtopic, the more important the reader will assume it to be in relation to the other subtopics. Therefore, by organizing your paper before starting the research, you can spend the greatest part of your research time searching for details on your most important subtopics, and less time on less important points.

Some of the material we presented in the preceding pages covers ground similar to that covered in Chapter 7; we intend to go over some of it once more in Chapter 11. Our reason is that we have watched so many beginning writers trip themselves up with sloppy or needlessly complicated organization. We hope you will simplify your writing tasks by sticking to simple and direct kinds of organization patterns whenever you have a paper to write. To help you accomplish that goal, we've prepared a checklist of some of the more popular patterns; you'll find it at the end of this chapter.

Types of outlines

The form in which you write your outline depends on your style (or your teacher's preference). Many people prefer a formal letter-and-number outline:

     I. Subtopic
        A. Detail
        B. Detail
        C. Detail
            1. Example
            2. Example
        D. Detail
    II. Subtopic
        A. Detail
            1. Example
        B. Detail

Others prefer an informal outline in which they jot down key words or phrases in the order the topics are to be covered.

Our own outline style varies depending on the complexity of our writing assignment and how familiar we are with the paper's subject matter. Often, before starting the research we jot down a word or two about each major subtopic. Then, after research is completed, we fill up two pages of a lined pad with a detailed outline that sometimes even shows where we'll put each of the quotations, statistics, and anecdotes we've amassed.

No matter which outline style you prefer, there are three things to keep in mind:

● You must be sure to write down every subtopic and each aspect of that subtopic that you intend to cover.

● If you have not included at least three levels of information in your outline (such as the I's, A's, and 1's in the formal outline presented above), you probably have not investigated your subject in enough detail.

● You must remain willing to shift the order of your outline if a better organization occurs to you during the writing, researching, and editing.

We have reprinted as Illustration 8/1 (at end of this chapter), the actual outline coauthor Kesselman-Turkel used when she wrote the study tips article reproduced earlier as Illustration 7/2 (Chapter 7). It shows how much detail she worked out before putting the first piece of paper into her typewriter. We've annotated the outline to show how she moved several parts around during the writing. Study both the outline and the final article to see how one follows the other.

Notice that Kesselman-Turkel's outline tells only what goes into the body. Although you can jot down possible leads, topic sentences, and endings on the paper you use for outlining, do not make them part of your outline. They are autonomous parts of papers and have to be treated that way.

8.4 THE ENDING.

It's self-evident that every paper must have an ending. But many writers don't understand what the ending is supposed to do. Here, for starters, is what it should not do:

- It should not contain any new ideas.
- It should not offer any new examples.
- It should not reach any new conclusions.

Everything you have to say—all of your proofs, specific illustrations, and conclusions—belong in the body of your paper. The ending merely wraps up the theme, ties it in a bow, and presents it to the reader one final time. It comments, in effect, "This was the point of what you just read." It must be strong, but it must not be long. A sentence or two is usually enough.

There are many ways to create a satisfying ending. Here are some popular ones:

- **Restate the purpose positively.** If you've offered directions for building a telescope, you might end, "Now you can build one yourself." If your purpose was to persuade that autos should use gasohol, you might end, "As the evidence shows, gasohol is a viable fuel for everyone."

● **Sum up.** Wrap up all the points you made into one general statement. This can be a restatement of your topic sentence or lead. For example, in "Flunk, Dick and Jane," reprinted as Illustration 7/6, the topic sentence reads, "But chances are, the books your children use are just as bigoted as that teacher." For an ending, Peterson chooses, "So far the report card on textbooks would have to be, 'Oh, see Dick and Jane flunk. Flunk, Dick and Jane, flunk, flunk, flunk.'"

● **Echo the lead.** Repeat an image or phrase that you used back there. If your lead was a question, answer it or refer to the fact that you answered it in the body. For example, John Hirsh's lead on his dieting article began, "I used to be a greaser. A food greaser." So he ended, "I feel more awake than ever before. And I can jog almost thirty minutes at a clip, which is pretty good for a greaser who couldn't walk one block without feeling totally exhausted."[22]

● **Incite the reader to action.** Tell what she can do to learn more or to act on what you've just written about. Or simply exhort, "Go out and build one yourself." For example, in the study tips article (see Illustration 7/2), Kesselman-Turkel ends by referring the reader to additional sources of information.

Your ending does not always have to be in your own words. If you find a quotation or anecdote that makes a good ending according to the criteria above, use it.

EXERCISES:

1. From at least three different popular magazines, copy the endings of five articles. For each, tell what kind of ending it is and the kind of feeling it left you with. Explain whether each is a good ending.

2. Duplicate Exercise 1, using at least three different scholarly publications for your sources.

3. While doing Exercises 1 and 2, accumulate at least five endings that you feel are inadequate. Explain what's wrong, and rewrite each ending to accomplish what it should do.

4. Write an ending for each composition you began as part of the exercises at the end of Section 8.2.

CHECKLIST: POPULAR WAYS
TO ORGANIZE PAPERS
OR SECTIONS OF PAPERS:

GROUP 1. In time sequence:

- in the sequence in which it was seen or done
- in the sequence in which it should be seen or done
- from cause to effect

GROUP 2. From general to specific:

- general topic to subtopics
- theoretical to practical
- generalizations to examples

GROUP 3. From least to most:

- easiest to hardest
- smallest to largest
- worst to best
- weakest to strongest

- least important to most important
- least complicated to most complicated
- least effective to most effective
- least controversial to most controversial

GROUP 4.   From most to least:

- most known to least known
- most factual to least factual (fact to opinion)

GROUP 5.   Giving both sides
(grouped or interspersed)

- pros and cons
- similarities and differences (compare and contrast)
- assets and liabilities
- hard and easy
- bad and good
- effective and ineffective
- weak and strong
- complicated and uncomplicated
- controversial and uncontroversial

NOTES: CHAPTER 8

1. John W. Knutson, "Controlling the Cost of Dental Health Care Insurance," *American Journal of Public Health*, July, 1979, p. 647.

2. Dan Carlinsky, "Weatherwomen," *Seventeen,* August, 1976, p. 180.

3. Bonnie Remsberg, "Love and Sex: The 10 Most Often Asked Questions," *Good Housekeeping*, July, 1979, p. 70.

4. Claire Safron, "How Children Feel About Their Bodies," *Redbook*, June, 1979, p. 21.

5. Ted Schwarz, "Buying a Condominium or Coop," *Physician's Management*, November, 1979, p. 114.

6. "Physicians Hoist the Media onto the Examining Table," *Physician's Management*, June, 1978, p. 25.

7. Alan D. Haas, "Buy That Bonanza V8 Convertible or a '55 Goldmine Coupe," *Science Digest*, March 1979, p. 8.

8. Marvin Grosswirth, "What Is a Doctor of Osteopathy?" *Science Digest*, March, 1979, p. 76.

9. Judi R. Kesselman, "It Costs Too Much to Go to a Museum," *New York Times*, Nov. 11, 1973, Sect. II, p. 21.

10. John L. Hirsh, "Food Greaser Loses 47 Pounds," *Milwaukee Sentinel*, January 11, 1979, p. 6.

11. Flora Davis, "How to Live with Stress and Thrive," *Woman's Day*, May 22, 1979, p. 76.

12. Franklynn Peterson and Judi R. Kesselman, "10-Year Paint Job," *Popular Science*, May, 1979, p. 112.

13. Vella C. Munn, "Early Reading," *Baby Talk*, June, 1978, p. 4.

14. Lee Edson, "Doctors Call Her the Miracle Girl," *Family Circle*, June 26, 1979, p. 28.

15. Franklynn Peterson, "Who Planned Apollo II, Von Braun or Verne?" *Science & Mechanics*, March, 1971, p. 88–89.

16. Franklynn Peterson, "The Nightmare of Nuclear Blackmail," *Oklahoma City Oklahoman*, *Orbit* magazine, September 21, 1975, p. 8.

17. Haas, see note 7.

18. Grosswirth, see note 8.

19. Remsberg, see note 3.

20. Davis, see note 11.

21. Edson, see note 14.

22. Hirsh, see note 10.

ILLUSTRATION 8/1

"How to study more effectively"

I. How to use study time
  A. Where to study
    1. Behavior modification
      a. Pavlov
  B. How long to study
    1. Efficient time use
      a. Value of cramming
    2. Ideal time periods
      a. research
  C. How to keep studying
    1. Study breaks
      a. As reward
      b. As necessity
        1) Pauk quote
  D. How to pace studying
    1. Hard to easy [Note: moved to C during writing]
    2. Separate similar subjects
      a. Radio waves analogy
  E. When to study
    1. Lecture notes
    2. For recitation class
  F. When not to study [Note: transposed with E during writing]
    1. Psychological research
II. How to use notes
  A. Note-taking organization
    1. Paper to use
    2. How to organize paper
      a. Clue technique
        1) Note and text related
        2) Note and text unrelated

B. Note-taking tricks
  1. Shorthand
  2. Clue words*
  3. Examples*
  4. Listen to the last * [*these last three items became hint 11, part of IV-B]
C. Use of notes in studying
  1. Palmatier technique
III. How to memorize
A. Use senses
  1. See
  2. Hear
B. Associate
  1. Mnemonics
  2. Acronyms
IV. How to use texts
A. Reading texts
  1. Pauk method
B. Note-taking in texts
  1. How
    a. Color system
    b. Sign system
  2. When

CHAPTER 9
HOW TO RESEARCH

The reason why so few good books
are written is that so few people
who can write know anything.
Walter Bagehot

If you expect readers to find your writing authoritative, valuable, and interesting, your research must uncover material for you to write about that is authoritative, valuable, and interesting. It should be self-evident that facts and figures must come from authoritative sources, sources that can be trusted to be accurate and precise. What is not self-evident to inexperienced writers is that the facts should be not only accurate, but plentiful. Some of the dreariest papers we've read are those in which the author tried to stretch too little research across too many pages.

As writers, we make it a rule always to collect more information than we think we're going to use, so that we can choose the best examples to make our points. We think of ourselves not as composers, but as arrangers who assemble other people's themes and counterpoints until they match the available instruments.

9.1 A FACT IS ONLY
AS GOOD AS ITS SOURCE.

When *Reader's Digest* editorial researcher Nina Georges-Picot read in a manuscript that George Washington stood 6 feet 3½ inches in his size 13 boots, she decided to check whether old George really owned boots that big. But how to find out? First she pored over sixteen volumes about Washington at the New York Public Library. Next she studied books, letters, and diaries of Washington's associates. None of them cared a whit about George's shoe size. The ardent fact finder called Mount Vernon to see if perchance George had left his boots under the bed. He hadn't, but somebody there knew about a statue of George made entirely from plaster casts of his body. The likeness was standing in the Richmond, Virginia, state capitol building. Ms. Georges-Picot called Richmond and prevailed on the building's superintendent to measure George's feet. With boots on, the right foot was 10 ⅞ inches long, the left 11 inches—a man's size 8 boot, not 13, if one is to believe the accuracy of the measurement.

The size of George Washington's boot may seem entirely too trivial to have been worth so much of the *Reader's Digest* researcher's time. But to the writer who evidently was caught with the wrong information in his article, it may not be. He probably went back and double-checked, figuring that, if it was true, the tiny foot on such a big man could make the basis for another George Washington article.

To get to the point of our anecdote, a fact is only as good as its source. There are at least three practical reasons why writers should stick to dependable sources and record them along with the information they elicit:

1. It's more efficient.
Let's say that you're researching a railroad crossing paper. From a chart of statistics, you extrapolate that 3,392 people are killed or injured at crossings every year. Then, while organizing or writing the article, you decide it will be more effective to separate

how many were killed from how many were injured. You'll waste a lot of time relocating your information unless you also made note of its source (in this case the U.S. Federal Railroad Administration's *Accident Bulletin* reprinted in the 1973 *U.S. Statistical Abstract*, p. 561).

2. It's more believable.

One author writes that "3,392 people are killed or hurt at railroad crossings every year." Another writes: "The Federal Railroad Administration tallied 3,392 deaths and injuries last year." Which sounds more like a fact? Which sounds more dramatic? If the source of your fact is authoritative, including it in your paper lends credibility.

3. It's safer.

If you say that 3,392 people a year are killed or hurt at railroad crossings, without attributing the number to anyone else, it's you who must stand behind the statement's accuracy. If, instead, you include the source of your data, it leaves you practically in the clear if somebody else got the numbers wrong. As we saw in the example about George Washington's boots, a fact is no better than its source.

9.2 DISTINGUISH BETWEEN PRIMARY AND SECONDARY SOURCES.

There are two basic kinds of sources. If you get your information directly from the expert's mouth (or his own written words), that's a primary source. If, instead, you take second-hand information reported in a newspaper story, an article, a book, or a movie, you're using a secondary source. This is not merely an academic distinction, as all too many writers have found out the hard way.

For example, Dick Kerckhoff, a professor at Purdue University, one day in 1971 came across a startling fact in *Today's Child:* "In a recent survey to determine the amount of time fathers spent with their 5th grade sons each week, the average time was found to be 7¼ minutes, reported the psychologist." That sounds authentic, doesn't it? Still, Kerckhoff was piqued by the statement. He wanted to verify its accuracy from its primary source. The article attributed it to a psychologist at a Florida college. The psychologist told Dick that she'd taken it from *The Father's Book* by Ted Klein.

Kerckhoff checked Klein's book, published in 1968, and found that the "fact" referred to seventh and eighth graders, not fifth graders, and to the time spent *alone* with their fathers. Klein's source: a speech by a psychologist reported in *Vital Speeches of the Day*, September 1, 1961. Reading the speech, Kerckhoff found it was 7½ minutes, not 7¼. The psychologist's source: an article by Philip Wylie, "American Men are Loving Fathers," which appeared first in *The American Weekly* and was condensed in the March 1956 *Reader's Digest*. There, in a short article connected to the main feature, were those elusive boys and their 7½ or 7¼ minutes a week with dear old dad. The source was listed: Gordon H. Schroeder writing in the *Christian Herald*. Professor Kerckhoff tracked the Reverend Mr. Schroeder to his church in Lincoln, Nebraska, only to learn that the minister wasn't the primary source either, and didn't remember where the fact had come from. He'd read it somewhere.

After arduous backtracking, Kerckhoff had established that the 1971 *Today's Child* article missed on every one of the four facts he'd checked: (a) there was no recent survey—the fiasco had begun at least sixteen years earlier, (b) it wasn't fifth-grade boys but seventh or eighth graders—maybe, (c) the time was not 7½ but 7¼ minutes—or maybe neither, and (d) no authoritative source could establish that there had even been such a survey.

As both anecdotes in this chapter make plain, you can't assume that a fact is a fact simply because the author of a paper says it is a fact. Every good factual writer monitors the accuracy of his information as closely as possible. These three guidelines will help:

1. Whenever possible, use primary sources.

2. When using a secondary source, try to double-check with at least one independent secondary source.

3. Always report your information accurately. Identify your source, unless there's an overriding reason not to.

9.3 HOW TO ASSESS THE FACTS YOU FIND.

There are five common reliability checks for assessing the facts you research.

1. Accuracy
If you have seen an event happen, and report it just the way you saw it, both you and your readers assume it's accurate reporting. An accurate report may not be precisely what did happen; six eyewitnesses to an accident often render six conflicting reports. But accuracy of reporting enhances both believability and reliability.

2. Authenticity
Authenticity means that the fact comes from someone who should know what she's talking about. If you can't confirm the data, you must be careful to present it as an authentic statement, not a verified fact. The Pentagon, for example, has authentic information about the number of missiles owned by the United States. At budget time, it claims there aren't enough missiles; when proving the good job it's doing, it has more than enough missiles in the ground. That's why good writers report that the missile figures coming from the Pentagon are authentic, but never assume their accuracy.

3. Credibility
The source's way of presenting his facts and proofs, or the source's proven track record, or both, make up his credibility.

If it's your subjective conclusion that a source's fact can be believed because of his credibility, present the information to your readers that way.

4. Plausibility

If you subjectively conclude that the fact makes sense to you, you are accepting its plausibility. You must report it not as verified fact but as plausible consideration.

5. Corroboration

If you obtain information from a separate, also believable, source that substantiates your first source's facts, you will have objectively demonstrated the reliability of your source and her information. This is one of the strongest indicators that your facts are correct; in reporting them, it is a good idea to mention both sources.

For most factual writing, it is necessary to research to acquire the facts you need and to verify them. The rest of this chapter will discuss many of the places where such research can be done.

9.4 THE LIBRARY.

The library is the major depository of secondary sources and historical primary papers and a useful lead to current primary data as well. We have found that most writers use the library poorly—if at all.

For any research project, your college or university library is the place to start. The larger the institution, as a rule, the larger its collection.

Many colleges have more than one library, a fact we've seen too many students overlook. At the University of Wisconsin, for example, Memorial Library is the major library. But the School of Engineering, School of Medicine, School of Agriculture, and such, each has its large library as well. A number of individual departments maintain smaller, specialized libraries, such as geology and Afro-American studies. The librarians at these places know their respective fields intimately and can be valuable guides to resources and to authoritative people.

A typical nonfiction novice enters the local library, heads for the card catalog, looks up the subject, checks out the available books, and calls it a day. But by the time a book is written, printed, and tucked away on a library shelf, its information is usually at least a couple of years old. The more enterprising beginner adds *Reader's Guide to Periodical Literature* (RGPL) to provide a more current overview of the topic; even this information is likely to be half a year to a year old. The brightest self-starter becomes familiar with the library and learns where the various little volumes of this and that are kept. He knows how to use the reference collection, the tools designed specifically for researchers. In some libraries, the most useful reference volumes are behind the reference librarian's desk.

The best researcher seeks out the librarian and explains precisely what he's looking for.

> Not: "Something on cars."
> Instead: "Something very current about pollution control systems on diesel cars."

> Not: "A book about protein."
> Instead: "Whatever is very new about high protein diets, and especially their hazards, for an exposé I am writing."

Years ago librarians realized that even the best budgeted libraries were not going to be able to purchase every book published. Eager to provide users with complete facilities, they developed interlibrary loan systems. Depending on what locality or state you live in, you may have easy access to almost any nonrare book and periodical in almost any public or academic library in the United States. Even part of the Library of Congress's collection is kept busily circulating to libraries across the country.

When you begin a major research project—better still, before you start one—ask your librarian about interlibrary loan procedures.

Periodicals

Many libraries maintain their periodical collections in their reference departments. Others keep them separate. In addition to the popular periodicals, the ones indexed in RGPL and such, there are the professional and scholarly periodicals. These are the keys to current thinking and the latest research. Some libraries' collections of both general and technical periodicals are extensive; some are inadequate. But most now have interlibrary loan facilities for getting needed periodicals within a week or two, and many libraries maintain lists of the other libraries in the state that do subscribe to them.

The readers' guides to professional journals are called indexes and abstracts. They are published by professional societies and by companies catering to the needs of the various professions. One of those needs is quick access to research data. Therefore, a great many professional journals and their matching abstracts or indexes are on library shelves within a few months after the scientists have completed their research papers. For nonfiction writers, timeliness is assured.

Aside from new, non-dog-eared pages of facts and figures, the journals are also useful for providing leads to primary sources—people doing current research, whom you can reach by mail or telephone for the most up-to-date information, interpretations, and opinions. These people are the papers' authors, whose professional addresses are usually noted in the journals.

An index is simply a categorized listing of article titles or topics plus authors' names. Using it, you can find journal articles on your topic by first locating the general subject and, second, singling out the titles that seem most appropriate. With your list of article titles, journal names, and page numbers, you can skim the journals in your library's periodical collection (or available from interlibrary loan) to pick out what you need.

An abstract does everything that an index does. In addition, it includes a thumbnail summation of the salient points covered by each indexed article. The summations generally save you from having to skim dozens of articles to locate the two or three that are right on target. Sometimes the abstracts are comprehensive enough that, for quick generalizations, you can work from them and not have to read the articles at all. Thorough research, however, calls for reading the article, not only the abstract entry.

Computer search services

More and more libraries are linking up to computers that store and sort out information for researchers. For a fee of from about $5 to $75, depending on the service you need, your library may be able to provide you with a computerized index or collection of abstracts to journal articles on the topic of your research. The type of information available on computers is growing all the time. With luck, you may even be able to find a library that's hooked into *The New York Times* computerized index—a dream tool for researchers of current events, humanities, and social sciences. It indexes a great many periodicals besides the *Times*.

Private libraries

Associations of professionals, businesses, and activists from the Administrative Management Society in Pennsylvania to Zero Population Growth, Inc., in California, maintain libraries too. Most of them feel it is part of their mandate to help serious researchers in their fields of interest. American Metal Climax, Inc., in New York City, for example, maintains a library of 10,000 books, 1,000 journals, plus sundry reports and other backup information. It is willing to make interlibrary loans. The Zator Company in Cambridge, Massachusetts, holds 4,000 technical reports, 400 books, 350 volumes of journals, and other data on artificial intelligence, computer program languages, information storage and retrieval, and so fourth.

There are indexes to these special libraries. Ask your librarian.

Not indexed among the special libraries, but valuable nonetheless to many researchers, are newspaper libraries, which have always been called morgues. Invariably crammed between the boiler room and the coal bin, a typical morgue includes 143 filing cabinets, two shopworn tables, and four intelligent, eager employees. Morgue librarians clip and file their newspapers on a topic-by-topic, name-by-name basis. Most permit access to researchers. Some also answer short questions by phone, and answer mailed requests by photocopying shorter files, usually for fees.

9.5 HOW TO LOCATE AND TAP LIVING PRIMARY SOURCES.

Although plenty of fine papers have been written from secondary sources located in college libraries, it's always better if you can get facts, figures, anecdotes, and quotations right from the living primary experts. Most students, we've found, try to get away with using secondary information until they're forced into more rigorous research by more demanding course requirements. Laziness alone is not the reason: they don't understand the importance of primary sources, and they don't know how simple it can be to find and tap them.

No matter where you live or go to school, we'll bet you can ferret out two or three authorities on almost any subject, no matter how specialized. If you keep your questions short and specific, they should be willing and maybe even flattered to assist you in any serious research, in person or by telephone.

The telephone is the fastest way to obtain information from primary sources outside your locality. But the mail is less expensive. To be successful at researching by mail:

● Address your letter to a real, live person (Mr. John Jones, Director of Research), not simply to a title (The Director of Research).

● Tell why you need the information.

● Tell how the information is to be used. (Is it for a class assignment? Are you asking permission to quote it in a publication? Is it background for a thesis?)

● Ask a specific question. If there's more than one, number them. Leave room in the margins of your letter for handwritten answers. Don't expect more than a few words for each answer—though you may be pleasantly surprised.

● Refer to your deadline. Allow at least a week after the letter is received for a reply.

● Keep your letter typed, businesslike, and short—no more than one page. (Chapter 13 shows how to write a good letter.)

● Enclose a stamped, self-addressed envelope for a reply.

Where can researchers get the names, addresses, and phone numbers of primary sources? Here are just a few of our own favorite aids:

1. Who's Whos and other biographical directories:

Almost every field of endeavor—science, medicine, psychology, journalism—has its own biographical directory. Addresses and phone numbers are usually included along with achievements. Many libraries maintain at least small collections of these tools among their reference works.

2. Journal articles:

After reading an article, you can get in touch with its author at the institution listed (along with his name and title) at the beginning or end of the article.

3. Professional and trade associations:

Executive directors of most associations know which members are experts or which member companies have experts on staff.

4. Public relations people:

Manufacturers and sellers of everything from nuts to education, hospital care, and peace are all out to promote their products. Many produce packets of information for writers (press kits and press releases) and for the general public (pamphlets, booklets, and such) that are often useful in researching papers and sometimes steer you to primary sources. But you must pay particular attention to evaluating the credibility of information provided by organizations eager to promote products and causes.

5. Federal, state, and local governments:

One of the largest sources of primary (and secondary) information is government. The *U.S. Government Manual*, an annual guide to the bureaucratic morass we call the federal government, is available at many libraries. Detailed though it is, it just touches the tip of the information iceberg. The names listed in the manual tend to be those of department heads and subheads who can refer you to more knowledgeable subalterns.

State governments, too, have matrices of informed individuals tucked into their political infrastructures. You can find them generally through the public information officers of the various departments; they're ready sources of current information and leads to other sources. Larger local governments have good resource people too.

For quotable facts and figures there is no library (except the Library of Congress) that contains as much up-to-date and often practical data as the huge library of publications ground out by the U.S. Government Printing Office and stored in pamphlet and microfiche form by depositories in selected libraries in every state in the United States.

When it comes to potatoes, weather, and census figures, you're on sure footing when it comes to government sources. But start to build a well-documented argument that relies on government figures and government officials' opinions in areas such as employment, taxes, or housing, and you may be in big trouble. To play it safe, ask yourself in advance whether, if you were *reading* instead of writing the paper, you'd have much confidence in the bearer of the information.

EXERCISES:

Answers to the following questions are available from standard reference books found in most college libraries and good-sized public libraries. Finding them will acquaint you with reference tools and test your persistence in tracking down sources.

1. Tell where you can write to Alex Haley.

2. List at least six books or research articles published during 1976 and 1977 on test-taking anxiety.

3. Find the names and addresses of four companies that manufacture atomic reactors.

4. Find the names and addresses of four companies that manufacture billiard balls.

5. Give the name of at least one bibliography of the writings *of* W. E. B. Du Bois.

6. Give the name of at least one bibliography of the writings *about* W. E. B. Du Bois.

CHAPTER 10
THE TECHNIQUES USED
IN FACTUAL WRITING

If you can't write your idea
on the back of my calling card,
you don't have a clear idea.
David Belasco

To people who haven't written extensively, one of the most mysterious attributes of the accomplished writer is the seemingly limitless number of words he manages to spin off on any topic he chooses. Even with good outlines, novices find it difficult to weave together more than 500 words about anything no matter how intricate or interesting.

But there's a key to spinning those reams of colorful words and phrases. The accomplished writer has learned that no outline, no matter how well thought out, can be converted instantly into a perfect paper. An outline is just a series of topics. For a finished paper, those topics must be fleshed out into general statements, and those statements must be explained and supported.

10.1 THE THREE BASIC TECHNIQUES.

In preparing the paper, a writer has only three basic techniques to choose from: exposition, quotation, and narration. These techniques are used not only in papers, but in all writing. Their differences are straightforward and logical when viewed from the perspective of writers. In brief:

● When an author *thinks* something, and reports that to readers, offering facts and figures (without attribution) when they're needed to prove it, that's *exposition*.

● When an author *hears* something worth repeating and repeats it for readers, that's *quotation*. (If the author repeats what someone has said in print, that's also quotation. To employ quotation, you do not always need to use quotation marks.)

● When an author *sees* something happen and reports it for readers as a story, that's *narration*. (When someone other than the author sees the event, tells her, and she reports it in story fashion, it is also narration. A synonym for *narrative* is *anecdote*.)

As with so many other aspects of good writing, however, these three techniques take on slightly different definitions when they're considered from the perspective of readers. These differences in meaning may sound arbitrary or illogical at first, but if you disregard them, you risk having your papers disregarded by readers. In brief:

● When a reader encounters *exposition*—your own words based on your own knowledge and backed up only by your own reputation—he is skeptical unless you are a currently renowned expert in the field about which you are writing, or one of those few writers who have mastered the English language so well that you can spellbind a reader into forgetting his skepticism. Because of its limited believability, exposition is limited by good writers to repeating information readers already believe, or to unifying and reinforcing passages based on the other two techniques.

Something else happens when a reader encounters exposition: he expects to be bored. That's largely because published examples of vivid exposition are so few and far between these days that most readers assume it's a dull technique. As a result, exposition is the most challenging of the three techniques for even experienced writers to use well.

• When a reader sees *quotation*—a reference to someone else who agrees with what you have to say—your own believability increases dramatically. We wish we could say that the increase is in direct proportion to the amount of genuine expertise your quoted source has attained. But watch your own reaction when you read a scholarly paper that frequently quotes other scholars: Do you pause to evaluate the respect given each quoted scholar in her own field? Or do you, like most readers, simply say, "Hmm, these scholars agree, so it must be true."

Writers who know the value of having agreement from anyone with a pedigree, use that technique, quotation, to enhance their papers.

• When a reader finds, in your writing, *narration* of real-life examples of what you're talking about, again your paper's credibility increases dramatically. The reader seems to assess believability more on the vividness of your anecdotes than on any other factor. Perhaps the reason for this is the same reason quotation lends credibility: the factor of safety in numbers. (Professional writers and editors have found that if they offer a reader three examples, quoted or anecdotal, of almost anything, she expects no further proof.) Or perhaps it's that seeing is believing, and that anecdotes generate strong visual images.

Whatever the explanation, experienced writers know for a fact that a reader finds anecdotes believable as well as exciting, and go to great lengths to include them in their papers.

These techniques are often intermingled in good writing. A quotation may be inserted within a sentence of exposition, or included within an anecdotal paragraph. An anecdote may follow hard on the heels of exposition, without even a period to separate them. The goal of all three techniques is the same: to present convincing evidence in an easy-to-read format.

In Chapter 7, we looked at these techniques in the most general way in discussing how to determine the purpose of your paper. In Chapter 11, we'll explain how to put all the techniques together to make a convincing paper. But first, it's important to learn how to recognize and work with each technique.

10.2 EXPOSITION.

Exposition is the presentation of your own thoughts plus the data that help the reader understand and accept them. The thoughts are offered in generalizations of fact and opinion (about which we'll say more in Chapter 11) with backup data such as specific facts, figures, and details that prove the generalizations without the need to call on other people's experiences (anecdotes) or authority (quotations).

The main strength of exposition is that it presents statements more concisely than either quotation or anecdote. However, if the writer isn't an accepted authority in the subject of his paper, the only statements he should make using exposition are those he can safely assume his readers won't quibble with; in other words, statements the readers can accept as truths. They can be:

● *Defined truths*, like the statement that a good writer is someone who writes well, or that a paper is a piece of written schoolwork (so defined by *Webster's New Collegiate Dictionary*, 8th edition).

● *Self-evident truths*, like the statement that dogs bark, cats purr, and writing must be legible if it is to be read.

● *Accepted as truths* by readers who are minimally informed on the topic. In writing to experienced mothers, for example, you don't have to explain or support the statement that every smart mother wants to avoid diaper rash, but you do have to explain the chemical composition of benzene. But in writing for chemists, the reverse is true.

- *Demonstrated truths* that you are carefully proving in your paper.

Most students know most of the fundamentals of expository writing by the time they get to college. It's the nonfiction technique used almost exclusively in grammar and secondary school to write papers on "What I Did during Christmas Vacation" and "How Shakespeare Showed That King Lear Was Mad." It's an adequate technique for learning to put nouns, verbs, and other grammatical parts together into workable sentences. It can—and should—be as accurate, precise, and vivid as the other writing techniques.

Yet vivid exposition is rarely achieved by student writers. Partly it's because published examples of vivid exposition are few and far between. Out of haste and laziness, many professional writers forget that they're competing for today's readers' attention, and because they churn out dull exposition, students may assume that exposition should be dull. We hope that, with the help of Unit II, you have learned the value of making your exposition as colorful as possible. Frederick Simpich's fine expository writing offers a goal to strive for.

Simpich's task, in writing about New York City for *National Geographic*, was to state that, on a hot day, the city consumes one billion gallons of water, and to make the reader understand and accept the statement. Here's how he met the challenge with expository writing that, half a century later, still has force and vividness:

> Can you imagine a man nearly a mile tall, with a mouth a hundred feet wide? A man who could wade across Lake Superior, which is 1,000 feet deep, and get wet only up to his knees? Such a monster, drinking night and day, could just about consume New York's water supply. On a hot day the city uses one billion

gallons. There are less than two billion people on earth;
so that is more than half a gallon for every person.[1]

We were faced with a similar challenge when we had to relate
to ordinary readers, concisely yet vividly, the following collection
of facts about common rust:

● The annual U.S. cost of corrosion is $70 billion.

● The National Bureau of Standards estimates that the
cost of metal corrosion in the United States in 1975
was 4.2 percent of the gross national product.

● Of all energy consumed in the country, 3.4 percent
is used to prevent, repair, or replace corrosion damage.

To find equivalents that readers could easily visualize, we used
the reference book *U.S. Statistical Abstracts*, and came up with
the following exposition:

Each year rust consumes enough of the United States'
iron to supply all of Canada's iron and steel needs for
a year. To prevent, repair, or replace rust, we consume
enough energy to supply all of New England with
electricity for a year. Rust costs every American man,
woman, and child $750 each and every year.

Pause right now to read the short paper reprinted as Illustration
10/1 (at the end of the chapter). In the space of a few hundred
words, the student-author of "Giant Junk Invades Wisconsin!"
attempts to defend her assessment of a large, multipartite tourist
attraction. Her paper fails because of its lack of specifics. Had
she worked hard enough to preserve the details of her sightseeing
trip, the author could have added pages of colorful exposition.
We visited the same place. Here are some details that caught our
eyes.

● In one room, whose floor, ceiling, wall, and railing are covered
with tan carpet, a wine-colored carpet is used to upholster a 30-
foot-long sofa.

● In the same room, a 20-foot-wide fireplace made of tan field-stone functions without a chimney, and smoke wisps out through a hole in the ceiling.

● The entrance to that room is through an almost round doorway made from carefully matched fieldstones that stay up with very little mortar.

● Among the automated musical instruments *not* mentioned in the paper are (a) a Mills Violano Virtuoso, one of the last remaining instruments of its kind, that pneumatically fingers and bows a pair of real violins through a Mozart violin duet; (b) a Hupfeld violin machine, large as a church's pipe organ, that plays an operatic aria by encircling five real violins with a circular bow that's hand-strung with horsehair. The bow automatically plays whichever strings are pneumatically thrust against it, while a second pneumatic mechanism fingers the proper strings; (c) a steam-driven calliope called the Gladiator, so large that its bass drum could conceal a gladiator's chariot while the low-F steam tube could swallow a gladiator whole.

EXERCISES:

By performing this exercise and subsequent ones in the chapter, you will totally rewrite the "Giant Junk" paper shown in Illustration 10/1. For now, do the following:

1. Reproduce the entire paper, as illustrated, and cross out any parts of this draft that you feel do not belong in the finished paper.

2. Using vivid exposition, add the six details we supplied above wherever you think they belong in the paper.

10.3 QUOTATION.

The technique of quotation sometimes hides behind tag-words like *testimony, citation, appeal to authority*, and *paraphrasing*.

Carefully used, quotations amplify generalizations the same way exposition does: they can define, compare, describe, detail, offer evidence, evaluate, and so forth. They present other people's knowledge, experience, opinion, expertise, or reputation when you believe your own may not be adequate to the job at hand.

When to quote (and when not to)

Too many students think that quotations are magic dust to be sprinkled frequently amid expository paragraphs to stir up excitement or lend weight to skimpy ideas. Quotations can enhance your papers but the fact is, a dull or incomprehensible or badly thought-out idea does not gain in credibility or excitement merely through being sandwiched between two sets of quotation marks. Improperly used quotations can say as much about your writing as improper table manners say about your upbringing. They can say, for instance, that you lack confidence to draw conclusions on your own, or that you lack originality to cast your own sentences, paint your own prose pictures, turn your own phrases. If you make a habit of quoting "in" intellectuals or obscure men and women of letters, sharp readers may suspect you of name-dropping in order to pad a poorly conceived outline or badly executed research.

The time to be on the lookout for effective quotations is while you're researching the paper. You must choose them as carefully as you choose the rest of your supports, being guided by two criteria: do they make your points, and do they make for good reading? If the authority you want to cite is long-winded in his statement, throw away the quotation marks and paraphrase him, giving him credit for the thoughts but not the exact words. That way, you can rest on his expertise without burdening your readers with his cumbersome choice of language. Keep in mind that quotation marks have no magic; they indicate only that the exact words between them have been borrowed. Nothing more. Nothing less.

To sum up, use a quotation (a) when you need the voice of authority for a fact or opinion, or (b) when someone's thought, conclusion, or way of saying something is important to the point or point of view of your paper.

Whom to quote

Writers have access to two basic types of sources, primary and secondary. The distinctions are described in Chapter 9. You are expected to signal to readers whether your source is primary or secondary and whether you've spoken to them or only read what they wrote. It is intellectually dishonest to imply that you have spoken to someone you've only read; on the other hand, if you received your facts straight from your authority, it's foolish not to take credit for that. Primary sources carry more weight with most readers than secondary ones, because the readers assume— not always correctly—that what you heard or saw directly is more precise and accurate than what you got secondhand.

Writers usually signal an interviewed source with words like, "He told me." Whether paraphrasing or directly quoting, it is important to give the basis of a source's expertise: her title, the agency she represents, the experience or reputation that makes her authoritative. When relying on secondary sources, writers signal the reader by giving not only the authority's name and credentials, but also the place where the writer got the information. First, it lends credibility to the citation. Second, it helps readers who want to research your facts further for themselves. (In papers that call for footnotes, both primary and secondary sources should be footnoted.)

Before you lean on testimony from any source, primary or secondary, use the following guidelines to consider whether it belongs in your paper.

● *Are the source's facts correct?* Especially in science, the "facts" are constantly being disproved by later evidence. In quoting an authority, it is your job to make sure his facts are still correct.

● *Is his authority still intact?* The heroes of one generation often become the villains of the next. It will do you and your paper no good to rest on the laurels of a 1960s hero if he's a villain to your contemporary readers.

● *Is his statement or opinion made in a field that's within the scope of his authority?* Jane Fonda on the rigors of acting is authoritative. You can cite her observations as fact. Fonda on nuclear energy is outside her field of recognized expertise. If you decide to cite her, you must signal that it's informed opinion. Why use it? Because, although it may carry little weight, it may perk the reader's interest.

● *Is the context of your quotation accurate?* A phrase, a sentence, or even an entire paragraph taken out of context can seem to mean something entirely different from what the expert intended. Even a paraphrased thought can be misinterpreted if it is detached improperly from the thoughts that have surrounded it.

● *Has the authority changed his mind?* Even a scientist refines his conclusions and evidence on the basis of new research. You have to reflect your source's viewpoint so accurately that, if he were to read your paper, he would approve. This is one very important reason why the best papers rely most heavily on up-to-date primary sources.

How to quote

Whether you borrow someone's exact words, or paraphrase, the reader follows more easily and with greater conviction if your attribution appears first and the attributed material comes second, instead of the other way around. It's a good habit to get into.

When should you quote, and when paraphrase? It's easy to decide if you keep in mind that, like every other part of your paper, whatever you quote must interest the readers. What isn't interesting, you are obliged to rephrase in your own more interesting words.

You may find that some parts of a quotation are interesting or said better than you could say them, whereas others are tedious or hard to understand. In that case, quote the good parts and paraphrase the rest. It's amazing how quickly this surgery improves a paper. But don't chop up the quotation, stringing bits and pieces of quotation together with a few linking words of your own. It distracts the reader from your point and tells other writers that you're too lazy or too timid to choose only the very best information to be quoted.

When you paraphrase, aim for economy of words. Don't ever quote a source directly and, in addition, paraphrase or summarize her words. If your source needs translation, she should not be quoted directly in the first place. Nothing exasperates a reader so much as redundancy.

Below we've reprinted part of a long passage on quotation in H. W. Fowler's *A Dictionary of Modern English Usage*.[2] Read the selection carefully, because the next page or so of comment rests on your understanding of it.

Quotation. . . . A writer expresses himself in words that have been used before because they give his meaning better than he can give it himself, or because they are beautiful or witty, or because he expects them to touch a chord of association in his reader, or because he wishes to show that he is learned or well read. Quotations due to the last motive are invariably ill-advised. The discerning reader detects it and is contemptuous; the undiscerning is perhaps impressed, but even then is at the same time repelled, pretentious quotations being the surest road to tedium. The less experienced a writer is, and therefore on the whole the less well read he is also, the more is he tempted to this error. The experienced knows he had better avoid it; and the well-read, aware that he could quote if he would, is not afraid that readers will think he cannot. . . .[2]

Mr. Fowler is authoritative and clear, so we might have just quoted his passage in our book and saved ourselves some writing effort. However, Fowler was British and his book was first published in 1926; his pace and style are different from ours and from our readers'. We would have risked losing your interest and, possibly, your comprehension as well.

We might have chosen to use the opening part of the excerpt, however, in this way:

> Language expert H. W. Fowler, in his *Dictionary of Modern English Usage*, finds only three appropriate reasons for an author to quote the words of others: "Because they give his meaning better than he can give it himself, or because they are beautiful or witty, or because he expects them to touch a chord of association in his reader . . ." We quibble with the second reason. In addition to wit or beauty, there must be applicability to the topic at hand.

Notice:

● We carefully cited the source from which we borrowed the words.

● Fowler's language does not refer to quotations in general, but only to the direct borrowing of words, and we carefully composed our introductory phrase to make that clear. Had we done otherwise, our own previous advice to you in this chapter would have seemed to contradict Fowler's.

● Nowhere does Fowler say, "There are only three appropriate reasons for an author to quote the words of others." Careful reading of the quoted passage, in context, convinced us that Fowler said almost—but not precisely—the same thing, and used several extra sentences to say it. So we paraphrased.

● We did not call Fowler a recognized authority or famous authority or any other of the redundancies students are fond of. If the source is famous or recognized, there is no need to say so. If you feel a need to say it, it may be because your source's credentials are not solid enough to begin with.

To show Fowler's authoritative endorsement of another of our points, while avoiding his meandering style, we might have linked his appropriate passages with our own words and then paraphrased the rest:

> H. W. Fowler, in his *Dictionary of Modern English Usage*, warns that an author who incorporates quotations merely to "show that he is learned or well read" is "invariably ill advised." He explains that the careful reader will spot the ruse and feel contempt for the author, and that the casual reader will be bored by it.

Notice that the good writer makes sure to have all her tenses and persons agree, when incorporating quotations:

• Because Fowler's first quoted phrase uses the singular, we word our own sentence in the singular.

• Our own sentence stresses *the technique of quoting*, a subject that requires singular nouns and verbs. The second of our citations was originally written in the plural. To avoid mixing numbers, we borrowed only as much as would fit comfortably into our sentence: "invariably ill advised," not "*are* invariably ill advised."

Well used, quotation is an asset. But, as you can see, it's a challenge to use it well. To avoid misuse, resort to direct quotations only when they're the best or only way to say what has to be said.

How much to quote

In their book *Plain English Please* (2nd edition), Gregory Cowan and Elisabeth McPherson say, "Never use more than three consecutive words belonging to another writer without putting quotation marks around them."[3] This is a sensible basic guideline. But it leaves unanswered the question, "How many words can I borrow?" To answer it, we must explain the difference between *information* and *expression*.

Once it is published, *information* becomes everybody's property. Legally, anyone can freely borrow the information another has collected. *Words*, on the other hand, are protected by law. You cannot copy another person's book or paper in its entirety without infringing on the author's copyright; you cannot even extensively copy it in your own words without committing plagiarism.

Copyright law is practical, however, and recognizes that authors and students must be given a certain amount of latitude in using other authors' works. Therefore the doctrine of *fair use* has evolved, which says in short that you may copy for publication as much of another author's work as will not diminish its commercial value. If that seems fuzzy, it's because it was intended to be; the framers of the law want authors to rely on common sense when weighing the pros and cons of borrowing someone else's words.

If you were to copy an entire paper, that would be copyright infringement or plagiarism. If you were to copy a few sentences out of a book, that would not be. What if you were to copy 100 words of a 30,000-word manuscript for your own 2,000 word paper? Obviously, there is room for argument here. (Centuries-old works are not copyrighted, and copyrights of somewhat newer works may have expired. There, you are legally free to copy; how much you borrow becomes a question of ethics.) To sidestep most of the problems in defining the parameters of fair use, we follow this guideline:

● Use another author's words or ideas sparingly, and only with credit, and then only if it's the best literary device available to make the point that has to be made.

You need not credit an author who has borrowed another author's ideas. For example, if we had written a book that sums up Einstein's ideas on relativity and you used our book in researching a paper on modern physics, we would not expect you to mention us when discussing the theory of relativity. On the other hand, if in our book we suggested the idea, "Einstein's theory of relativity changed the foundations of physics as completely as Darwin's *Origin of Species* changed those of biology," we'd expect you to credit us if you borrowed that idea for your own paper.

When in doubt, be generous in crediting other authors. If

you've researched your subject well, and have something original to say yourself, your citations will be regarded by readers as a sign of your own confidence and intellectual strength. If you've researched poorly, or have nothing new to contribute on the topic, no amount of covert borrowing is likely to save your paper anyway.

EXERCISES:

1. Here are exact quotations taken from an illustrated guidebook to the House on the Rock, the tourist attraction depicted in "Giant Junk" (Illustration 10/1). Indicate which of them (or which parts of longer passages) you will use as direct quotations, which you will paraphrase, and which you will use for information only. (You may completely discard one or two of these citations, but no more.)

> a. *"The Gladiator* calliope originated in the fancy of Alex Jordon. The Sousa and Dixieland the machine plays conjures visions of a Mississippi steamboat."

> b. "The Rock [that the house stands on] is a sturdy sentinel, sightless, voiceless, alone—seeming to guard the invisible gates of the extraordinary Wisconsin countryside. The Rock had withstood relentless onslaughts of glacial torrents that swept away comrades made of lesser stuff. It withstood vast ages of capricious winds that probed and swept the remaining soft spots and abated only when satisfied that solid rock remained."

> c. "The first construction was one of necessity—a haven from the coming fury of a Wisconsin winter. It was to be a studio and workshop, cozy and rustic, with a man-sized fireplace to warm his [the architect-owner's] zeal—and his supper. To most men such a beginning need only be primitive and temporary. But

he stayed with his covenant and initiated the work with infinite skill and care. From the beginning each stone represented a distinct part of a master composition. It was quarried, cut, laboriously carried to the site and wrestled into position. It was prodded this way and that until the esthetic eye was satisfied. Only then was the mortar applied to permanently cement this extraordinary relation of man to Nature."

d. "There followed seven additions in seven years, with every stone, every timber, every length of cable that would lash segments of this precarious aerie to its mother stone—was carried up The Rock without mechanical aid of any kind."

e. "Left: The House on the Rock boasts the largest collection of Bauer and Coble lamps in the world. The management considers them finer and expects them to be more valuable than Tiffanys. Here are two beautiful specimens. The sunflower shade features an edge that outlines the petals and leaves in natural fashion."

f. "Below: An original Mills Violano Virtuoso—one of the few known to still exist. For all its rarity and age, the Mills has lost none of its ability to charm listeners with skirling reels and furious fiddle favorites. The enduring craftsmanship of [this instrument] predates the transistor by more than half a century."

2. Here are quotations gathered during our own trip to the House on the Rock. Indicate which of them (or which parts of longer passages) you will use as quotations, which you will paraphrase, and which you will use for information only. (You may discard one of these items.)

a. John Korb, general manager of the House on the Rock, said, "Alex Jordan, creator of the House on the Rock, is a bit reclusive. He likes his privacy and won't even consent to give interviews to newspaper reporters who might write up his architectural wonder."

b. Korb also told us, "Many people in the art and business community around here are jealous of what Alex has accomplished. They're forever looking down their noses at him as a painter and potter. But Mr. Jordan was a recognized artist before he started the House on the Rock. In fact, he conceived the House as his studio, and it just sort of grew like Topsy from there."

c. An employee of the House on the Rock told us, "Mr. Jordan likes to keep an eye on what goes on, and likes to see and hear what tourists think of his House on the Rock. So he wanders around looking like one of the maintenance workers, even pausing to answer questions for interested tourists."

3. Insert the quotations, verbatim or paraphrased, in the rewrite you began as part of the exercises at the end of Section 10.2.

4. Using the *Encyclopedia Americana* entry on *fluorine* as your sole resource, write approximately 200 words about fluorine. Concentrate on where it can be found and how it is used. Borrow at least two quotations, giving appropriate credit; one must be a direct quotation, and another must include parts of two different sentences from the encyclopedia, with paraphrasing where needed, worked into a single sentence in your exercise paper.

5. Using the *Encyclopedia Americana* entry on *the Spectator* as your sole resource, write approximately 400 words about the publication, Addison's background, and the relationship between Addison and Steele. Incorporate every quotation you find in the entry, giving proper credit. Also select at least two other passages to quote, crediting them to the entry's author, Caleb T. Winchester. One of these should be a direct quotation and the other should consist of parts of two different sentences from the entry, worked into a single sentence in your exercise paper.

10.4 THE NARRATIVE
OR ANECDOTE.

The technique that we know as narration gives relatively few people problems when they talk about or write fiction. But we've found that in writing nonfiction, too many students narrate only *what* is happening. They forget to include who it's happening to, when and where it's happening, and all the other story-telling elements that make good narration the factual writer's strongest technique. To remind learning writers that there's more to nonfiction narration than just recalling what's happened, we'll use the synonym that's preferred by professional nonfiction writers—*anecdote.*

An anecdote has most or all of the following attributes:
- It is a complete story in miniature.
- It has a beginning and an ending.
- It takes place in a particular setting, and the scene usually has to be described in brief.
- It shows a real person or real people.
- It shows something happening to the people—or shows them making something happen.
- It shows time passing or people moving about.
- Its setting, action, or dialogue singly or together make a point that belongs in the paper.
- It is nearly always told in the past tense, unlike the rest of the paper which is usually in the present, or sometimes future, tense.
- Its power lies in the fact that everyone loves a good story.

In conversation, we call on stories frequently to keep our listeners interested in what we have to say, and to help them understand—maybe even agree with—our generalizations. We saw an example of that recently in our living room when a young writer friend was trying to convince us that our criticism had changed his life. When we seemed dubious, he narrated how he'd shown his sister what we'd written on his manuscript. He told us that she'd noticed our praise of his dialogue and our comment that the story could be turned into a film script, and she'd urged him, "Why don't you take a filmwriting course?" He'd signed up for one and had enjoyed it so much that he was now off to Hollywood to try his hand at it in earnest. "So if I become a famous screenwriter," he added, "you can take the credit for it."

The above is actually an anecdote within an anecdote: we narrated the story about the young man who narrated a story about his sister. Effectively used, the anecdote not only whets the reader's interest in the subject, but conveys information the reader needs in order to understand the paper's point. Like the quotation, it generally takes the place of exposition. The point it makes should not be summarized afterward (or in advance) for the reader. If you feel your anecdote's point isn't made adequately, the remedy is to fix the anecdote.

Learn to look for anecdotes when you research. If the subject of your interview generalizes, ask, "Give me an example of how you applied that idea," and "Tell me about a time when that fact helped you." Call on your own experiences, and those of people you know, for anecdotes that fit into your writing projects. Sometimes even secondary sources contain anecdotes you can borrow—with proper credit.

Anecdotes, unlike quotations, rarely depend on the authority of the people whose experiences are being used. Professional writers often use just first names, or even false names where embarrassment or invasion of privacy is a consideration. The fuller the name, however, the greater the sense of authenticity the reader feels.

Calling it "new journalism," some writers openly (and sometimes not so openly) invent settings, people, and situations for their anecdotes. As expected, the people described usually sound like stick figures and the anecdotes ring false. The true new journalists, who make heavy use of anecdotes, always describe real people involved in real happenings. Sometimes these writers set their subjects in their natural milieus even though the interviews may have taken place somewhere else. That might be considered invention. It works because during an interview, as a rule, the successful journalist—old or new—has made enough astute observations and solicited enough facts to reconstruct the subject's natural habitat.

In learning to write with this technique, you must be sure that each anecdote you create contains all or most of the elements we listed. Then as you sit at your writing desk, you must dovetail them smoothly into the rest of your writing. For maximum effect, all three writing techniques have to work hand in hand.

We have seen too many students finally grasp what anecdotes must contain, only to slip up by putting them down as if they were no more than interesting asides to the main thrust of the paper. You can learn to use them with finesse by studying the published writing of experienced authors. Illustration 10/2 (end of this chapter) reproduces an article we wrote for *Family Health* magazine. In it, we switched from exposition to quotation to anecdote to enliven and support our explanation of CAT scanners, which had to include price, size, theory of operation, duration of a scan, medical benefits, and more. To grab readers' attention at the outset, we chose the strongest technique, anecdote, for our lead. The long narrative not only sharpens reader interest in a subject most people don't understand or care about, but gets across the following information: (a) CAT scanners are new, (b) CAT scanning is painless, (c) traditional X rays have trouble distinguishing between healthy and diseased soft tissue, (d) CAT scanners provide pictures that distinguish the difference. Our anecdote also describes what the machine looks like, and a patient's-eye view of how it works.

EXERCISES:

1. Rewrite as an anecdote the author's passage, from the "Giant Junk" paper (Illustration 10/1), about driving to the tourist attraction and seeing the billboards that announced it. Add whatever information you care to from your own or others' experience.

2. Rewrite the following information, obtained during our own visit to the attraction described in Illustration 10/1, as one or more anecdotes that fit into your rewrite of the "Giant Junk" paper.

> a. While we were looking at the panorama of hills and valleys seen from a terrace alongside the studio building, a tall, slightly stooped, graying gentleman of about sixty walked up near us. He had a belt laden with tools, and resembled an electrician. (You can describe which tools he might, in your mind's eye, have had in his belt.)

> b. Several tourists, inferring that the gentleman was a maintenance worker, inquired about names for the various peaks and valleys they could see.

> c. The gentleman answered the questions knowledgeably and in a distinctive, soft-spoken, well-educated manner. He pointed out that the Mississippi River Valley was to the west and the ancient Baraboo Hills to the north.

> d. As he turned to leave, we recognized him as Alex Jordan, creator of the House on the Rock. He seemed to sense our recognition and quickened his pace.

> e. We noticed then that the sun was beginning to set and a wind had sprung up.

> f. As we left the terrace, a bunch of high-schoolers came running along and nearly knocked the man over. He straightened up, dwarfing them with his height, and gave them a sobering look. They quieted down, and walked—at least till he was out of sight.

3. At home or in the library, read through popular magazines until you locate four different anecdotes. Be sure they come from at least two diverse publications. Photocopy the page on which each anecdote appears, and draw a box around the anecdote.

4. Read through scholarly journals until you locate four different anecdotes from at least two diverse publications. Photocopy the page on which each anecdote appears, and draw a box around the anecdote.

5. Discuss in class or in a paper of about 500 words (depending on teacher preference) what you learned about anecdotes and their uses while searching for the answers to Exercises 3 and 4. Be sure to include answers to these questions:

> a. Did the articles in popular magazines offer more or less exciting reading than the journal articles?

> b. Did the anecdotes in the scholarly papers add to or detract from the effectiveness of the papers? Their credibility? Their scholarliness? Their entertainment?

> c. Did the anecdotes in the popular magazine articles detract from or contribute to the believability of the articles? Their effectiveness? Their entertainment? Their authority?

> d. Would it have been possible to use more anecdotes in the scholarly papers you chose?

6. Make a photocopy of Illustration 10/2.

> a. Circle all quotations, direct and indirect (para-phrased). Box all anecdotes. Underline all exposition. Explain the technique used in any passage you have not circled, boxed, or underlined.

> b. List the paragraph numbers and, for each number, the technique most used in that paragraph. For each, explain why this was the best way of making the point or argue why another technique might have worked better.

NOTES: CHAPTER 10

1. Frederick Simpich, "This Giant That Is New York," *National Geographic* magazine, November, 1930, p. 563.

2. H. W. Fowler, *A Dictionary of Modern English Usage*, 2nd ed., rev. by Sir Ernest Gowers (New York: Oxford University Press, 1965), p. 498.

3. Gregory Cowan and Elisabeth McPherson, *Plain English Please*, 2nd ed. (New York: Random House, 1969), p. 324.

ILLUSTRATION 10/1

Giant Junk Invades Wisconsin!

When I left Los Angeles, I thought I left the world of kitsch and chachkas (a Yiddish word meaning junky figurines) behind me. But I wasn't prepared for the "House On The Rock" in Spring Green, Wisconsin. One Sunday, I packed a picnic lunch and drove out to that part of the country—lovely scenery, warm day (a hint of Indian summer) and uncrowded roads. About four miles before this major attraction, signs announced its appearance. Serious.

The approach is lovely—a two lane tree-shaded road and leaves turning with their golden nipples and jade skin. As I walked to the entrance, I saw the sign with the admission price: $6.00 for adults. What a steep price considering I had just returned from Washington, D.C., and did not have to pay admission at the National Gallery East or the Hirshorn Museum with their outstanding collections of art.

I steeled myself, paid the admission, and started walking the long ramp into the house (self-guided tours only). It is now privately owned and while it might have been beautiful at one time, the interior was covered in Shag Rug or "early Hollywood star"—not just the floor, but railings and ceilings. No money was spared (or perhaps it was) to make the inside hideous. There were additional shoddy touches: near the piano was a machine which played the Hungarian Rhapsody for twenty-five cents, plastic pine trees and plants, pseudo-Tiffany lamps in religious reds, bawdy blues, and outrageous oranges. The beautiful Oriental dolls were so out of place I wondered if one might not mistake them for Bucky Badger dolls.

There were other parts to this set-up—the Mill On The Rock with the enchanting streets of yesteryear and marvelous calliopes (although one entitled "The Mikado" did not play anything from that operetta, but a Khachaturian composition).

If this "attraction" could have been described as "Midwestern Kitsch," "Giant Junk," or "The Big Hype," my shock at its ugliness in this pristine setting would not be so great. But, oh, Wisconsin, how you disappointed me . . . and what about Frank Lloyd Wright.

ILLUSTRATION 10/2

Miracle Machine*

¶1   Wade Barnes is a big, likable middle-aged man who used to make television commercials before he became a successful New York real estate dealer. Despite the pressure of his current job, he is usually in excellent health—except for periodic, but painful, gallstone attacks. The last time he had one, the standard gallbladder dye tests failed to produce positive findings and Barnes's doctor, concerned about ulcers or colitis, ordered a complete GI, or gastrointestinal, series. Barnes obediently swallowed some evil-tasting liquid barium and posed in a variety of uncomfortable positions as technicians took X-rays of the thick fluid passing through his intestinal tract.

¶2   When the radiologist examined the X-rays, he suddenly became less interested in Barnes's gallbladder than in a peculiar shadow he spotted on the pancreas. He told Barnes's doctor, "I don't like it. Looks like there might be something growing in there." The physician passed the bad news on to Wade Barnes. *Something growing? Cancer!* was Barnes's first, frightened thought.

¶3   But how were they to find out for sure? X-rays, like the ones Barnes had just had, can hint at a pancreatic growth, but cannot define it. The reason? Unlike bone and other hard body tissues, which reflect radiation onto an X-ray plate, soft body tissues, such as the internal organs, absorb almost uniform amounts of radiation. Thus, the differences between diseased and healthy tissues in an organ like the pancreas will be barely distinguishable even to a specialist's trained eye. Barnes would have to undergo risky, expensive and painful exploratory surgery so that a doctor could see with his own eyes if there was, indeed, a growth.

¶4   Fortunately, however, Barnes was acquainted with a team of radiologists who had recently bought themselves a fancy new machine that was capable of taking readable X-ray pictures of parts of the body never clearly photographed before. Barnes called the radiologists at their Queens, New York, office and asked if their machine could help him. He was told it could, so he made an appointment.

¶5   The doctors, however, couldn't see him for two weeks and, during that time, Barnes lived with fear of the disease and apprehension about the complicated new machine that would determine his fate. His nervousness didn't abate when he walked into the scanning room, changed into a paper examining gown, and was asked to lie on a table and insert the lower half of his body through a donut-like ring and into a huge, rectangular steel device. He was prepared for the worst—certainly for more discomfort than a GI series.

¶6   Instead, as the noisy machine started up and the rectangle began clicking and circling around his stomach like a robot from some science fiction novel, the only discomforts Barnes experienced were those of having to remain motionless for several minutes at a time and of holding his arms stiffly behind his head. After half an hour, the technician who'd helped him onto the table helped him off. It was all over and, by the time Barnes had dressed, the radiologists, Drs. Herbert Rabiner and Jeffrey Kaplan, were ready for him. "Wade," Dr. Rabiner said, "there isn't a thing wrong with your pancreas. It looks as healthy as mine."

¶7   The machine that saved Wade Barnes from exploratory surgery is called a CT or CAT whole body scanner. (There are also scanners designed to photograph only the head or the torso; the whole body scanner, however, does both.) The initials stand for Computed Tomography or Computerized Axial Tomography, different terms for the same process. The *computing* is done by mini-computers similar to the ones used in rocket ships. The word *axial* refers to the fact that, unlike conventional X-rays that produce a two-dimensional, lengthwise picture, CT scanners use the patient as an axis and rotate the machine around him. The result: a crosscut image. And *tomography* is a Greek word meaning "to write a slice," which is exactly what the CT scanner does—it writes a detailed description of what a thin slice of the patient would look like if a doctor could section him the way a cook slices tomatoes.

¶8   But when Barnes had his pancreas scanned, he wasn't even poked. Instead, the CT scanner made a series of 180-degree arcs around his stomach, pausing every so often to direct a tiny amount of radiation—no greater than that of conventional X-rays—through him. The X-rays were then fed through an electric eye into a computer terminal, where the information was translated into a front-to-back photo of the inside of Barnes's torso, as well as a numerical printout and a magnetic tape to be filed for future reference. Within seconds, a slice of Wade Barnes could be viewed on a TV screen—either in black-and-white or, with the press of a button, in psychedelic colors. His pancreas, his stomach, and his backbone and spinal cord were all clearly distinguishable. And with assurance of 95 percent accuracy, the radiologists could tell Barnes that his pancreas was not malformed, that it was not diseased, and that there were no blood clots or other foreign bodies that shouldn't be there. Only surgery could give more precise information—but that, fortunately, was no longer necessary.

¶9   The CT scanner can bring to light organs other than the pancreas, too. It can examine the liver for hematomas (tumors containing effused blood). It can detect benign cysts in the kidneys, which can then be drained to cure the patient without surgery. And it can show the extent of cancerous tumors and ascertain whether or not they've spread. For example, after an ordinary chest X-ray, one patient was told that she had a lung tumor. An operation would have followed almost automatically, except that a CT scan revealed that the tumor had spread to the chest wall, making surgery useless. Although the woman wasn't cured, at least she was spared a needless operation.

¶10   Surgery isn't the only unpleasant diagnostic tool that CT can replace. A patient suspected of colonic tumors, polyps, or diverticula (sacs produced by abnormal protrusions through organ walls) may be scanned instead of having to take an uncomfortable barium enema. Scanning is also a possible alternative to tests involving the injection of dyes or radioactive materials via painful catheterization of the artery that supplies blood to the liver, pancreas, spleen, or kidneys. (Sometimes dyes *are* used in conjunction with CT scanning but, on those occasions, comparatively small amounts are administered by simple needle injections.)

¶11   Valuable as it is, CT body scanning is only a babe-in-the-woods compared to its older sibling, CT head scanning, which has revolutionized the diagnosis and treatment of brain disorders.

¶12   Until seven years ago, a doctor had few alternatives—none of them pleasant—if he wanted to find out what was happening in the soft tissues hidden behind a patient's skull. He could order an encephalogram, a technique that involves forcing air into the patient's brain to outline the convoluted tissues on an X-ray plate. (The patient would suffer excruciating headaches for days afterward.) He could perform an angiogram by injecting dye into the arteries that supply blood to the brain—a procedure that sometimes triggered convulsions, stroke, or even death. Or, if he was associated with a major research center or teaching hospital, he could request what was then called a brain scan. With this method, radioactive liquid, injected into the brain, is charted as it makes its way through the soft tissues. Not only are these techniques painful and/or dangerous, but they cannot be counted on to detect anything more subtle than a major stroke or a large tumor.

¶13   For years, medical researchers had played with the idea of a device that could collect a series of soft tissue X-ray pictures, and with the aid of computers capable of differentiating minute shadings, combine them into a well-visualized "slice." Little had come of it beyond one experimental machine that worked too slowly and projected too much radiation to be practical. But in 1970 an English scientist, Godfrey Hounsfield, who had been working on a CT scanner for three years, turned on his brand-new machine in a London hospital—and twenty minutes later gave the startled doctors mankind's first clear, detailed look at the tumor deep within the interior of an uncut human brain.

¶14 Three years later, improved, faster-operating versions of Hounsfield's invention—capable of illuminating for the first time the soft tissues of the eyes, nasal passages, and larynx—were introduced to American hospitals and laboratories and hailed as wonder tools.

¶15 According to Dr. Marvin E. Haskin, chairman of diagnostic radiology at Hahnemann Medical College and Hospital of Philadelphia: "The head scanner brings medicine out of the Dark Ages. Now we not only can look directly at the brain but we can do it so easily and safely that even a newborn infant can be scanned. With CT, we have picked up correctable abnormalities in children as young as four days old."

¶16 Dr. Haskin and his team of radiologists at Hahnemann have done much of the pioneer work in brain scanning and have written definitive medical texts on the subject. Since July 1974, when their hospital purchased a head scanner, they have examined over 6,000 patients, many of them youngsters.

¶17 Haskin's associate, Dr. Patricia D. Laffey, chief of Hahnemann's section on noninvasive imaging, department of diagnostic radiology, sees many of the pediatric patients. Recently, she examined a four-year-old boy who was behaving erratically following a fall and a sudden blackout. Positioning the child in her scanner, she discovered not only the blocked brain ventricle (cavity) that had caused the boy's blackout but a benign tumor the size of a tomato that nobody had known about. Had the child not been scanned, the tumor could have gone undetected until it caused irreparable brain damage. The boy might have grown up deformed or retarded—or he might not have grown up at all.

¶18 "As a result of our scan," Dr. Laffey says, "the doctors knew just where to operate to remove the tumor." And after the operation, a follow-up scan made sure the entire growth had been removed. The small amount of X-ray exposure each CT series entailed—about as much as a dentist's X-ray—seemed a reasonable risk to take in return for what Laffey calls "every chance of complete recovery."

¶19 Scanning also led Drs. Laffey and Haskin to discover a surprising number of cases in which children, diagnosed as retarded, turned out to have unsuspected brain tumors or hydrocephalus (water on the brain). They promptly arranged to scan thirty children from St. Elizabeth's Home, a school for the educable and trainable retarded in West Philadelphia. Fully twenty percent of the young-sters—a much higher figure than anticipated—were found to have tumors, cysts, water on the brain, congenital malformations, or structural abnormalities that could have caused the mental prob-lems. Unfortunately, the diagnoses were made too late to help most of the St. Elizabeth children. But Haskin feels that, as head scanners become more accessible, many similarly afflicted young-sters will be discovered in time to be treated. "My experience has convinced me that every hospital with a patient load of over 100 should have a head scanner," Haskin says.

¶20   Dr. Stephen Rothman, director of computerized tomography at Yale-New Haven Hospital in Connecticut, agrees. He recalls the case of Chuck, a little boy whose only symptom was that he "behaved strangely." When Dr. Rothman settled Chuck into the head scanner, the TV screen promptly revealed a benign tumor as large as a grapefruit. "I not only could tell the surgeon there was an operable tumor but from the computer printout—which provides exact positions to within a millimeter—I could tell him just where the tumor was placed," Rothman says. "Today Chuck is alive and normal, but he would have had a dim prognosis before CT scanners came along."

¶21   Even more dramatic was the case of the adult patient rushed to Yale-New Haven's emergency room with a stroke. As the staff worked over the fifty-year-old man, his vital signs deteriorated rapidly. Then, on impulse, the doctors rushed him to radiology and shifted him to the CT scan table. While residents stood by, Dr. Rothman set his instruments in motion, and in less than a minute a "slice" of the dying patient's head appeared on the TV screen. Clearly visible were the eyes, both sides of the brain, and the ventricles containing the cerebrospinal fluid that transports nutrients to the brain and toxic materials away from it.

¶22   Dr. Rothman's trained eye isolated the problem at once: A blood vessel in the brain had burst and was bleeding into a ven-tricle. The surgeon watched closely as Rothman pinpointed the endangered area. Right there in the CT scan room, the surgeon drilled a hole through the man's skull, inserted a needle and drained the cavity. "If that ventricle had filled with blood," Rothman says, "the patient would have died within minutes. Instead, he left the hospital some days later, completely well."

¶23 "After I did a thousand head scans I was excited by the tool," Dr. Haskin says. "Now that I've done six thousand, I'm six times more excited—and that's rare in medicine. This machine is revealing pathology we could only guess at before. And although no indirect diagnostic tool is 100 percent accurate, the CT scanner's record of 95 percent accuracy makes it 25 percent better than any other radiologic instrument!"

¶24 So enthusiastic is Haskin that he recommends a head scan if any of the following symptoms occur: sudden-onset recurrent headaches, seizures, sudden and continued behavior changes, concussion, sudden symptoms of senility, an accident followed by loss of consciousness, or abnormal childhood development. Each of these, he points out, could indicate a brain injury which, if diagnosed and treated in time, could be reversed.

¶25 But just how easy is it for an ordinary person to get a CT scan?

¶26 The answer depends, in part, on the patient's ability to pay for it. A CT scanner can cost a hospital, laboratory, or private physician from $300,000 to $650,000 to purchase, $30,000 a year to service, $5,000 a month in electric bills—plus the salaries of the highly trained technicians and radiologists who operate the machinery and interpret the results. Since newer models appear frequently, offering medically valuable reductions in the time it takes to obtain and produce a picture of a squirming child or a throbbing organ like the heart, scanner owners must replace obsolete equipment or update it with add-on units. And these may cost as much as $200,000. The price of being scanned is, as one might expect, proportionately high: anywhere from $125 at a hospital to $450 at a private radiology lab. Medical insurance will often pick up part, but not all, of the charges. In many cases, of course, the expenditure seems reasonable when compared to the alternatives. Wade Barnes, for example, paid $300 for his scan, but considered it cheap in comparison to the price of the two-week hospital stay that exploratory surgery would have entailed.

¶27 But money is not the only barrier to scanning: Access is another. Considering how new and expensive the devices are, head scanners are surprisingly ubiquitous. Hundreds are in use in hospitals, diagnostic centers, even private physicians' offices, throughout the country. The construction of the human head—not

very large, relatively uncomplicated and bilaterally symmetrical—
makes it exceptionally amenable to scanning. "We use a shotgun
technique," says Dr. Rothman, "and in four scans we have all the
information we need!" As a result, CT scanning is rapidly becoming
the diagnostic tool of choice for disorders within the head and
some doctors report that patients must wait as long as four weeks
for an appointment. "We find ourselves having to decide," says
Dr. Laffey of Hahnemann, "which is more important, the patient
with a concussion or the patient with recurrent headaches. Too
often a headache case is bumped so an emergency concussion
can be scanned, and it's the headache victim who turns out to
have the rapidly growing tumor!"

¶28   Body scans, however, are far less popular with physicians,
and they are often used only when standard diagnostic techniques
fail to produce results, when confirmation of other tests is required
or when—as in Wade Barnes's case—a very specific question
about a particular organ must be answered. This reluctance is
based on the fact that the body is difficult to scan because it is
long, crowded with diversified tissues and asymmetrical in the
interior. It takes as many as four hundred scans to achieve a total
body picture—and that requires too much valuable time on the
machine, and too much expense for the patient, to be practical.
What's more, four hundred pictures provide too much information
for one human mind, no matter how experienced, to digest, recall,
and comprehend. "Remember," says Dr. Rothman, "the machine
only provides the information. It's still the doctor who must interpret
it for signs of tissue malfunction or malformation."

¶29   Some medical facilities that own torso scanners as well as
head scanners report that their machines are used nine times
more often for head diagnosis than for body work-ups, and, as a
result, it seems likely that many institutions will phase out their
body scanning equipment. In fact, there is a movement underway—sparked by the high price of scanning and its potential in-
flationary effect upon medical costs and insurance—to discourage
"excessive" purchase of scanners, or even limit acquisition by
state legislation! Dr. Julius E. Stolfi, writing in the *New York State
Journal of Medicine* in July 1976, said of the CT scanner, "This
remarkable instrument could bankrupt our institutions if we do not
exercise good judgment in its use."

¶30 There is, however, considerable dispute over just what constitutes an "excessive" number of CT scanners or "good judgment" in their use. Some researchers believe that future applications of body scanning must be explored eagerly. Scientists are experimenting with body scans for diagnosing spinal disc diseases, and they're investigating the possibility of connecting whole body scanners to radiation-therapy units in order to more accurately direct electron beams to tumors and thus avoid the danger of radiation scatter to healthy tissues. Drs. John R. Haaga and Ralph J. Alfidi of the Cleveland Clinic Foundation in Ohio are researching the use of CT scanning in conjunction with biopsying tumorous tissue. The physicians have already reported, in the March 1976 issue of *Radiology Magazine*, their belief that "localization by computed tomography is the single most accurate method for performing biopsies." In the future, it is not inconceivable that CT-guided needle biopsies, which accurately guide the needle to the site of the newest tumor growth, may do away with costly and deforming surgical biopsies.

¶31 Last April, in an article in the *New England Journal of Medicine*, Drs. Stuart Shapiro and Stanley Wyman, referring to the astonishing number of scanners on order or already in service across the country, coined the phrase "CAT fever—a feverish impulse to own, operate, exploit. . . . Computed Tomography." They may be correct. Certainly, like any other sudden and unusual condition, "CAT fever" must be kept within appropriate bounds. But under the right circumstances, it may turn out to be the healthiest fever the American public has ever suffered.

* Judi R. Kesselman and Franklynn Peterson, "Miracle Machine," *Family Health/ Today's Health,* January, 1977, pp. 28,30,57,59–60

CHAPTER 11
HOW TO PRESENT
YOUR EVIDENCE
MOST EFFECTIVELY

*I never desire to converse
with a man who has written
more than he has read.*
Samuel Johnson

How many times have you read through something that was so well written you applauded the author's style and so well researched you marveled at the author's persistence in pursuing obscure facts, but finished reading and thought to yourself, "But what's the point of it all?" Even if you've mastered the three techniques of writing and organized your research into the four sections of a classic nonfiction paper, you may still not fully achieve the purpose of your paper unless your tools are used to present your evidence as effectively as a skilled debater.

It is easy to lose sight of your paper's goal as you wrestle with procedural details. For an example you have only to look at the Constitution of the United States. None of its authors, the likes of Benjamin Franklin, Alexander Hamilton, and Thomas Jefferson, noticed until it was already ratified that they'd left out all the important parts, the guarantees of personal freedom that had led them to found the United States in the first place.

They had the luxury of quickly drafting ten amendments. Most of us don't get a chance for addenda. What's handed in the first time has to cover it all—and cover it well. That's why we urge you to work at your first draft from an outline of the body of your paper (see Section 8.3). When writing the draft, simply convert each subtopic in your outline into an autonomous, carefully reasoned paragraph that presents all your exposition, anecdotes, and quotations—the evidence that will convince your readers you know what you're talking about. Don't worry now about paragraph length or connecting words and phrases—only about making each paragraph complete.

To be sure that you don't make the blooper our founding fathers did, remember the following tenets as you convert your outline into your first draft's paragraphs:

- Make your point and stick to it.
- Acknowledge your point of view.
- Generalize, but avoid generalities.
- Support your generalizations convincingly.
- Separate fact from opinion.

11.1 MAKE YOUR POINT AND STICK TO IT.

It's a rare student who, like the framers of the Constitution, turns in a paper that misses the point entirely. The common scenario is to find a point after meandering around for about a thousand words and then, so thrilled at having found it, to make it with a flourish and call that the last paragraph. A typical example is Illustration 7/1, whose author starts with a walk through the woods, is sidetracked into following the trail of a deer from a deer's-eye view, and finally launches a defense of deer-hunting. Asked why he tacked on the defense, the writer said, "I suddenly realized I needed a point."

Sometimes even a professional writer doodles with words on paper, typing sentence after random sentence until she sharpens the focus of her thoughts. The difference is, once she finds her point, she knows it's necessary to go back and begin again.

The main point of your article must be stated in your topic sentence. Begin with it, once you've written your lead. When you've finished your first draft, check back and make sure that everything you wrote after that main point has to do with it, and that even your ending refers to it. But that's not all. All your secondary points, and all your evidence for these points, must keep building up the validity of your theme, which includes both your subject and your purpose in writing about it. In addition, your point of view must never veer from the original stance you took toward your topic.

For some subjects, you will have to consider both the theme and its counterarguments. But unless you are assigned specifically to explore a controversial issue while remaining neutral, you must present a well-established case favoring your chosen side.

11.2 ACKNOWLEDGE YOUR POINT OF VIEW.

It is impossible to write any paper without a point of view. No two writers take the same subjective approach to any theme. In organizing, in researching, in choosing the lead, the ending, and the words in between, each writer has his own particular way of going at things. Between the gathering of material and the actual writing comes another process—forming an attitude toward what you've found. Only when you know your attitude, or point of view, can you select from your research and arrange it to have its desired emotional or intellectual impact.

It is this nebulous, all-pervasive point of view that makes the writer a powerful person. With it, he leads the reader to assume his way of seeing the theme. He can make the reader care or be concerned, doubt or disbelieve, accept or act, reject or recoil, want to know more or feel he knows it all. He can be the reader's friend or an impersonal voice of authority. He performs this feat (a) by selecting the material that enhances his point of view and that ignores or demolishes other points of view, and (b) by artfully choosing his words.

We were once assigned by *Seventeen* magazine to prepare an article on the theme "Ways to Win A's in School."[1] One of the ways we included was "Be nice to the teacher." From our point of view, it was a fact of human relations that some students knew and the rest ought to learn. But the editorial staff of *Seventeen* did not want to endorse the point of view that good grades aren't always achieved solely on merit; they eliminated the offending paragraphs.

It is important to recognize that every published nonfiction work has a point of view, and that you bring your own attitudes to everything you write. To affect a stance of total diffidence toward your theme is deceitful. Fairness to the reader demands that you acknowledge forthrightly your point of view.

11.3 GENERALIZE, BUT AVOID GENERALITIES.

● A generality is a vague or inadequate statement.
● A generalization is a general conclusion drawn from specific examples.

It's not difficult, given these dictionary definitions, to understand why you must steer clear of the first and aim for the second. It is the good writer's primary job to find interesting specifics, to study and evaluate them, and finally to use them to draw—or have the reader draw—general conclusions. In the actual writing, we usually generalize first and then supply the specifics. Experienced writers sometimes offer the specifics and let the reader make the generalizations. That's even more effective.

Here is a generality:

1. We studied the Jones, Smith, Watson, Johnson, Olson, and Rogers families and concluded that residents of Shaker Haunts Houses are pretty decent poker

players and lousy backgammon players, and let their kids play games on the lawn.

And here is a generalization, followed by the situational specifics that support it:

> 2. The Watsons are typical of the families residing in Shaker Haunts Houses. They manage to win a few dollars at Friday night nickel-stakes neighborhood poker games, but lose it all at Saturday night backgammon club. Sundays, they try to mow the lawn. It isn't easy, because Shaker Haunts is the local Frisbee-tossing arena.

The first example is devoid of specifics. The second example is vividly specific. There's no doubt which one more quickly catches the reader's attention and remains longer in her memory.

One student chose for his paper the premise that a guerrilla war is being fought between smokers and nonsmokers. To cover the subtopic *public places* he wrote the following, and then went right on to the next point in his argument.

> 3. In public accommodations, nonsmokers are less less and less being discriminated against as greater numbers of nonsmoking sections are being established.

There's a generality for you! How much less discrimination? How many greater numbers? Which public accommodations? The student should have stated his point and offered the specifics that back it up.

Let's assume that the student's research was thorough enough to get the facts that led him to his conclusion. (It's the poor writer who solidifies his conclusions *before* he checks them out and who doesn't arm himself with backup data.) Let's call on hypothetical data to show how he might have more effectively convinced the reader:

> 4. In public places nonsmokers are breathing easier.
> So far twenty-seven states have enacted laws that re-

quire nonsmoking sections in public areas of restau-
rants and retail stores. In 1979, federal legislation out-
lawed smoking on interstate buses, trains, and planes.

Poor writers often use generalities to avoid the need for proof or
to hide the fact that no proof can be found. The truth is, generalities convince nobody. Nowhere in his paper did the student
just quoted prove, with evidence, his generality that smokers are
discriminated against, so his readers refused to take him seriously.

Writers who sprinkle their papers with generalities also tend
to misuse words. The good writer chooses his words to mean
what he wants to say, and knows the accepted meaning of all the
words he chooses. Notice that our last rewrite changed "public
accommodations," a term limited mainly to hotels and res-
taurants, to "public places" to reflect what the author really
meant.

Let's look at another paragraph in the student's paper. See
how many generalities you can spot, and how many misuses of
the language. (There are a lot of trite phrases, too.)

5. Smoking did in fact for a period of time become
such an emotional issue that children and parents
would have bitter quarrels over the smoking habits of
parents. Husbands and wives at times would become
angered beyond despair at the disagreements generated
in households where one person was a militant non-
smoker and the other a militant smoker.

The intent here was to prove the generalization that families were
torn apart by the smoking issue. Instead of offering evidence,
however, the student piled generality on generality. For example,
his statements about "children and parents" and "husbands and
wives" apply the point to nearly everybody in the world. Two
possible reasons for his lack of evidence come to mind: first, that
he didn't do enough research to back up his hunches; second,
that he hasn't yet learned the power of using anecdotes, quota-

tions, and specific facts to bolster his generalizations. We've rewritten the above paragraph, limiting the generalization just to families that house nonsmokers with smokers. Our rewrite makes a generalization, not a generality, because it paints a general principle derived from particular examples.

> 6. During the seventies, when a smoker lived with a nonsmoker the living wasn't easy. Ned and Ellie, for example, had smoked all their lives. Suddenly their two teenaged children began to harass them like angry parents every time Ned or Ellie would light up. They began a guerrilla war, too, soaking cigarettes in soapy water, putting chalk in the filters, dumping unopened packs in the toilet tank. The tension became so keen that Ned's and Ellie's smoking almost doubled. In the case of Ernie the smoker and his wife Susan the militant nonsmoker, the attacks were more subtle. Susan would only make nasty remarks in front of friends. Ernie retaliated by refusing to entertain or go visiting, and the couple saved their marriage only by . . .

EXERCISES:

For each entry below, indicate whether the information, as presented, is a generality, a generalization, or a specific:

1. In Topeka, families don't often catch colds.

2. The Kansas Board of Health reports that Topeka residents catch colds at a rate 27 percent below the national average.

3. The Board of Health has started a research project in which they hope to show that the reasons Topekans get fewer colds is that they eat more beef.

4. Families who eat more beef than the national average also have fewer colds than the national average.

5. In a six-month period after the price of beef goes up, the incidence of reported colds in Topeka also goes up.

6. If you want fewer colds, eat more beef.

7. Six beef taste-testers said they never had colds.

8. The incidence of colds among professional beef taste-testers is 30 percent below the national average.

11.4 SUPPORT YOUR GENERALIZATIONS CONVINCINGLY.

To be convinced of your evidence, the reader must understand it. That goes without saying. But writers often forget that understanding must extend to every word in the specific and to every image it creates. They sometimes grab for images that prove their own knowledge or wittiness, forgetting that the first goal of writing is reader comprehension.

In some cases, knowing what your readers understand is easy. When communicating with third graders, most writers know enough to avoid words like *philistine* and *plebian*, and most know that concepts like *euthanasia* and *adultery* are probably beyond the reader's comprehension. Because all of us have been third graders, we can put ourselves in their shoes.

It's not so easy to guess at what's stored in the head of a stranger or someone you merely nod to in class. Professional writers are most successful when they either write for people who share their interests and experiences or, like George Plimpton, investigate and experience everything about the subject that the readers are likely to know. Students can accomplish the goal vicariously through lots of reading. By reading the books, magazines, and newspapers their readers have probably read, they acquire a pool of *universal images* that can be called on to make their points. For example, a writer who knows her readers are all college graduates can assume that they share her images of cramming for exams, writing overdue papers, and registering late for a favorite course. However, she can't assume that they all know who George Plimpton is, because his writing is not generally studied in college.

The Wisconsin student who wrote the paper on "Giant Junk" (Illustration 10/1) included the following sentence:

> The beautiful Oriental dolls were so out of place I wondered if one might not mistake them for Bucky Badger dolls.

Other Wisconsin students probably would have known what she meant, because Bucky is the University of Wisconsin's mascot. Her image would have been lost, however, on readers who live in other states.

Another student set out to write a persuasive paper on the lack of women's rights in Brazil. For her lead, she deliberately chose a universal image—the picture most Americans see when that country is mentioned:

> When one speaks of Brazil, the mind's eye sees Carnaval, samba, and sandy beaches filled with beautiful women.

Then she made this transition to her topic:

> Next to the beaches, women are the second biggest tourist resource.

She led readers from a familiar old image to a transition filled with new information. Because the image was one the readers could accept, the fact was accepted as well—without any proof. That's the power of a universal image.

Keep in mind that a universal image is not an image that everyone in the world, or even in America, is expected to know—only one that everyone (or nearly everyone) among your *readers* can be expected to understand. Also keep in mind that it is sometimes necessary to call on images that the readers don't know. If you are forced to do that, you must also take the time to explain the image (as we did with our image of Plimpton), and that will slow your paper's pace. In general, your writing job will be easier if you keep your readers in mind while researching, and look for specifics that don't rely on images they can't be expected to understand.

EXERCISES:

1. In the article "12 Ways to Get More out of Studying" (Illustration 7/2), locate the following images and tell, from the context, whether the author thought they were universally understood by her readers. Do you agree with her conclusions? Why?
   a. Pavlov's dogs salivating on cue
   b. Learning in short takes
   c. Radio waves are like brain waves
   d. Staying on after the bell

2. In the article "Miracle Machine" (Illustration 10/3), written for a health-conscious portion of the general adult population of the United States, locate the following images and tell, from the context, whether the authors thought they were universally understood by their readers. Tell whether you agree with their conclusions, and why.
   a. Clicking and circling . . . like a robot from some science fiction novel
   b. Mini computers similar to the ones used in rocket ships
   c. The way a cook slices tomatoes
   d. Only a babe-in-the-woods
   e. Out of the Dark Ages
   f. A . . . tumor the size of a tomato
   g. A squirming child

11.5 SEPARATE FACT FROM OPINION.

The necessity for separating fact and opinion ought to be self-evident. Unfortunately, we've seen many otherwise fine papers fall apart when their authors attempted to substantiate generalizations with people's opinions and called it fact. It is the writer's job to signal what's fact and what's opinion, and to indicate the limits of each fact.

If an economist tells you that the gross national product is $47 billion, and you or he verify the figure, that's a fact. (If he says it's $47 billion and it isn't verified, it may be an *incorrect* fact.) But if the economist says it ought to be $47 billion, no matter how many other opinions concur, it's still an opinion, not a fact. And if he says it's somewhere under $47 billion, it's not $47 billion no matter how much you might like it to be. You may overlook the important difference a word makes, as you rush toward a writing deadline, but your readers may not be in a hurry. If they notice that your specifics don't fully support a conclusion, they'll mistrust your credibility throughout the rest of the paper.

The easiest way to signal others' opinions and the limits of your facts is with *qualifiers*, words like *most*, *possible*, *probably*, *can*, *may*, and the like. But that's not the only way. Carefully selected nouns and verbs can also do the job. When we wrote about cancer immunology for *Science Digest*, credibility was a big factor because the article's point of view was at odds with the public's. One section of the article answered the question, "Are viruses a cause of cancer?" There, it was especially important to separate fact from opinion. (We'll underline the nouns, verbs, and qualifiers that signal opinion in both excerpts that follow.)

> 7. You <u>may</u> have <u>heard</u> that viruses cause cancer. <u>Suggested</u> by researchers as a <u>question</u>—not an answer—some years ago, this <u>theory</u> quickly was <u>espoused</u> by physicians, patients, and especially the popular press. It was a pleasant <u>theory</u> to <u>believe</u>; <u>if</u> a virus caused cancer, an inoculation that <u>would</u> prevent or cure it <u>had to be</u> just around the corner. . . .
>
> A virus has the ability to sneak in beside a normal cell's DNA and unite with it at a point or two where the DNA is particularly vulnerable. Aided by enzymes, the virus then alters the composition of the normal cell's DNA.

Notice the phrase *a point or two* in the second paragraph of this excerpt. The *or two* was purposely inserted to show the limits of this particular fact.

An author has to make the point she sets out to make, and our point was the opinion, based on our research, that viruses probably don't cause cancer. When we presented the specifics for our generalization, we labeled every tentative conclusion with a qualifier and chose our verbs and nouns with care:

> 8. Many private physicians still support the viruses-cause-cancer theory. And some clinical researchers are still searching for viruses they can link to human cancer. But almost without exception, the basic scientists we interviewed and those whose papers we studied doubt that viruses are (or will ever be found to be) a significant cause of human cancer. Dr. Temin states simply, "Most human cancers appear to result from genetic changes that are not a result of viral infection."

Earlier in the article we identified Dr. Temin as having won a Nobel Prize for his work on viruses in cancer. So it was not chance that led to our choosing his quotation to settle the argument we composed out of irrefutable facts laced with strong opinions held by authoritative individuals (some of whom had already been mentioned by name in the article).

When choosing from your collection of specifics, keep in mind that the same piece of evidence, whether fact or opinion, can be used in several ways. How you use it should depend on your purpose. How well you mold it to your purpose determines your success as a factual writer.

For an example, let's take the fact (supported with statistics) that children are influenced more by television than by anything else. You can use that fact to support a contention that children's TV viewing should be monitored carefully, or to support the entirely different contention that advertisers should put their money into children's TV shows. Or you could use it in a simple explanation of the things that influence modern American children. But if you present it as an alarming fact in a paper that's a simple explanation, you may confuse your readers.

Most readers believe that numbers, at least, don't lie, and because of that they're the most convincing facts in a writer's arsenal. The fact is, numbers can be as opinionated as prose. They can be reported with complete accuracy, and still say nearly anything you want them to say.

Examine the following article, reproduced from the *Madison* (Wisconsin) *Capital Times* of September 26, 1977:

> 9. CITY'S SERIOUS CRIME UP 3%, STATE REPORTS
> The state's "serious crime index" for Madison jumped three per cent in the first six months of 1977, the State Justice Department reported today.
>
> Violent crimes increased five per cent, while property crimes jumped three per cent.
>
> The Justice Department figures are based on statistics for the first six months of 1977 compared to the first half of 1976.
>
> The largest jump occurred in reported rapes. This year the city had 33 reported rapes, 57% higher than the 21 in the first half of 1976.
>
> No murders were committed, compared to two in the same period a year ago. Robberies were down from 55 to 51, while aggravated assaults dropped from 14 to 13.
>
> Burglaries were up two per cent to 1,226, while car thefts were up one per cent at 231.

The information in the above article appears straightforward until we analyze it. Then we find:

● The article doesn't define "serious crime," and the statistics don't make clear whether property crimes, burglaries, and car thefts, for example, are included.

● Although "violent crimes" increased, three of the four types of violent crime have actually decreased. Only rapes rose in incidence.

● Considering all the statistics, the article's title and lead may be unduly alarming; so may the use of the point-of-view word *jumped*.

● If you read the excerpt as quickly as most newspaper readers, you probably missed the significance of the phrase *reported rapes,* a term that explains most directly why some of the statistics, although accurate, are practically meaningless. It was because of the dramatic increase in reported rapes (57 percent) that the "violent crime" rate rose. But having lived in Madison during the period covered by the statistics, we are aware that community organizations undertook massive antirape campaigns in early 1977, in which rape victims were urged to come forward and file formal complaints. So the increase in reporting may have had nothing to do with an actual increase in rapes, and it is therefore possible that the "violent crime" rate and "serious crime index" both decreased, contrary to the report.

You can't always verify the accuracy of statistics by having lived through the making of them, but it is important to evaluate the source of your statistics as carefully as you evaluate every other primary and secondary source of your facts. Averages and percentages can deceive. Poll questions can be asked in a way that achieves the responses the poll-taker wants. Samples can be too small for meaningful generalization. We know a famous behavioral psychologist who was able to make his reputation with a weight-loss experiment that involved less than a dozen overweight women, simply because the reports of his success neglected to mention the small number of people who achieved the remarkable results. Putting down the facts accurately is only a small part of your job as a writer. Evaluating them is your most important job.

But numbers, like all facts, must be not only accurate but

easily understood. Sometimes, especially when dealing with percentages and large figures, this means you must search for accurate comparisons. The more vivid your examples, the more quickly the readers will grasp the figures. Here's how Joseph E. Brown made his readers understand the meaning of 50 billion tons of salt:

> There is enough salt in the sea alone—50 billion tons— to cover the earth's land mass to a depth as high as the Washington Monument.[2]

Notice that the comparison must be as accurate as the numerical figure.

In this entire section on separating fact and opinion—in fact, in the entire book—we have not told you where to put your own opinions in writing the paper. That's because opinion is the ghost of writing: although it pervades your paper from beginning to end, the reader shouldn't be able to see it anywhere.

Whatever a paper's purpose—to give directions, to report, to explain, or to persuade—it doesn't achieve that purpose unless it convinces the reader that you know what you're talking about. Whether on your authority or on the authority of your sources, the reader must be able to accept what you're saying. If your facts and ideas are no surer than his own, then reading what you have to say is a waste of his time. That's why you must never let "I think" or "I believe" creep into your writing (although if your sources only think or believe, that's quite all right). That's also why your opinion on anything doesn't count, but only gets in the way, unless you're an expert in that field.

EXERCISES:

1. For each entry below, indicate whether your hypothetical paper would present the given information as fact or opinion.
    a. This year 28,045 babies were born in Wisconsin.
    b. Health department experts estimate that 29,450 babies will be born in Wisconsin in 1990.

c. Hank Hero hit 34 home runs during the 1978 season.

d. White Sox manager Gail Glorious said, "Hank would have hit at least 40 homers if he hadn't broken his toe."

e. Nobel laureate Dr. Arthur Perkins says, "Once we learn the mechanism that links viral infections with interferon production, we'll be able to cure the common cold."

f. The price of flour has risen to 87 cents a pound, and peasants are therefore unable to eat well-balanced diets, according to a UNESCO report released today.

g. Dr. Jones, professor of physics at City College, says, "Einstein's Theory of Relativity proved that traveling at or near the speed of light will slow up apparent time inside the spaceship."

h. In his later years, Einstein worked with anti-nuclear-weapons organizations in an attempt to halt the proliferation of A-bombs.

2. Use information presented in the CAT scanner article (Illustration 10/2, Chapter 10) to write a paper of at least 500 words on the theme "The Medical Benefits Offered by CAT Scanners," based on your own hypothetical conclusion that the high cost of scanners far outweighs their medical benefits. You should incorporate most of the information from paragraphs 7, 8, and 25–31 of that article, part of the anecdote contained in paragraphs 1–6, and part of the paraphrased quotation in paragraphs 23–24.

NOTES: CHAPTER 11

1. Judi R. Kesselman and Franklynn Peterson, "12 Ways to Help You Win A's," *Seventeen*, April, 1978, p. 168.

2. Joseph E. Brown, "Exploring a Watery Planet," *Science Digest Special*, Winter, 1979, p. 12.

CHAPTER 12
PARAGRAPHS AND
TRANSITIONS: BUILDING
STONES OF GOOD PAPERS

*The art of literature, vocal
or written, is to adjust
the language so that it
embodies what it indicates.*
Alfred North Whitehead

We recently heard a conversation between a three-year-old and a six-year-old as they animatedly discussed their most recent birthday parties. We've reproduced it here to illustrate both the paragraph's place in speech development and its importance to speech and writing.

The younger one began, "We had a big cake and mom put a lot of candles on it and someone turned the lights out when she carried it in and all the kids sang happy birthday and I got a million presents and one of them was a dump truck and . . ."

A gasp of breath interrupted his flow of words, and the older child jumped in with her report: "That was nothing. You should have been at my party. My dad made a cake that looked like a rocket ship. We had a thousand balloons strung around the room. My mom put up streamers. I opened my presents after everybody left. I got clothes and games and even a bicycle my grandparents sent from California. And let me tell you about this one neat game. You get a bunch of horses and dogs and cows and things and a great big board. You put the animals on the board and . . ."

The younger child speaks at the word stage; he hasn't yet learned to make sentences. The older one has learned to organize her words into sentences, but her thoughts flow like a flooded stream. She hasn't yet put them into thought units. If she had, she would have recognized that she wanted to jump from telling about the party to telling about the new game. She would have indicated, by pausing slightly, that she was now going to introduce another theme—and would have begun her next topic with a transition, something like, "I got one game at the party that's real neat."

You may not think of these speech units as paragraphs, but if it weren't for them, and the clues given by their separating pauses and transitions, people would end up having to interrupt one another rudely to insert their own thought units.

Some people never learn to speak in paragraphs and transitions, and must be interrupted if the monologue is to become a dialogue. Next time you meet one of these frustrating people, listen closely to the way he strings his thoughts together, leaping from one theme into the next without pause.

If it weren't for written paragraphs and transitions, reading someone's writing would make you as exhausted—and, finally, as bored—as listening to one of these nonstop talkers. That's why learning to use paragraphs correctly is essential to good writing.

The written paragraph, like the spoken thought unit, serves three important functions:

- It fully expresses one, and only one, thought.
- It organizes the paper into short units.
- It incorporates transitions that lead readers from the previous thought to the next one.

You may have seen the paragraph defined as a unified, logical amplification of a theme. It's a definition that is precise and concise, but hard for most people to visualize. It lacks vividness because all of the key words in the definition are abstractions. If you enjoy word exercises, you can use your dictionary and thesaurus to trace each of the four terms (*unified*, *logical*, *amplification*, and *theme*) to a more vivid synonym. Our own efforts led to this expanded definition:

• A paragraph rolls into one neat package (unifies) the widening, stretching, beefing up, working out, unfolding, and rewording (amplification) of what we're writing about (theme) with a firm leg to stand on (logic) so that we make sense and present a good case.

That's a tall order for a paragraph. But it's not hard to fill. In fact, you've already learned most of the mechanics in earlier chapters of this unit. The paragraph has a topic phrase and a body—an organizational structure that corresponds, in miniature, to the topic sentence and body of a paper. And the paragraph, like the paper, fully expresses one theme. The only difference is that the theme of a paragraph is less extensive than the theme of a paper.

12.1 A PARAGRAPH FULLY EXPRESSES ONE THOUGHT.

Every good paragraph must have a theme, and only one theme. Otherwise, according to definition, it's not a paragraph. Every good writer has to decide what her theme is before she begins to write the paragraph. Usually, she gets the theme from the subtopics listed in her paper's outline.

The topic phrase states the theme.

In a paper, the topic sentence (see Section 8.2) expresses its theme early on. In a paragraph, the theme may be revealed to readers in a full-blown topic sentence, but as often as not the writer uses only a topic phrase. It is almost always a generalization. Although it is often the first sentence of the paragraph, or part of the first sentence, it needn't be.

The following paragraph is part of a high school student's paper: (All the paragraphs excerpted in this chapter are numbered for ease of referral.)

> 1. Though people yell about nuclear energy, the atrocities of the coal companies have been forgotten. Who will shout for the homeless, or mourn for all the dead? We need your help. A few scattered people can't fight huge corporations. Join the fight to stop the rape of the land.

Is there a theme in this paragraph? If so, what is it? Where has the author shared his theme with readers? We'd say that the paragraph lacks a unified theme. Each sentence is a separate generalization, and not one is clearly an amplification of any other. It makes for confusing reading.

Contrast the above paragraph with the following selection from "Down Home in the Ozarks" by Bern Keating. Make note of themes and topic phrases as you read.

> 2. Viewing the Ozarks from the air at sunrise, I was impressed by the prevailing presence of water in what I had known as a long, low mountain range drained only by trickling brooks. Now, rays of the rising sun glittered off streams running between every pair of hills, and gleaming sheets of light flashed from vast lakes built up behind hydraulic power dams. That network of water supports a tourist industry serving 50 million Americans within a day's drive of the Ozarks.

> 3. Once a sea covered the land. Then the earth heaved up the sea bottom and formed about 55,000 square miles of plateau, a flat sheet of rock the size of Georgia. Rain and ice eroded the rock; the runoff formed streams that carved the tableland into mountain ranges and over the ages wore down those lofty peaks to the

gently rounded hills that today roll across southern Missouri, northwestern Arkansas and a small area of northeastern Oklahoma.

4. The region was not kind to early settlers. They retaliated by stripping its tree cover through wasteful logging. By the turn of the 20th century, the Ozarks had been ravaged. The hill folk who hung on made a poor living. During the Depression, even those few diehards began drifting to the cities, and large areas reverted to wilderness. Because I was a student at the University of Arkansas deep in the Ozarks during the Depression, I have been a witness to the region's near death and resurrection.

5. First came the dam builders in search of electricity. They blocked the White River—at three places—as well as the North Fork in Arkansas, the Sac River, the Pomme de Terre and the Osage in Missouri to form thousands of acres of lake and thousands of miles of shoreline. Resort and real estate promoters saw the possibilities in the new water bodies. Fishing lodges, marinas and resorts mushroomed around the shores. Tourist dollars spread across the hills and made them burgeon again.

6. Not all the development has been guided by sophisticated taste. The occasional theme park and roadside mart is painfully quaint, with overalled actors and clerks laboring mightily to re-create a past that perhaps never existed. The cuisine in the most garishly cute of the hillbilly stops can bring on an acute attack of grits intolerance. But anybody with antennae the least sensitive to synthetic charm can avoid such traps.[1]

Did you recognize that the first sentence in every paragraph but one contained Keating's topic phrase? In paragraph 2, it is *the prevailing presence of water*. Does he talk about anything but that topic in the paragraph? (Be as careful in your answer as Keating was in his writing.)

The topic phrase in paragraph 3 is *the land*. Does he stray from that topic?

In paragraph 4, Keating's topic phrase promises readers information about *early settlers*. Does he deliver? Does he stray off the topic? If you think he strays in his last sentence, you've probably picked the wrong topic phrase for paragraph 5. It isn't *first came the dam builders*, because the last three sentences in that paragraph are only distantly related to dams. Keating wraps up paragraph 4 and introduces his topic for paragraph 5 with one stroke: *the region's . . .resurrection*. It takes an experienced pro like Keating to orchestrate paragraphs so skillfully. By studying them, you can learn to bring a similar charm to your own writing.

Until you have successfully written as many papers as Keating has, you will probably be most comfortable putting your topic phrases at the beginnings of your paragraphs, as Keating did again in his paragraph 6. Wherever you put them, you must amplify their generalizations convincingly with specifics.

The paragraph contains only one theme.

Even when you begin with a well-stated topic phrase, extraneous generalizations or specifics can creep in to defeat its unifying purpose. This student's paragraph is an example:

7. Have you ever wondered why some therapists do not answer questions about themselves? If a therapist does not answer one's questions directly, it may be because he or she is interested in the concern that lies behind it. Answering a question directly can kill curiosity; and if you want a major guideline to this process, it is to be curious about one's self. That is why a therapist takes nothing for granted. One person's experience of a situation and of people is different from anyone else's. The movie you saw or the book that delighted you is not the same one I saw or read even though they were the same material.

The paragraph does have a well-stated theme: "Why some therapists do not answer questions about themselves." Then it attempts to amplify the theme with a generalization that shows its possible cause (sentence 2) and one that shows its effect (the beginning of sentence 3). (Notice how the author offers us no specifics, quotations, or details to support her generalizations.) Then she gets derailed into another theme (the therapy process) and still another one (different perceptions of the same experience). Even though the individual sentences make sense, the paragraph ends up having no coherence. Because the theme is not kept *unified*, it ends up being illogical.

Here's an example of a student paragraph that begins with a well-stated topic phrase and adds lots of specifics. Still, it becomes illogical when the author forgets to keep on the topic. It's from the first draft of a paper on how business owners can save energy dollars.

> 8. Walk around your shop with your eye cocked toward maintenance. Any cracks around windows and doors that need repair, caulking, or weatherstripping? Can you see how much insulation is in attic and walls? "But for most businesses, the large cost of adding insulation is way down on the list of improvements," says a top energy consultant. "It's more productive to work in areas where you'll have fast payback, in one year. Rather than buying insulation, I'd put that money into inventory."

The writer's topic phrase, in the paragraph's first sentence, tells business owners to look for shop areas that need fixing. By the middle of the paragraph she's moved from fixing up to adding something new, and by the end of the paragraph, she's on to another topic. Her first three sentences deal with one thought; after that, she should have begun a new paragraph.

The paragraph fully amplifies its theme.

The writer of paragraph 7 crams her paragraph with theme after theme because of a misconception that, perhaps more than any other writing error, separates the poor writers from the good ones. She assumes that just stating an idea makes it clear to the reader, and that the reader will quickly become bored unless she moves right on to the next point.

In fact, the opposite is true. It's with your generalizations, which are always abstract and sometimes also hard to grasp, that you stand in danger of boring the reader. It's the specifics, which amplify your generalizations and subgeneralizations, that add vividness and interest to your writing.

The length of your paragraph depends on the complexity of the theme and the knowledge your readers bring to the subject. (It also depends on visual considerations that will be discussed in the next section. Those other considerations must not come into play until the final typing of your manuscript.) To amplify fully, you can choose to (a) reword the thought in terms the reader can visualize, (b) work it out in detail, (c) unfold it so the reader can see it from all angles, (d) beef it up with lots of supports, three being the ideal number, (e) widen it, stretching it to its maximum limits; or you can combine several of these devices. Not every theme needs the same amount of amplification. The best guide is to include as much as you need to make readers understand and accept the point you're attempting to make.

The following three paragraphs are from a two-part article for *Popular Science* magazine in which we used about 5,000 words to explain how wood products can be manufactured from scraps:

9. All the manufactured boards are produced in basically the same way once the raw material is prepared. The wood fibers, shavings, or chips are mixed with about five percent synthetic resin and about one percent wax, then subjected to intense heat and pressure.

10. In the Forex Leroy particleboard plant, for example, a mixture of 85 percent wood shavings and 15 percent sawdust is laid out on 8-by-20-foot steel plates, then spread with a mixture of urea formaldehyde resin and

wax. A dozen plates at a time are fed into a press, where the mats are subjected to about 300 psi at 300 degrees F. for five minutes. The resulting panels, ⅜ to two inches thick, cure for four days. Prefab-home builders use the large panels for one-piece walls or floors, but Forex Leroy saws most of the sheets into smaller panels or into precut furniture parts.

11. Hardboard goes through a similar process, but a different resin is used: Waterproof lignin, the natural glue that holds trees together, is mixed with about one or two percent phenolic resin. [2]

If this article had been written for, say, *Country Gentleman*, our amplification of the theme, *how the manufactured boards are produced*, would probably have been limited to Paragraph 9. We would have included hardboard in that paragraph and used the general word *glue* instead of specifics such as *resin* and *lignin*. For those readers, precise details would have confused, not clarified, our point.

Sometimes, especially in school, amplification is limited by assigned length. It is often more difficult to write effective paragraphs in a short paper than a long one. Remember that, no matter how many ideas you need to cram into a paragraph, you must relate them to one another for the reader. We were once assigned 800 words by *McCall's* magazine in which to discuss the history, methods, successes, and authoritative evaluation of a North Carolina screening program that offered physical and psychological screening to preschoolers (see Illustration 12/1 at end of this chapter). Because of the restrictive word limitation, we were forced to deal with many ideas all in the first paragraph.

Read the reprint now. Notice that the first idea, a generalization that introduces the program and its purposes, fills up the first sentence. Sentence 2 is awkward, but it is jam-packed with general and specific amplification: it gives a thumbnail history, defines the project's scope, introduces its leader, and begins to describe how it works. The next sentence continues that last generalization, and the paragraph's final two sentences cover a sixth idea: how screening results are used.

The rest of the article focuses on what the reader really wants to know about the program: specifics about what is tested, what the results are, and whether it's available for their children.

Does the first paragraph contain only one theme? Surprisingly, it does, but that theme is a very broad one: a general overview of North Carolina's screening program. Does it fully express the theme? Fully enough for its readers.

A paragraph is logical.

Above all, you must make the logical progression of your information clear to the reader. This can be accomplished only if you move one step at a time. Poor writers often make the mistake of assuming that if one idea leads to another through a third idea which is common knowledge, the reader doesn't need to be reminded of the intermediary concept. Excerpt 8, which jumps from *areas that need repair* to *buying insulation isn't wise*, is an example. The writer assumed that readers would supply the connecting question: "If making insulation repairs is wise, is it also wise to add more insulation?" Ask the reader to supply your missing links, and you convert your paper into a puzzle. Remember, for effective communication to take place, the reading effort must never stand between the reader and your ideas.

Because the writer of Excerpt 8 failed to consider the relationship between her ideas, she makes a glaring error that undercuts the entire authority of her article. She calls her readers' attention to insulation as a way of saving energy dollars—and then she jumps to a quotation that not only leaves her idea unsupported, but actually denies its validity. An intermediate sentence (for example, "If you need just a little insulation, it may pay off to add some") would have gone a long way toward eliminating the illogic.

12.2 PARAGRAPHS ORGANIZE
THE PAPER INTO SHORT UNITS.

As we have pointed out time after time, a good writer has to be perpetually alert to his readers' demands. One of those demands is that the reading process should be as effortless as possible so that attention can be concentrated on the ideas expressed. Paragraphs organize reading into short units that enable the reader to pause, to react to what has been written, and to shift his focus to the next idea.

In addition, paragraphs serve a more subtle function. As school reading increases in difficulty from Dick-and-Jane books to Emerson and Thoreau, students can't help noticing that paragraphs get longer and longer. Independently but universally, they reach the conclusion that short paragraphs signal easy reading and long paragraphs warn of difficult concepts. They discover a quick and easy way to tell the length of paragraphs at a glance: by the amount of white space on a page. So when a reader picks up what you have written, he judges the difficulty of the reading by how dense the page's type looks.

To a limited extent, this assumption has some validity. Complicated generalizations do require lengthy amplification, and that generally leads to longer sentences and longer paragraphs. But the media control their white space, and you can control yours.

Newspapers have very narrow columns of type. In order to keep their articles from appearing visually ponderous to readers, editors require reporters to write very short paragraphs. This restriction suits the medium fine, because news reporters seldom produce in-depth articles and, when they do, those articles often appear in magazine-like format. Notice, in the newspaper excerpt in Chapter 11 (see subhead 11.5), what happens to logical relationships between complicated concepts when paragraph length is kept very short.

Magazines have wider columns of type, and they run longer articles than newspapers do. Writers are given more flexibility in paragraphing. Still, some magazine editors like their pages to promise easy, fast-paced reading, and they aim for the white space that signals short paragraphs.

Books have the widest columns of type of most media. Paragraphs taken from newspapers and magazines seem very short unless they are reprinted in bigger type. Readers expect more depth of detail in books, and normally long paragraphs don't dismay them. Still, some textbook writers and editors go to great lengths to cut paragraphs into visually appealing segments, to persuade students that the subject matter is easy to understand.

Many of the illustrations, subheads, and other graphic devices found in books, magazines, and newspapers are put there not so much to elaborate on the printed material as to put white space around paragraphs. If you think this phenomenon is new, examine some of the hand-copied manuscripts for which monks spent weeks on end elaborately illuminating the pages.

But paragraphing doesn't help just the reader. It serves as a gauge for the writer, to help show at a glance how much has been said. If you do as we suggest, and allot each paragraph of your paper to one subtopic (or sub-subtopic) of your outline, a visual check of your first draft should give you a rough feel for how well each idea has been amplified in relation to the others. Keep in mind that the reader gauges the importance of an idea by how much space is devoted to it—how many sentences or how many paragraphs—so don't give short shrift to an item just because you think its supports are obvious.

When you type your final draft, you may decide that some of your paragraphs are too long visually on the page. Those paragraphs probably call on a lot of amplification techniques—redefining, offering examples, considering from several perspectives, quoting authorities, and using anecdotes. Once you learn to separate one device from another, it's easy to divide the paragraphs right where you switch technique.

You can break one long thematic paragraph into component paragraphs, but you must never amalgamate two short paragraphs with unrelated themes unless you can rework the sentences to include a bridge that shows a relationship.

EXERCISES:

1. Browse through popular magazines, scholarly journals, or other sources of printed information (besides books and newspapers) until you locate at least two pages on which the type looks so dense that the reading seems formidable, and two on which the type looks so light or the paragraphs so short that the reading seems trite. Photocopy each of the four pages and jot down its source.

2. Choose any two consecutive paragraphs from each of the dense pages, and rewrite them as four paragraphs. Choose any two consecutive paragraphs from each of the sparse pages, and make them longer either by adding information or combining them. (If you need more information to properly divide, expand, or amalgamate any of the paragraphs, you may invent reasonable sounding facts, quotations, or anecdotes.)

3. Make a copy of Illustration 12/1. Using the editing symbol that shows where a paragraph indentation is to be added (¶), locate and mark at least five places where new paragraphs could begin. You may indicate one-sentence paragraphs if you can show that the themes in these sentences are capable of expansion or that they can stand alone without support.

4. Study Illustration 10/2, and find at least two places where you could divide a long paragraph effectively so that each new paragraph has at least two sentences. Copy (photocopy, type, or neatly hand-write) the new paragraphs you've made. Then explain, for each:

    a. Why the paragraph can be divided there.
    b. What rewriting, if any, is needed to make each half a complete paragraph.
    c. Whether, and how, shortening the paragraphs changes the effect of that portion of the article.

5. Again using Illustration 10/2, locate at least two places where you could amalgamate two existing paragraphs. Copy each (photocopy, type, or neatly hand-write) as one paragraph. Then explain, for each:

a. Why the original authors (or the publication's editors) may have chosen to make two paragraphs instead of one.

b. Whether you prefer them as one paragraph or two, and why.

12.3 TRANSITIONS PROVIDE THE BRIDGES BETWEEN OUR THOUGHTS.

One unifying theme has pervaded all the chapters of this book: that good writing communicates a relationship between ideas. So far we've focused on the ideas that are expressed. Now let's examine the transitions that bridge those ideas.

Because the paragraph is, by definition, a thought unit, most people think of transitions as phrases that relate one paragraph to another. But the sentence is also a thought unit; the phrase is a thought unit; even the paper is a thought unit, since it deals exclusively with one theme. Obviously, thought units come in many sizes. It's not surprising, then, that transitions do too.

- Punctuation is used for transition.
- Words and phrases are used for transition.
- Sentences are used for transition.
- Even paragraphs are used for transition.

Here's how one series of thoughts would look if we omitted most of the transitions:

12. Here it is winter again. Some people in your family have colds. You saw that they got all their vitamins. You saw that they got lots of rest. You kept their feet dry. You kept their rooms free from drafts. You avoided germ-filled crowds. You must have overlooked something.

13. You won't overlook anything. You'll ply them with aspirin. You'll give them antihistamines. You'll give them hot chicken soup. You'll keep them warm.

You'll keep them dry. You'll sterilize all the dishes. You'll cure them. You'll keep their germs from spreading.

14. Doctors don't know how you can completely avoid colds. Doctors don't know how you can contain colds. There is a cure in the works. The cure will be marketable in a few years. The hunt for a cure has been proceeding for a steady quarter-century. Here are a fascinating array of facts about just what is the "common cold." Here's an up-to-date profile of Public Enemy Number One.

Now read the passage as we actually wrote it for *Weight Watchers* magazine:

15. Here it is winter again, and some people in your family have colds. You saw that they got all their vitamins and lots of rest, you kept their feet dry and their rooms free from drafts, and you avoided germ-filled crowds— but it was all to no avail. You must have overlooked something, right?

16. But you won't overlook anything now. You'll ply them with aspirin and antihistamines and hot chicken soup, you'll keep them warm and dry, and you'll sterilize all the dishes. That should cure them and keep their germs from spreading, right?

17. Wrong, on all counts. The truth is that doctors still don't know how you can completely avoid colds or contain them and, although there is a cure in the works, it'll be years before it's marketable.

18. The hunt for that cure has been proceeding for a steady quarter-century and has unearthed a fascinating array of facts about just what is the "common cold." On the theory that forewarned is forearmed, here's an up-to-date profile of Public Enemy Number One.[3]

The reader rarely notices transitions. But without them, we're sure you'll agree, communication becomes primitive.

Punctuation shows transition.

Most people don't think of punctuation as transition, but it gives readers quick and important information about how thoughts are related to one another.

- A *comma* can link two separate thoughts to show the reader they are equal in strength and closely related.

- A *semicolon* shows an equal relationship that isn't as close.

- A *colon* signals an unequal relationship in which the thought after the colon defines or explains the first thought, often with an example.

- *Parentheses* enclose a weak and unrelated thought.

- *Brackets* enclose a weak and unrelated thought.

- *Dashes* surround a parenthetical thought that, while weakly related, is also nearly as important as the enclosing thought.

- A *period* shows the end of a relationship. It provides a gap between separate thoughts. That's why, if you want to show that sentences are related, you must use transitional *words*.

- A *paragraph's end* signals an even greater gap. To show that the next paragraph's thoughts are related, you may be able to make do with a word. But a phrase or sentence may be needed to bridge the gap. If the relationship is tenuous indeed, it may take an entire paragraph to relate what you've said to what you're about to suggest.

In your reading, notice the transitions shown by punctuation marks.

Words and phrases show transition.

Words and phrases are the transitions most often used to link two closely related paragraphs or two ideas within a paragraph. Many of these transitions are obvious and pose no problems for writers. But sometimes getting from here to there is a perilous process. To make it a bit easier, become familiar with Illustration 12/2. That chart includes just some of the many transition words in our language and the relationships these words usually show. After you've gotten the knack of varying your transition words to keep the reader's interest, you won't need the chart any longer.

Another way of showing transitions with words and phrases is to *echo* the previous thought in the one that follows. The link is strongest if you repeat the exact word (usually a noun or verb), but synonyms and even antonyms may provide adequate echoes. The subtlest echoes repeat not words, but thoughts.

It is important to keep echoes from sounding forced. They're fun to use, but if you find yourself struggling to make one work, throw it out and try another kind of transition.

In general, the less obviously related are the thoughts in your paper, the more words you'll need to make your transitions. Look again at Excerpt 15-18, while we describe our thinking as we wrote it.

In the first paragraph, the only transitions needed are some *ands* and *buts*. The theme (cold-preventing actions you tried) is closely related to that of the next paragraph (actions you'll try), so only a *but* and a *now* are needed to show that. However, look at the next paragraph's thought (that doctors still can't avoid, contain, or cure colds). To show its relationship to what went before requires a sentence and a half: *Wrong on all counts. The truth is that* . . . For an extra clue to the reader that paragraphs 15 and 16 are to be related to paragraph 17 we actually went back in our editing and added the word *right*—the opposite of *wrong* and an echo also of *truth*—at the ends of paragraphs 15 and 16.

Sentences, and even paragraphs, show transition within papers.

The good writer is like a master map-reader: she identifies her start and finish, and then charts a course from here to there. To get there *quickly* is a consideration, but more important is to get there *smoothly* and *interestingly*. That may require several sentences, or even several paragraphs.

Paragraphs 15 and 16 are the article's lead, in the form of an anecdote that lures the reader doubly by making her the real person in the story. (We based our fabrication on the assumption that we were describing a universal experience of our readers.) But now we must show a relationship between the lead and the article's topic sentence—an up-to-date factual account of everything that's known about the common cold. And everything between the end of paragraph 16 and the topic sentence, *here's an up-to-date profile of Public Enemy Number One*, is all transition.

Let's retrace the way we got our reader from her family's colds to *all about colds*:

- from *you don't know how to avoid, contain, or cure them* to *nobody* (here personified as *doctors*) *knows how to avoid, contain or cure them*;

- *from lack of* a cure to *research on* a cure;

- from *research* to *the facts* research has unearthed;

- from *the facts* to *here are the facts*;

- and then, for good measure, a transition that hearkens back to *you* and your unavoidable, uncontainable, uncurable colds.

Transitions are learned best through observation and practice. After a while, they become instinctive and, like the transition we just traced, they take longer to explain than to create. The following exercises are designed to help you practice using them to advantage.

EXERCISES:

1. Photocopy Illustration 10/2. Underline all the transitions, excluding punctuation. If you find a paragraph that provides transition between topics, underline all of that paragraph.
2. From Exercise 1, choose six marked transitions, each of which shows a different relationship. (Refer, if necessary, to Illustration

12/2.) For each example, write at least 100 words that tell:
   a. Why the transition is required.
   b. How the two linked pieces of writing relate to one another.
   c. How the author could have shown the transition differently.

3. Write a second draft for Exercise 2, combining the six critiques into one essay. Then underline all *your own* transitions in the essay, and edit them so they are smooth and interesting without being wordy.

4. Locate a paper that you've written for this class or another. Make a copy of it and go through the copy carefully, underlining all the transitions. Mark, with an *X*, all the places that need more or better transitions. Rewrite the paper, fixing these spots, and bring both papers to class.

12.4 VARIETY IS THE SPICE OF GOOD PARAGRAPHS.

If you like ice cream, imagine having ice cream every day. After a while, we're sure, the sight of ice cream will cease to make you salivate. Now imagine ice cream one day, strawberry shortcake the next, then watermelon, and blueberry pie the day after. You may not enjoy them equally, but when ice cream comes around again it'll sure taste good.

The good writer knows that variety prevents boredom. She uses this fact to keep readers interested. She puts variety into her writing in one or more of four ways:

- by varying writing technique
- by varying words
- by varying sentence structure
- by varying mood.

Let's see how it's done.

You can vary your writing by selecting
from among the three writing techniques:
exposition, anecdote, and quotation.

Insert a quotation in the midst of a long anecdote, and it will grab the reader's attention. Inject a little factual story to illustrate an expository fact or idea, and it will help the reader remember the generalization or specific fact. Stop in the midst of a long quotation to explain one of its points, and that too will get more than usual attention, nudging the reader out of her passive word gathering.

The following excerpt, from an article on assertiveness training, shows how Neal Ashby uses variety in technique to keep reader interest high:

> 19. Be persistent. Repeat your statement. Don't get upset about angry responses or hostility toward you—anger is the problem of the person feeling it, and that's not you. Actor Tony Randall provides a good example of the hard line. "I don't let anyone smoke around me," he declares, "on the set, in the theater, anywhere. I think smoking is a killer, and I don't like the smell or anything about it. They think I'm a crank, but I just keep at it."
> If persistence doesn't work . . .[4]

In the above excerpt, a quotation is used to provide variety. In the next, from the same article, an anecdote follows some exposition:

> 20. Ironically, many who are submissive finally—after being frustrated repeatedly—explode into aggressiveness, and still their needs go unmet. They overreact, scream, curse, and threaten, before receding back into meekness and further frustration. Dr. Goldfried relates an example. At a Broadway play recently, a man in the audience grew increasingly angry as another man, sitting in the row behind, continued to make audible comments about the action on stage. The offended patron said noth-

ing—until intermission, when he suddenly rushed up to
the talker in the crowded lobby and shouted:

"You've got a hell of a nerve disturbing all of us with
that blabber!"[5]

Reread Excerpts 19 and 20, noticing what happens to your atten-
tiveness when Ashby introduces the Randall quotation and the anecdote. In each case, the shift from exposition doesn't waste a bit of
space, and both the quotation and the anecdote present new information (in the first case, what is meant by *hard line*, and in the second, what overreaction means in specific terms). If you'll remember
to call on all three techniques in writing your first drafts, you'll
achieve this kind of variety almost effortlessly.

You can vary your writing by varying your choice of words.

The good writer avoids using the same word over and over in a paragraph unless he does it deliberately for emphasis. Instead, he finds
a synonym.

In Unit II, a great deal of space was devoted to the variety of
words that writers can call on, and the usefulness of the thesaurus in
locating them. Let's look at an excerpt from a student's paper that
questions the value of prisons, to see what word variety does for writing. Here's the paragraph prior to editing:

21.   The second justification for punishment is to say that
it serves as a deterrent, to persuade a man not to commit
a crime because he has seen others punished for the same
crime. The punishment is supposed to incite fear and hes-
itation in the criminal's mind. The fact that crime still exists, after thousands of lives have seen that the only exit
from prison is death, makes one wonder just how effective punishment is as a deterrent.

Underline and count all the words with the roots *crime*, *punish*, and
deter. (We count ten.) Now read an edited version in which we've

concentrated just on word variety. (In the actual editing, other faults would be corrected.)

> 22. The second justification for seeking imprisonment is that seeing others punished keeps a man from committing that particular crime. Incarceration is supposed to incite fear and hesitation in the criminal's mind. The fact that crime still exists, after thousands have seen that prison's only exit is death, makes one wonder just how effective a deterrent punishment is.

Notice that adding word variety often points up redundancies that can be eliminated.

You can vary your writing by varying your sentence structure.

If you write a succession of sentences that are all structured the same way, you may lull readers to sleep no matter how important your subject. In most cases, sentence variety keeps readers on their toes.

The following quickly written paragraph suffers from unvaried sentence structure:

> 23. Strip mining has been practiced throughout the United States. Three hundred thousand acres of Pennsylvania have been stripped. Forty percent of Iowa is being torn away to yield 24 billion tons of coal. Eleven thousand acres of Iowa were dug up for coal by 1964. Thirty-three thousand additional acres of Iowa were dug for clay and stone by 1964. Pennsylvania and Iowa are two examples of strip-mined states.

The student who wrote the excerpt considered word variety; he substituted *torn away*, *dug up*, and *dug* for his initial word, *stripped*. If he had also tried for sentence variety, he might have written:

> 24. Strip mining has been practiced throughout the United States. In Pennsylvania, three hundred thousand

acres have been stripped. In Iowa, forty percent of the topsoil is being torn away to yield 24 billion tons of coal. By 1964, eleven thousand Iowa acres had been dug up for coal, and another three thousand for clay and stone. Pennsylvania and Iowa are only two of the strip-mined states.

Notice that the rewrite (excerpt 24) retains parallel construction in sentences 2, 3, and the opening of 4, while making their structure quite different from sentences 1 and 5. The new repeating rhythm, or parallelism, helps make the subtle point that these examples fortify the first sentence's generalization.

The only time the good writer deliberately avoids varying sentence structure is when he wants parallelism. This device tells the reader, "These ideas are tied together." The rhythm of several parallel sentences builds a tension that the writer can relax with a climactic statement; the more parallel sentences (or sentence parts), the greater will be the climax when the writer changes rhythm. If your final statement doesn't warrant the buildup, however, your reader won't take kindly to the drone of parallelism.

Here's how a student used parallelism to begin the first draft of a paper:

25. He is a super human being.

He flies around the country helping Indian tribes to take or reject this money or that money from Uncle Sam.

He gets government money to get Indians into graduate school or to get jobs for Indians on reservations.

He helps Indians accept white medicine with dignity when they are suffering.

He is a professor who lectures, who makes speeches and writes articles.

He is the first Indian to get a doctorate in social work.

But only one writer in a million turns out a perfect paper on his first try. Notice what a bit of editing did for his effect:

26. He flies around the country helping Indian tribes to take or reject this money or that money from Uncle Sam.

He finds government money to get Indians into graduate school or to create jobs for Indians on reservations.

He helps Indians accept white medicine with dignity when they are suffering.

He lectures, makes speeches, and writes articles.

He is the first Indian to get a doctorate in social work.

He is a super human being.

Notice that our rewrite tries for word variety—except when it comes to the word *Indians*, which is a major theme of the article. It also strengthens the rhythm by offering readers four successive sentences with parallel beginnings: *He* followed by an active verb that tells what *he* does. The two-sentence climax reveals, finally, who *he* is.

When using parallelism, it's a good idea to introduce your ideas in the order of dramatic impact, even when you offer no immediate punch line. Trude B. Feldman, writing about Rosalynn Carter, constructed a fine paragraph that illustrates this point. Notice that Feldman uses the magic number, three examples, to support her generalization.

27. Most of us know paragons of female virtue and achievement who manage to make the rest of us uncomfortable in their presence. Their homes are sparkling and neat while ours have too much clutter and need a painting. They make their own clothes while we lack the skill or time. They are in harmony with their children while we scream at ours.[6]

In this excerpt, as in Excerpt 26, the sentence structure creates a rhythm in the writing. This sense of rhythm is not accidental, but put there on purpose by a good writer. Author Willa Cather once told television interviewer Dick Cavett that before she attempts a day's worth of writing, she first spends some time reading the Bible. She does it to pick up the cadence of its natural rhythms, which she then transfers to her own pages.

Try to develop an ear for writing's rhythms by reading poetry or fine prose, or by listening to rhythmical music. If you can put rhythm in your own sentence structure, your writing will improve tremendously.

Everyone has his own most preferred writing rhythm. Learn to use yours. With time, you'll find, it will sound just like you.

You can vary your writing by building moods.
Your writing expresses a certain mood to readers, whether you like it or not. If you write carelessly or too quickly or with your own concerns more in mind than those of your readers, the mood you express may be one of sterile unconcern. On the other hand, if you choose powerful words, take care to construct varied sentences, and weave them into well-orchestrated paragraphs, you can create moods of pleasure, excitement, horror, concern, contempt, or consternation.

Weaving a mood with words is even more subjective a skill than making writing rhythms. Like rhythm, its effect in good writing is akin to its effect in music. It's so intangible that there are many different terms for it. (*Tone* and *texture* are commonly used in composition books.) If you learn to tune in to the moods your writing creates, you will achieve the maximum return for investing the time and effort that writing demands of all of us.

Good writers use moods in somewhat the same way they effectively present their evidence. For example, they don't shift mood in mid-paragraph except for a very good reason. And they build crescendos in mood from the beginning of a sentence to its end, from the start of a paragraph to its climax, and from the introduction of a paper to its finale. Used self-consciously by a beginner, these mood crescendos may make the paper seem choppy or melodramatic. But they're worth the trial and error that lead to effective use.

Critical reading, of your own words and others', is an effective way to learn how to use mood. To start you off, here's a paragraph by Rob Schultheis that describes a bus trip through a strange land.

> 28. A whole continent is eviscerated for you: a veiled, dark jinni of a woman, floating down a sun-blanched street; a grinning, white-bearded man in robes, pointing a Sten gun at you and then waving hello; a line of camels loaded with opium or guns or gold, strutting off into a setting sun the color of a persimmon; a voice crying out the call to prayer, dipping and soaring over a mud warren of a city hardly changed in its 3,000 years; sea-green minarets and dark green trees full of pigeons, in a park where the fortunetellers sit in the cool of the dusk. Dysentery, dust, pickpockets and all, the bus is well worth it. It is the only way to go.[7]

The very long, loose, complex, yet parallel sentence builds the mood of lushness because of its detail, of strangeness because of its slightly unfamiliar words, and of beauty because of the sound of those soft words, some of which almost rhyme. The reader nearly overlooks the fact that some of the images are ugly. But then the mood changes abruptly to unpoetic words we know (dysentery, dust, pickpockets) put in a short, punchy sentence— and then, for climax, an even shorter sentence with short, everyday words. Read the excerpt again, and see how closely rhythm is related, here, to mood.

Mood is not an afterthought of writing. It creeps in, assisted or unassisted. Let it lead you, and your writing will suffer. Make it your friend and servant, and it will help you communicate from the first paragraph of your paper to the last.

EXERCISES:

1. Reread Excerpt 28, and write a well-constructed essay of at least 250 words that includes all the following information:

a. How many, and which, writing techniques are used.

b. The number of generalizations and specifics used, and their effect on the reader.

c. The variety of words, or their lack of variety, and its effect.

d. How well you guessed at the meanings of unfamiliar words, and the effect on your reading of having guessed wrong or right.

e. The effect of pleasant and unpleasant images.

2. Read the following excerpt by Lewis Mumford, and write a well-constructed essay that answers the following:

a. Is there variety in words and sentences? To what effect? Is the effect achieved, and why or why not?

b. Does Mumford approve of electro-mechanical advances? How does he make the reader know his opinions?

c. How does the final sentence compare to everything that precedes it?

d. What is the mood of the paragraph? How is it achieved? How well does it contribute to or hinder your understanding of the theme?

Are not refrigerators, private motor cars and planes, automatic heating systems, telephones and television sets, electrically driven washing machines worth having? And what of the drudgery-eliminating achievements of the bulldozer, the forklift truck, the electric hoist, the conveyor belt, and a thousand other serviceable inventions? What of the appalling mental burdens in bookkeeping that have been lifted by the computer? What of the exquisite arts of the surgeon and the dentist? Are these not colossal gains? Why weep if some of the old goods and enjoyments have fallen through this electro-mechanical mesh? Does any sensible person mourn the passing of the old Stone Age? If all these goods are in themselves sound and individually desirable, on what grounds can we condemn the system that totalizes them? So say the official spokesmen.[8]

3. Read through nonfiction magazines, journals, and books until you locate four paragraphs, each of which shows one of the following: variety in words, variety in sentence structure, variety in technique, variety in mood. Copy the paragraphs and, for each, write 150 words explaining how that particular device contributes to or detracts from the writer's communication with readers.

4. Read the following paragraph from a student's paper about getting around Brazil as a sightseer. Write a 250-word analysis that includes the following information:

a. Compare the topic phrase with the last sentence.

b. Describe whether there is variety of words and sentence structure, and whether it helps or hinders effectiveness.

c. Discuss the mood the writer tries for, and evaluate her success.

d. Suggest any changes that strengthen the paragraph.

You have a fifty-fifty chance of finding an honest cobrador, or independent cabdriver. Dishonest cobradors try to shortchange you or, depending on the rates, play a kind of shell game with the customer. If the fare is Cr $2.90 and you give him Cr $3.00, he may not have any more 10¢ pieces left for change. If you inquire you'll be asked for a 10¢ piece and in return should receive the correct change of 20¢. But this little game becomes complicated with a sharp cobrador who knows how to ask for coins to confuse the issue. Even if you lose 10¢, you can console yourself with the thought that it's worth one-fifth of a U.S. penny, you'd have been in worse shape at a cabbie's mercy, and the money is going to a good cause—the cobrador. A cobrador makes the equivalent of U.S. $86.00 per month for working a 10- to 12-hour day. After living in Rio for even a few days you won't begrudge him the con.

NOTES: CHAPTER 12

1. Bern Keating, "Down Home in the Ozarks," *Travel & Leisure*, September, 1979, pp. 128–29.
2. Franklynn Peterson and Judi R. Kesselman, "New Generation Particleboard," *Popular Science*, December, 1979, p. 96.
3. Judi R. Kesselman, "Colds: Catching Them, Curing Them," *Weight Watchers Magazine*, December, 1974, p. 40.
4. Neal Ashby, "Stop Putting Up with Put-Downs," *Today's Health*, July–August, 1975, p. 17.
5. Ibid., p. 17.
6. Trude B. Feldman, "Rosalynn Carter," *Woman's Day*, February, 1977, p. 72.
7. Rob Schultheis, "Bus Tripping," *Mother Jones*, June, 1979, p. 37.
8. Lewis Mumford, *The Pentagon of Power* (New York: Harcourt Brace Jovanovich, 1964), p. 333.

ILLUSTRATION 12/1*

Detecting Learning Problems
Before Children Start School

A statewide program in North Carolina helps ensure that youngsters enter kindergarten both psychologically and physically prepared to learn. Three years ago, under the direction of psychologist Mary Haynes of the North Carolina Developmental Evaluation Centers, a network of twelve screening programs in which four-year-olds are given free comprehensive examinations were set up throughout the state. Trained examiners spot hidden problems that could hinder normal development or progress in school. Then they tell parents how to have those problems solved. They also pinpoint gifted children, so that parents and schools can provide adequately for them.

Dr. Haynes says, "About twenty-five percent of the youngsters have serious disorders that could handicap them in education or growth. Ten percent have vision defects, and eighteen percent have hearing loss. We detect hints of serious emotional disorders, learning disabilities and even incomplete immunizations."

Besides these problems, another 25 percent of the examined children have correctable weaknesses that could slow them down in school. "We find weak pencil skills, poor language skills, poor eye-hand coordination and socialization problems," says Dr. Haynes. "Often they can be remedied."

Dr. Haynes believes that North Carolina's figures probably reflect the percentage of preschoolers all over the country who have undetected handicaps. She says, "The irony is kindergarten teachers used to complain that half their students began school with problems. We're finding they were right. But our job isn't just to diagnose; it's to correct the problems before the children start school by guiding their parents to the proper help."

Parents learn about North Carolina's Statewide Preschool Screening Program (SPSP) through TV, radio, and newspaper ads, brochures in pediatricians' offices, letters from preschool centers and word-of-mouth. Children may be taken to one of the state's twelve centers for screening by appointment, but the program's screeners also go into nursery schools, Headstart programs, and community centers. So far, about 20 percent of North Carolina's four-year-olds have been screened.

A reporter recently observed while one little girl was being tested at the Asheville Center. Four-year-old Lauri was led into an office by screener Katrina Wilson. The two played various games involving matching pictures and then letters. Eventually Ms. Wilson held up a card printed with the word *NO*. Lauri incorrectly matched it with the card saying *OZ*. But she found the correct match for the next word *EAT*. Ms. Wilson spent about an hour testing and evaluating the child's memory, perception, reasoning ability, balance, coordination, and so on.

In the meantime, Lauri's mother was being interviewed about her daughter's behavior at home and at nursery school. Afterward Ms. Wilson told her how Lauri's performance stacked up against that of other four-year-olds. Lauri, as is true with most children, came out above average in some skills, average in some, and below average in others. Her mother was told about games she could play with Lauri that would help correct two of the child's weaknesses—pencil skills and hand-eye coordination. Mrs. Wilson made a note to follow up on Lauri's progress in two months.

How did Lauri's mother react to the exam? "You have no idea how good it is to have somebody assure you your child is normal!" she said.

If, in the preliminary screening, children are found to have more problems than Lauri has, they are tested further by one or more of the center's specialists. (They include a psychologist, psychiatrist, pediatrician, physical therapist, social worker, educational psychologist, nurse, and speech pathologist.) Since few children turn out to have only one problem, the eight professionals hold frequent case discussions. Then they refer the children to public or private counseling facilities, where payment is scaled to the family's income. If the staff has time, it treats low-income children at the center.

Several other communities have screening programs like North Carolina's, but nowhere is there another statewide effort. Illinois experimented with a similar plan, but ran into administration problems and dropped it, although the city of Evanston retained its program. A suburban St. Louis school district tests its preschoolers. The large, western-based Kaiser-Permanente prepaid health organization routinely screens its subscribers' youngsters.

Unfortunately, the North Carolina screening program may be limited to screening only a small percentage of preschoolers because of monetary reasons. But at least one child expert believes such an economy would be shortsighted. A pediatrician, psychiatrist, and former director of HEW's Office of Child Development, Dr. John Meier, says, "Many of us tend to get our commitments backwards. We spend all that money on college when spending more on young children would bring the most long-term rewards. North Carolina has put together one of the most comprehensive programs I've ever seen. It not only informs parents but pursues them to ensure that the uncovered problems are taken care of."

Dr. Meier would like to see programs like North Carolina's developed all over the country. "If a national network of screening centers had been funded after World War II the average IQ in America today would be one hundred thirty instead of one hundred. We'd have very little illiteracy, fewer school dropouts, less juvenile delinquency. In general, we'd have a lot more happy adults."

*Franklynn Peterson and Judi R. Kesselman, "Detecting Learning Problems Before Children Start School." *McCall's,* August, 1977, pp. 69–70.

ILLUSTRATION 12/2

Relationships Described by Transition Words and Phrases

THE RELATIONSHIP	SOME WORDS THAT SHOW IT	
Add one thought to another	also and and so as well as at the same time besides finally furthermore in addition	moreover next not only . . . but second so then therefore with
Subtract one thought from another.	although but despite however in spite of nevertheless	or or else still whereas yet
Compare or *contrast* one thought with another	accordingly because (of) by the same token conversely either . . . or for in comparison instead likewise	neither . . . nor of course on the other hand similarly that these this those

THE RELATIONSHIP	SOME WORDS THAT SHOW IT	
Show a time change from one thought to the next.	after afterward before begin finally first	from then on last next then until then
Show a place change from one thought to the next	above across behind beyond down in in back of in front of	meanwhile next to on on top of over up within
Show a *change in purpose* from one thought to the next	after all on the one hand . . . on the other hand otherwise	
Show that one thought *results* in the next.	as a result based on consequently from that	furthermore thereby therefore when
Show that a thought is an *example* of the previous one.	for example for instance in this instance to demonstrate to illustrate	
Show that a thought is a *stronger version* of the previous one.	again indeed in fact in other words	
Show that a thought is a *summation* of the previous one.	in brief in conclusion therefore to conclude to summarize to sum up	

CHAPTER 13
HOW TO WRITE
AN EFFECTIVE
BUSINESS LETTER

*The writer does the most
who gives his reader the
most knowledge, and takes
from him the least time.*
Sydney Smith

Near the beginning of the book we wrote that a personal letter is in a class of its own. Because it's a communication between friends, it doesn't need logical organization, careful choice of ideas, examples, transitions, or even precise words. It can be poorly punctuated, badly spelled, and scarcely legible, and neither sender nor receiver will mind.

Business letters, however, are pieces of factual writing. Just as unplanned papers turn out weak and unconvincing, so do disorganized business letters. They are subject to all the rules and guidelines of factual writing. In addition, they must adhere to rigid rules of structure.

13.1 THE STRUCTURE
OF A BUSINESS LETTER.

Business letters should be typed. Whenever possible use white bond paper, 8½ × 11 inches in size. Type only on one side of the paper, and keep a carbon copy. Use No. 9 or No. 10 envelopes so that you can fold the letter into thirds.

Every business letter must have all the following elements:

1. An accepted form

The traditional business letter is typed in *indented form*. Your address and date of writing reach to the upper right-hand margin of the letter, with your recipient's name and address below it but flush with the left-hand margin. A two-line space separates that from the salutation, and another two-line space comes next. Each paragraph is indented, with double-spacing preferred between paragraphs. Indentation is usually five spaces, but flamboyant writers prefer ten. The closing matter lines up with your name and address, on the right-hand side of the page.

Many businesses now prefer *block form*. All the elements discussed below are lined up on the left-hand margin, and even paragraphs are generally not indented. They are always separated by double-spacing.

Whichever form you choose, the letter is always typed single-spaced, with double-spacing between elements.

2. Your full address

To ensure ease of reply, the address is generally placed conspicuously at the very top of the letter. For the same reason, some people type their names along with the address. Because so much business is transacted on the phone these days, your telephone number (complete with area code) should be included, too. Of course, whatever information appears in the printed letterhead need not be repeated.

3. The date

By dating the letter, you can accomplish two purposes. First, you and the recipient can both refer to the letter by date, if you've written several, to make sure you're considering the same one. Second, it reminds a busy paper-shuffler how long the letter has lain in his in-box.

4. The full name and title of the recipient, and the organization's name and address

Showing the full name of a living, breathing, thinking individual gets your letter right to the person who can act on it. Besides, most people feel anonymous enough in their jobs without the reminder of being addressed just by job title. (Refer to Section 9.5 for assistance in finding real names.) Showing the title helps route the letter to the right department. That way, if the addressee has moved on, her replacement may feel obliged to read it.

It's customary to put in the organization's full name and address. It helps you, since it's useful to have the data on your carbon copy, and easiest to find while you're working with the papers that pertain to the letter. Then you can just copy it when typing the envelope.

5. The correct salutation

If you've got a name, use *Dear Mr. Smith:* or *Dear Ms. Smith:* (Ms. is correct unless you're certain it's Miss or Mrs.) The colon is traditional, but some organizations have switched to the less formal comma. If you haven't got the name, use the traditional *Dear Sir or Madam:* or *To Whom It May Concern:* The variant *Dear Mr. or Ms.:* is little used.

6. The body

The body is always typed single-spaced, with double-spacing between paragraphs. In indented form, you must always indent paragraphs; in block form it's optional.

7. The closing

There are a number of traditional closings. Unless you deliberately want to appear eccentric or unbusinesslike, choose one like *Cordially, Sincerely, Yours truly, Very truly yours.* Start the closing with a capital letter and end it with a comma.

8. Your signature

Save fancy flourishes and brightly colored pens for personal letters. A businesslike signature is best. But some business people have taken to arbitrarily prejudging personality by signature; you can foil them by using a fairly broad, dark, felt-tipped pen that makes your signature seem confident and assertive.

If you've included your name at the top, it's optional to type it again. However, since most people's signatures can't be read, it's a courtesy we strongly recommend. Type your name four spaces beneath your closing, and sign the letter in the space between.

9. Additional touches

One element often found way down in the bottom left-hand corner of business letters is a set of initials such as JKT/FP. These tell the boss (JKT) which secretary (FP) typed the letter. If you don't have a secretary, don't put initials down there.

If you are enclosing additional material with your letter, that lower left-hand corner is the place to write *Enclosure*, *Encl.*, or *Encls*. If you're sending copies of the letter to people other than the named recipient, business tradition dictates that you name those people in that lower left-hand corner. Format is: *cc: John Jones*. If copies are going to several people, put the second and subsequent names underneath John Jones's.

13.2 THE CONTENT OF A BUSINESS LETTER.

Like all factual writing, the business letter has a subject and a purpose. Like most factual writing, it has to compete for the reader's time and attention. Therefore, most successful business letters are tightly written, with lead, topic, and purpose in a punchy, explicit beginning sentence or two, and one sharp summary sentence at the end. In other respects, the writer follows all the rules for preparing factual papers.

The opening: lead, topic, and purpose

Most letter-writers know the topic they're writing about and state it quite clearly in the first sentence. Fewer writers begin with a purpose in mind. Unless you state clearly what you want of the recipient, she probably won't bother to try to figure it out. If you attempt to cover more than one purpose with a single letter, you may confuse her into inaction on all fronts. If you have two separate purposes, it's best to write two letters, even if they're sent to the same person.

The lead of a business letter may be just a word or two, but it has the same purpose as any lead—to catch the attention of the reader. A reply letter assumes the reader's interest; a lead isn't important, and is often dispensed with.

Here are some examples of actual openings that give the lead, topic, and purpose as quickly and clearly as possible. (We have underlined the lead and put the purpose in bold type, and numbered the excerpts for ease of referral.)

1. Your new do-it-yourself handyman club <u>does sound</u> like an <u>exciting</u> project, and **I'd like to become involved** as the free-lance writer and editor you've advertised for.

2. Thank you for your notice concerning an ASJA Board of Directors' meeting in New York on September 13. Our local chapter has some **suggestions to offer** for the agenda.

3. I'm enclosing a brochure for the <u>spectacular</u> Writers' Conference taking place in Madison, Wisconsin, on May 11–12, in the hope that you will **mention** the conference **on your radio program**.

4. I am a lawyer in New Orleans who is presently handling a lawsuit in which the design of a small Briggs & Stratton engine is involved. <u>Your expertise</u> on engines can **help** . . .

5. To follow up our phone conversation of March 9, and to answer more formally your letter of February 23, let me briefly list those of my credentials that **may be of benefit to you** in the barge case.

6. A parking ticket, violation #713030, was issued to me 11/22/80 in the Memorial Union parking lot. The following information will **demonstrate** <u>my innocence</u>.

7. I am enclosing a sampler of PhoneScan articles we prepared for *Physician's Management* magazine over the past two years. The series <u>won this year's</u> *American Business Press* <u>award</u>. **We'd like to design a** PhoneScan **package for you,** too.

In every one of the samples above, the author plunges right into the subject with no more personal introduction than is absolutely required for the opening to make sense to the reader. In that way, once the recipient reaches the end of the first sentence (or, in the last example, the first paragraph), she knows if she's the right person to help. If she is, the momentum of the first businesslike sentence keeps her moving through the rest of the letter. If she's not, the opening contains enough data so she can redirect the letter before her interest flags.

Years ago, business letters often began with the abbreviation *re:* and then a formal statement of topic and purpose. This type of opening is practically obsolete.

Organizing the body
Just as the body of a factual paper must be outlined, so must the business letter's body. Before you write a word, decide on the subtopics you want to cover—the points you want to make—and collect the evidence you're going to use. Then arrange your subtopics according to the purpose of your letter.

For example, if your purpose is to report an incident or a theft, use time sequence. If it's to describe how you used a toaster that burned out, use step-by-step sequence. If it's to extend an invitation or to explain an idea for conserving energy, use a logical progression. If it's to complain about a faulty product or to argue for a political candidate, present your persuasion from a definite point of view. (For a complete review of organizational techniques, see the checklist that follows Chapter 8.)

Writing the body

Writing the body of a letter is just like writing a paper. It follows the rules for good paragraphs and good sentences. Mostly, it calls on facts, but quotations and anecdotes should be included where they make your points better than exposition. You should write naturally, honestly, from your experience, and always with your reader in mind.

In much nonfiction writing, vividness is more important than conciseness. In business letters, conciseness is as important as accuracy and precision. Business people rarely peruse more than two pages of any letter, and even two-pagers are often put aside to be read after the others have been answered. To attain conciseness, keep these guidelines in mind:

● Say only what has to be said. Personal information about yourself doesn't belong, unless it supports the topic of your letter. (Excerpt 7 contains personal information that does belong.)

● Avoid the empty phrases that many people think are part of a letter-writer's vocabulary: "I am writing this letter to . . ." "In closing I would like to say . . ." "Enclosed herewith . . ."

● If documents or examples are essential to your letter's effectiveness, don't restate their content in detail in the body of the letter. Sum them up, or simply say that the proof of your point is attached. Then staple or paperclip photocopies (never originals) of the appropriate papers behind your letter. (Excerpt 7 shows how brief a reference is needed.)

13.3 WRITE ASSERTIVELY.

It's your letter, you're in charge, and obviously you want something from your recipient or you wouldn't be taking the time to write. Assume that you have the right to whatever it is you're asking for. On the other hand, be sure that your tone sounds truly assertive, not grabby, hostile, insincere, or tentative.

Don't beat around the bush. It wastes everybody's time. Tell what you need and, succinctly, tell why. "I have a February

1st deadline to meet" will get much faster action than "I'm hoping for your earliest possible reply."

Keep a file of carbon copies of your letters. Notice which devices bring results, so you can use them again. When you write a letter similar in content to an earlier one, save time and energy by copying appropriate passages.

If an important letter brings no response, don't drop the matter. Write to remind the intended recipient that you've received no reply. We often attach a Xerox copy of our carbon copy to jog the recipient's memory and to avoid having to cover the same ground one more time. If you're writing as an adversary—let's say to get a company to fix a defective typewriter—establish a reasonable deadline after which you will address your complaint to some higher authority.

On the other hand, if your unanswered letter was sent to ask a favor, for example to get information for a paper, there's a more diplomatic form of assertiveness than imposing an arbitrary deadline. We sometimes attach a stamped, self-addressed envelope to a follow-up letter, and suggest the recipient "just jot down your answer in the margin and slip this letter in the attached reply envelope." Other times we say, "Why don't you call us collect at . . . ?" Both techniques show that you appreciate the demands on the recipient's time but are serious about needing a reply.

In some tough cases, we initiate the telephone call. The one thing many procrastinators hate worse than answering mail is talking to the author of unanswered mail; if the recipient's secretary tells you his boss is out of the office, be sure to leave your name and the purpose of your phone call. You're likely to get your answer by return mail.

EXERCISES:

1. Rewrite the business letter on page 318 to accomplish all of the following. (Note: Its indented form is correct. Retain it.)

    a. Make it as concise as possible.

    b. Be sure the tone is assertive.

    c. Keep in everything that belongs in, and remove everything that doesn't.

2. Rewrite the business letter on page 319 to accomplish all of the following. (Note: Its block form is correct. Retain it.)

    a. Make it as concise as possible.

    b. Be sure the tone is assertive.

    c. Keep in everything that belongs in, and remove everything that doesn't.

    d. Add whatever is needed to make the letter as effective as possible.

87 Wingra Court
Paducah, Kentucky 44859
(407) 999-8765

January 18, 1981

Timothy Trane
Director of Public Relations
The Triad Trampoline Corporation
818 First Street
Akron, Ohio 33845

Dear Mr. Trane:

    I have always highly regarded the Triad trampolines. Therefore I am writing this letter to you in the hopes that you can help me. I am a student at Kentucky State College (home of the Terrible Tigers) and have to do a paper on exercise equipment for Phys. Ed 27.

    How many are sold every year?
    How much do they cost?
    Who invented them?
    Do you plan to make any changes in them?
    Who says that trampolines are worthwhile pieces of exercise equipment?

    I hope you can answer these questions as soon as possible.

Very truly yours,

Jeffrey James, Jr.

19 80th Street
Port Edwards, WI 53825
(717) 234-5678

January 18, 1981

Professor Jennifer Richards
Psychology Department
University of Wisconsin
Madison, WI 53308

Dear Prof. Richards,

The women's movement has changed everybody's life. But
I don't have to tell you that, do I?

I am in the Women's Studies Department at U.W.–Stevens
Point. I'm a junior and so far have a 3.4 gpa. The head of
our department isn't as dynamic as I've heard you are, but
then Stevens Point isn't as big a campus either.

I've been assigned a paper on how assertive training has
changed American families. Actually, it deals with formal
assertiveness training—through courses, or on-the-job, or
places like that. I can't cover, much as I'd like to, informal
groups that often deal with assertive training of one sort or
another. You know more about them than I do, I'm sure.

Since you're one of the big guns in formal assertiveness
training—you get all those contracts for running seminars
and things for big business—I'd love to find out from you
everything you know on this subject.

I'm in a hurry since I let this paper go to the last minute.

Yours in sisterhood,

Angela Ames O'Connor

Encl.: stamped, self-addressed envelope

UNIT IV

HOW TO BECOME A BETTER WRITER

CHAPTER 14
EVERY GOOD WRITER
IS A GOOD EDITOR

You become a good writer
just as you become a good joiner:
by planing down your sentences.
Anatole France

Students come into our writing classes with a lot of fanciful notions about the craft of writing. Some they've inferred from novels and movies about authors. Many they've picked up in classrooms. The misconception most damaging to the writing skills of students is also the most widespread of all myths about the writing process: that fine writing flows like magic from the pens and typewriters of a few special people who have been blessed with the gift of effortless creativity.

During your school years you've probably read some factual writing by classical authors like Thoreau, Swift, Huxley, and Shaw. If you've encountered teachers who enjoy modern writers, you may have read Dee Brown's *Bury My Heart at Wounded Knee* or Rachel Carson's *Silent Spring*. No doubt you studied them for style, content, and excellence of expression. But we'll bet that nowhere along the way has a teacher pointed out that what you were analyzing did not spring from the mind ready-to-read. All these works were rewritten, edited, and perhaps revised again before their authors felt they were effective enough to publish.

If you haven't been told before, let us be the first to announce: most writers, even the greatest—no, especially the greatest—work very hard to achieve their masterpieces of prose. What often separates a great work from a hack job is the amount of time spent revising the first hasty sentences. If God did, in fact, smile on certain writers, it was to give them strong lower-back muscles suited to the chore of sitting for long hours to edit and rewrite.

Caskie Stinnett, in an article titled "It Wasn't As Easy As It Seemed," reports that when *Walden* was in the works, "Thoreau produced seven different versions of the book during the six years he spent writing and revising it." Stinnett continues:

> The reader of *Walden* today, enchanted by the clarity and beauty of the prose, would do well not to glance at the early versions; it is better not to see the wheels spinning and hear the motor grinding. . . . The tangle of handwritten scraps of paper with their abundance of corrections shows how persistently Thoreau pursued purity and his own peculiar literary style. Whether he was leading his readers on a bucolic ramble or writing a dialectic that would hold up with the passing of time, it's impossible to say, but he stopped and started, tinkered and rearranged, selected and discarded, chose and reconsidered, and fought with the English language until he forced it to come to terms with him. . . .
>
> Thoreau prevailed until he got what he wanted. It's hard to imagine how long he looked at the sentence "The mass of mankind lead lives of quiet desperation" before he decided it gave off a hollow ring and that there was a better way of saying it. He finally found it in "The mass of men lead lives of quiet desperation"; cleaner, more pungent, more to the point.[1]

It's important to realize that editing is as much a part of any writing process as writing the first draft. Unfortunately, it's rarely taught, and most students go through school thinking it's just a matter of cleaning up spelling and punctuation errors so that a neat final copy can be typed. Let's examine all that it really entails.

14.1 HOW TO PREPARE YOUR FIRST DRAFT.

Editing really begins with the way you prepare your first draft. Let's assume that you've selected a topic, done all your research, and are ready to start writing. What then? We suggest you get in the habit of going through all the following steps:

1. **Sharpen your theme.** Be sure to include both your topic and purpose. Review and improve your working title.

2. **Outline your paper's body.** Write down every subtopic and every specific you plan to use to amplify the subtopics. Select one or more patterns of organization, and alter your original outline, if necessary, to conform to these patterns.

3. **Decide on a lead and a topic sentence.** But don't worry about the ending until you've written the rest of the paper.

4. **Now write your first draft.** Start with the lead and topic sentence, and then write the body, working from your outline. Last, write the ending. Work with thought and attention to your ideas, but not to the mechanics of writing. At this stage you must simply get it all said with as few stops and starts as possible. Don't type precise, detailed references to all your sources, or bother with footnotes. But do key your research material to your manuscript as you go along so you won't waste a lot of time later tracking down where various pieces of information have come from. Sometimes we type sources' names and page numbers in our margins; other times we type sketchy clues in parentheses at the ends of passages that rely on research notes.

In writing your first draft, don't worry about correct spelling, punctuation, or grammar. Don't hunt for the right word or phrase either. If you feel you need reminders, you can type question marks near words or phrases that you're not certain of or would like to take more time with. The emphasis in this draft should be to put all your material down on paper as logically and as quickly as you can. Mull over ideas, not their best execution. That's what editing is for.

We recommend that you use a typewriter for your first draft. We know some writers who do well writing longhand, but we've found that students who learn to think of words at typewriters learn to write well faster, because they can see full pages at a glance.

If you type (or hand-write) your first draft double-spaced or even triple-spaced, you'll have room between the lines to make revisions. If you leave wide margins (a professional inch-and-a-half at the left and an inch each at the right side, top, and bottom) you'll be able to use the margins to insert notes to yourself and longer corrections that don't fit between the lines. (The page or two that you save now by typing from edge to edge will be lost later when you have to tear up and start again on the final draft because of confusing insertions.)

After finishing your first draft, it's good to put it aside for a while so you can get some psychological distance before re-reading it. (That's one good reason for getting an early start on papers.) Another way to gain some valuable perspective on your freshly written first draft is by reading it aloud. The aim is to become, as nearly as possible, "the reader" as you examine the words.

14.2 HOW TO EDIT
YOUR FIRST DRAFT.

It's the care you take with editing, not only with your first draft, that makes or breaks the effectiveness of your paper. The first step is to check the first draft against your outline and your research notes to make certain that you have put down all the information you should have, and that all the evidence is presented in the most effective sequence possible. It is counterproductive, during this preliminary reading, to fix sentences and choose better words, because you may have to edit out some of the sentences you're now inclined to start fixing.

Few writers organize all the information in the very best order in the first draft. That's because when you've forced yourself to write intelligent conclusions based on your collection of notes, you've forced yourself to think analytically about the various subtopics in your paper. Often that has brought you to a conclusion that some subtopics have more importance than you initially thought, whereas others have faded almost into oblivion. Often heretofore hidden relationships become obvious as you reread those changes. You may have to reposition paragraphs, maybe entire pages, so they match your reevaluated plan of organization.

On this first rereading of your first draft, you may also find that some weakly made points require additional amplification: more specific facts, anecdotes, or a quoted voice of authority. To make your presentation of evidence as logical and well-reasoned as possible, you may have to add a sentence or two here and there, or even a paragraph or more.

After a while, you'll devise shortcuts to the mechanics of editing. Some writers use scissors and tape and actually cut and paste to rearrange their first drafts into the best logical order. For people who have trouble visualizing rearrangements, it's the best way. We often rearrange by keying the sentences or paragraphs we want moved: we write a large A in the margin, circle it, and next to it write, "move A to p. 4." Then, on page 4, exactly at the place we want the copy moved to, we write in bold letters "PICK UP A FROM P. 6." If something else is to be moved from page 6 to somewhere else, we label that B and key it the same way. We always key in both places—where it moves from and where it moves to—so that we won't forget to type it in on the next draft.

We use carets for short insertions, as you see in our reproduced manuscript (Illustration 14/1 at end of this chapter). In addition, we key long insertions that are written in along the margins, so we know just where they belong. We use paragraph marks (¶) to break long paragraphs into smaller pieces, and write "no ¶" or an arrow to the margin to show elimination of a paragraph. Any method you devise is equally good if it works for you.

The best way to make revisions is with a pencil or a pen. We like red pen; it's easier to follow those tracks through our original words. Use anything you can read easily when typing your next draft. At all stages in the editing process, choose methods and tools that work best for you.

Only after you feel confident that the content of your paper is well in hand should you start to concentrate on how well you've said what you meant. It is best to assume, along with the rest of us writers, that few of your words have fallen onto the paper just right on your first try. There are too many words in the language, too many shades of meaning, too many opportunities to be just a bit more precise or vivid. In the good company of Thoreau, you must tinker and rearrange, select and discard, choose and reconsider, and fight with the English language until you, too, force it to come to your terms.

Your editing will go more smoothly if you have the right language tools to help you. A good thesaurus is mandatory. A dictionary is helpful. And you can get good mileage from compact, up-to-date books of grammar and English usage to help you sort out the correct preposition and get all your agreements right. Without such guides at their elbows, many beginning writers choose grammatical safety instead of reaching out for tougher-to-write sentences that make their points more effectively.

Some people edit by rewriting and re-rewriting the entire manuscript. But if you do that, be sure that you examine more than just words and phrases. Look at words in their sentences, sentences in their paragraphs, and paragraphs in the context of what goes before and after.

Because you often change words as you edit, you may find that on reconsideration, in context, the original words were the best way to make your statement after all. If you edit by rewrite instead of by marking the draft, you'll have to hunt through the previous draft if you want to pick up discarded words. (We find our first drafts so full of valuable clues to stages in our thought processes that we never destroy them until we're sure the final manuscript has been accepted by its editors for printing. We suggest you hold onto your first drafts until your finished papers have been returned to you.)

How to become your own best editor

Because most students never get to see the editing that's done by working writers, we've reproduced—just the way she typed it—several pages of the first draft of coauthor Kesselman-Turkel's article, "12 Ways to Get More out of Studying." (The manuscript is Illustration 14/1. Earlier you saw the published version of the article in Illustration 7/2 and the outline in Illustration 8/1.) Study these manuscript pages. See if you can figure out why each change was made.

Notice that some blanks were left on the first draft, to be filled in later so the author didn't have to stop in midstream. She did this because, in the course of writing, she realized she needed some concrete examples of some specific points. Also notice that, in the editing, the order of the various points was rearranged. Do you agree it's a better arrangement?

To show how writers think when they edit, let's examine together page 7 of the first draft. (We've numbered, so you can follow, every line but the top line of identification that separates this paper from the morass of other papers on our desks.)

Line 1: We added paragraphing here because we decided that in magazine format the original paragraph would look formidably long. We added the phrase "in your note-taking" partly as a transitional phrase from the previous paragraph, but also because we wanted to make sure the reader understood what "pay closer attention" referred to. We changed "even closer" to "closest" because, even though grammatically less correct, it was stylistically more forceful. (This is an example of how the experienced writer, like the experienced painter and potter, is able to break the rules with impunity.)

Line 2: We eliminated the last phrase because (a) it was extraneous, and (b) it weakened the force of the sentence, coming last as it did.

Lines 3, 4: On the first run-through, we grabbed at the thought. In editing, we refined it to say exactly what we meant.

Line 5: Notice the spelling correction: *hour's*.

Line 6: We got rid of a dash. We tend to write with too many dashes, so during editing we look for ones to eliminate.

Line 7: Again, we deleted the unneeded thought. It only got in the reader's way, as she stopped to figure out why "a few minutes" was significant enough to be included. (Our enforced objectivity was needed here.)

Line 10: We edited in a thought, then moved it to where it belonged.

Line 12: Notice that we began a thought in the first draft, rethought quickly and changed it, then refined it in editing. The change was a quick decision, in contrast to the carefully considered decisions made while editing. First draft rethoughts can be seen also on lines 2, 7, 8, 16–17, 20 and 24.

Lines 13, 14: Grammatical corrections.

Lines 18, 22: Again, a new thought was inserted during the editing. But then, as the editing continued, it was moved to where it really belonged. (Notice our search for the proper words.)

Line 28: We changed "look up" because it was confusing. We were afraid the reader might think we meant "check out the meaning in a dictionary" when what we really meant was "put aside the text."

Analyze the other first-draft pages we've reproduced here. Once you've decided why we made each change, compare the segment with its corresponding section of the final article (Illustration 7/2). Notice that there were more refinements made while typing the second draft (which, in this case, was the final draft) and that in editing we discovered that our material broke down into 12 points, not 10. We even re-edited the final draft for smooth flow and typing accuracy before we sent the article to *Seventeen* magazine, whose copy editor also made several changes before publishing it.

It's easier to learn good editing skills on somebody else's manuscripts. You can assume an objectivity difficult to achieve with your own precious words. The following exercises will help you learn how to attack your first drafts as ruthlessly as we attack ours. In preforming these exercises, you can use the Editing Checklist that follows this chapter, the Sentences Checklist at the end of Unit II (page 133), and and the Good Writing Checklist at the end of Unit I (page 52). In editing, it pays to use all the help you can find.

EXERCISES:

1. Illustration 14/2 (at end of this chapter) is an unedited page from one of our manuscripts. Photocopy it and edit it. When you think you've got it whipped into shape, compare your editing to ours (reproduced in Appendix B). If your changes don't match ours, don't assume that yours are wrong. Like writing, editing is a personal craft, and there may be a hundred correct ways of solving any one problem.

On the photocopy, number every point where your editing and ours are not identical. For each, write a line or two (more if absolutely necessary) explaining the difference. Include whether you prefer your change or ours, and whether it is a personal preference or justification can be found in a writing reference book. (If so, cite your evidence.) Bring photocopy and explanation to class.

2. Repeat Exercise 1 for Illustration 14/3, another unedited page from one of our manuscripts. (Our editing is reproduced in Appendix C.)

3. Repeat Exercise 1 for Illustration 14/4, another unedited manuscript page. (Our editing is reproduced in Appendix D.)

4. Bring in a nonfiction paper of between 750 and 1,250 words that was produced either for this class or another. Make sure the paper is double-spaced (even if it's handwritten) so that there is room to edit. Exchange papers with a classmate and edit thoroughly. Number each place where you make changes and, on a separate paper, justify each change. If you use reference books, cite your sources as evidence.

5. Now you're ready to tackle a nonfiction paper that shows off your writing skills from beginning to end. Select a theme suitable in size for a 1,250-word paper. Do all the necessary research. Make an outline. Write your first draft, being sure to double-space even if you write by hand. Write *First Draft* plus your name and telephone number at the top of your paper's first page; then photocopy the entire first draft. Bring the photocopy to class and exchange it with a classmate.

6. From the materials in Exercise 5, edit thoroughly both the original copy of your own paper and the photocopy of your classmate's. (You may seek clarification from the writer during your editing.) Return the photocopy to its author.

7. Selecting from both your own edited first draft and the edited photocopy, prepare a double-spaced second draft. Write *Second Draft* at the top of the first page. Make a photocopy and exchange that one with a different classmate.

8. Once more, edit your own second draft and your classmate's, and return the photocopy.

9. Again selecting from both your own and your classmate's comments, prepare a double-spaced final draft, following the format suggested in Section 14.3. Neatly correct any last-minute errors you catch.

14.3 HOW TO TYPE
YOUR FINAL DRAFT.

If your copy is heavily edited, you may have to type an intermediate draft between the first and final. This is usually the case in students' first several papers. Then we hope you'll edit the second draft, too. (The checklist at the end of this chapter seems very long now, but after a few editing sessions, much of it will become second nature.) When you've typed your final draft, do read it over. The polish of a careful typing job is lost if typos haven't been corrected.

Unless your teacher tells you otherwise, use this professional method of typing your final draft:

1. Use only 8½- × -11-inch white unlined bond paper, in a 16-pound or 20-pound weight. (Avoid paper so thin you can see typing on the page beneath it, or so thick it's heavy to carry around. Steer clear of obviously expensive paper that has a pattern or gaudy watermark.)

2. Use only black ribbons that are still dark. (Save your old ribbons for first drafts, and odd-colored ribbons for personal letters and love notes.) Clean your typewriter with typewriter cleaner when the *e*, *o*, or *d* starts to fill up with lint.

3. Pica type is preferred to elite, but not enough for you to scrap your elite machine. Don't use a fancy typeface (italic or script).

4. Set margins of 1½ to 2 inches at the left and 1 inch at the right (about 20 and 75 on your pica carriage).

5. Leave a margin of about 1½ inches at the top of your page and an inch at the bottom, so that you get about twenty-six lines per manuscript page. (Setting all your margins as we suggest will give you an average of about 260 words per pica page, for a quick way to figure approximate word length.)

6. Always type on only one side of the paper.

7. Double-space unless instructed to do otherwise.

8. Make a carbon or photocopy. (Papers do get lost.)

9. Indent five spaces for paragraphs, and for the entire text of long quotations (without quotation marks).

10. Indicate italics by underlining, and dashes by two hyphens with single-spacing before and after (--).

11. Footnote only if the paper calls for footnotes.

12. At the top left-hand margin of page one, put your name and whatever other information is required. Halfway down the page, put the title of your paper. Begin your first paragraph several line-spaces below that.

13. At the top left-hand margin of every page after the first, way up near the top, put your last name, the title (or an abbreviated version), and the page number.

14. For correcting final drafts while they're being typed,

invest in correction fluid or correction paper. Everyone appreciates neatness.

15. Make last-minute corrections on your final draft neatly in blue or black pen. If there are more than a few corrections on a page, or a lengthy insertion, retype the page. (How many are "a few"? It depends on your standards and your teacher's.)

EXERCISES:

1. On an assigned topic, or one of your own choosing, research and write a paper of from 1,500 to 2,000 words. Edit your own first draft. Type an intermediate draft unless you are thoroughly convinced that you do not need one. Prepare your final draft according to the format enumerated in this section. Retain your copy; bring the original to class and exchange it with a classmate.

2. Thoroughly evaluate the strengths and weaknesses of your classmate's paper in the paper's margins or on a separate piece of paper. For every comment you make on a strength or weakness, offer at least one of the following as support:

   a. A page number and paragraph number (or checklist entry number) from this book.

   b. A dictionary or thesaurus.

   c. A grammar or word usage book.

   d. A reference book or other authoritative source.

Strive to point out (a) at least two overall strengths of the paper as a whole, (b) at least two weaknesses of the paper as a whole, (c) at least four particularly strong paragraphs, and (d) at least four particularly weak paragraphs. But if you feel you cannot find all of these, write at least 250 well-written words that explain why you cannot.

NOTE: CHAPTER 14

1. Caskie Stinnett, "It Wasn't As Easy As It Seemed," *The Atlantic Monthly*, April, 1979, p.28.

study... 6   that takes the most time and is least well retained --

is to simply read something over and over again.

~~Foreg~~ Forget it if that's the way you memorize. Instead,

use as many of your senses as possible, and as many of
Don't just read it: try to visualize it in concrete terms, to get a picture of
your reflexes. In addition to sight, use sound: say it in your head.

the words out loud, and listen to yourself saying

them. Use association: relate the fact to be learned to
personally significant, or ~~a logical~~ find a logical tie-in.
something you-know-already;-try-to-visualize-it
timewise
for example, when memorizing dates, relate them to important

events whose dates you know already. Use mnemonics, like using
"Every Good Boy Does Fine" to remember the names of
the notes for the treble cliff spaces in music, .. or acronyms,
remembering
such as SKIR for the reading method outlined in point 8 below. And

be sure to <u>overlearn</u>, to memorize <u>beyond</u> perfect recall. Walter

Pauk says, "overlearning is one of the most effective ways to

insure remembering."

⑥ ~~8~~. <u>Study similar subjects at separate times.</u>

~~The brain is~~ Brainwaves are like radio waves: ~~in that two~~
the   ~~similar~~ input ~~isn't spaced~~ enough;
~~stations~~ if ~~you put~~ the stations/~~too-close-together~~, you get

interference. The more similar the kinds of learning taking
has
place, it been shown, the more interference. So space out your

study for courses with similar subject matter. Follow your hour
a
of German with an hour of chem or history, not with ~~your~~ Spanish.

⑪ ~~8~~. <u>Clue your lecture notes.</u> Underline, ~~or~~ star the ideas that
or otherwise mark
your prof says are important, thoughts/that he says you'll be coming

back to later, items that he says are "common mistakes." Watch for

words that tell you he's summarizing: "so that," "~~finally,~~" "therefore,"

"In essence." Always record his examples; in fact, in such subjects

as math and chem your notes should consist mainly of the examples

1 And pay ~~even~~ closer attention ^ST^ to the last few minutes *in your note-taking*

2 of class time, ~~than/to the first thirty, or s half hour.~~

3 Often a teacher gets side-tracked and ~~doesn't~~ *runs out of* time *for all* his

4 projected session content, ~~well.~~ He may jam into the

5 last five or ten minutes up to half the hour's content.

6 Get down those packed few minutes, if necessary, *after the bell*

7 stay on ~~a few minutes~~/to get it all down.

8 ⑦ ✗ 7. ~~Think before you read.~~ Take more time for

9 your reading. *And read with a purpose.* It really takes less time in the long

10 run! Instead of just starting a book or chapter or

11 original source paper at the beginning, and reading

12 through to the end, you'll ~~remembe read~~ *really do the assignment* a lot faster

13 and remember a lot more if you first take the time to

14 do the following (this technique has several variations.

15 We prefer the OK4R method suggested by Walter Pau**K**l.)

16 O: Overview: read the title the ~~first and last~~
   introductory and summarizing

17 / paragraphs (the first and the last few), and all the

18 headings included in the reading material. Now you

19 have a general idea of what/ the author will be discussing.
   topics

20 K: Key ideas: Go back and skim the text for

21 the key ~~iea~~ ideas (usually found in the first sentence of

22 every paragraph). Now you'll know what the author is *Also read the typesetter's clues -- italics and bold type in the text, bullets, itemizations, pictures + tables,*

23 saying about his topics.

24 RI: Read ~~the entire assigned~~ your assignment from

25 beginning to end. You'll be able to do it quickly now,

26 because you'll already know where the author is going

27 and what he's trying to prove.

28 R2: Recall. ~~Look up~~ *Put aside the text* and say or write, in a few

29 key words or sentences, the thrust of what you've read.

30 (This is the time to put down reading notes, ~~if~~

study...8

in your loose leaf book. It's been proven that
most forgetting takes place immediately after
initial learning. In one psychological study it
was shown that the best way to retain information is
to try to recall it immediately: to recite or write
in your own words what you've n̸ just heard or read.
Walter Pau͠l̸ says that <u>one minute spent in immediate</u>
<u>recall nearly doubles re͠tention</u> of that piece of data!

R3: Re̸flect. The last step helped to fix the
material in your mind. To really ~~have~~ *keep* it there
forever, relate it to ~~what~~ other knowledge: find
relationships and significance for ~~you~~ what you've read.

R4: Review. This step ~~takes place~~ doesn't take
It should be done
place right away. ~~Do it weeks later,~~ for the next
short quiz, and then again for later tests throughout
the term. Several reviews will make that knowledge
indelibly yours.

⑪ ⍿ ∅. Avoid ~~your sleepy~~ studying in your "sleepy" times.
Psychologists have found that everyone has a certain
time of day when he or she gets sleepy. $ $ Don't try to
that
study during ~~your sleepy~~ time. (But don't go to sleep
either. It ~~doesn't~~ hardly ever refreshes.) Instead,
~~sheedu~~ schedule physical activity for that period *such as*
or chopping instrument practice
recreation, ~~or~~ if you've a pile of schoolwork, use
that time to sort your notes or clear up your desk/ and
get your books together, ∅r ~~use that time~~ to study with a friend.
can
⑫ ∅. ~~If you- If you/- underline in your books~~ ⎰Beware

study...9

the underlined textbook. Of course, if ~~it's not~~
the book doesn't belong to you, you won't be underlining at all. But if you can underline, do it
sparingly. ~~To~~ And ~~O~~ver-underlining is a common fault
of students; only the most essential ~~key~~ words in
a paragraph should be underlined. ~~And it shouldn't
be done until you've~~ It should never be done in pen
(something you think is important at the time may not
be at all), and it should ~~never~~ be done only after
you've done the "OK" part of your OK4R reading. (The best
underlining is not as productive as the worst note-taking.)
If you're buying your books second-hand, never
buy one that's already been underlined. You'll tend
to rely on it -- and you have no idea whether the
hand that underlined got an A or an F in the course!
                    For marking up
10. ~~In~~/your personal books and hand-outs,
devise a color-and-sign system. ~~for p For~~ One example,
suggested by Robert Palmatier: red for main ideas,
blue ~~b~~ for dates and numbers, yellow for supporting facts;
                    in the margin
circles, box~~s~~es, stars and checks/can also be utilized.
to make reviewing easy.

11. ~~Foreign-language study should be~~
     Review lecture course material right after
class, and recitation course material (language for
~~example) right before class.~~
     Study at the most productive time.
/If it's a lecture course, do your studying ~~right~~ soon
after class; if it's a class in which ~~your e~~ students are
                to
called on ~~the~~/recite or answer questions, ~~do your~~ studying soon.
~~just~~ before class. After the lecture, you'll be reviewing,

ILLUSTRATION 14/2

++ But your education got in the way of
your learning how to write well.

In many ways, we look upon this as a brush-up
course for you. You might want to view it similarly.
You see, you almost learned how to write perfectly
well once before -- ~~when~~ (as) you learned how to speak.
If you'd been encouraged to write as instinctively
as you talk, you ~~might~~ not be enrolled in this course now. ++

+ Our language is so logical that even an infant
can learn ~~how to speak it~~ (its fundamentals) by the age of three. Most
people speak well by the time they leave high school
(unless they have an impediment). This is not to say
every high school graduate (speaks well enough to be) another Sarah Bernhardt
or John Gielgood, but well enough to get across the
meaning of even fairly complex ideas with a minimum of
effort. Than's universally true even though few/rhetoric oral
or public speaking courses are taught in schools these
days. People learn naturally not only to express
themselves clearly but to keep their listeners interested
in what they have to say. (Good speaking habits become ingrained) Through consistent positive
or negative feedback, mostly in the form of attention
from friends when they're (speaking is) interesting and clear, and
yawns when they/aren't it isn't.

Good speaking comes about only if there's someone
listening, someone providing feedback. Until then,

ILLUSTRATION 14/3

HOW TO ACHIEVE A TEN-YEAR PAINT JOB

If you're ~~one of those~~ like most home-owners, dreading

the next time you either have to shell out a lot of

cash to get the outside of your house painted, or

go through the mess and agony of doing it yourself,

take heart! At l~~e~~ast somebody has ~~scientifically~~

attacked the problem with scientific acumen, accumulated

actual research data to show how best to paint ~~the~~

our aging castle, and -- best ne~~w~~ws of all -- they

say that a properly done paint job sould last for

10 years!

The U.S. Forest Products Laboratory/, , affiliated in Madison, Wisconsin, is

both with the U.S. Dept. of Agriculture and the University

of Wisconsin.   It's staff of ___ scientists, technicians,

and backup staff conduct research into virtually

every aspect of wood and its thousands of uses. The

FPL's ~~has/finally/tackled~~ research includes a ~~they~~

thorough study of ~~paint~~ not only wood, but types of

paint used to protect wood, reasons for/paint failures, premature

how paint weathers as it protects, and even ideal

painting techniques. When they found paint materials

lacking in several ar~~d~~eas, they developed formulations

that are now commercially available.

Incidentally, the paint techniques developed at FPL

for wood siding, ~~works/on/any~~ will prove valuable even

if your house is covered with one of the other kinds

of siding that needs periodic painting or staining.

ILLUSTRATION 14/4

How many of us can survive enough falls off 28-
storie buildings, or ~~can~~ recover from enough near-
fatal illnesses, to make a living at writing personal
experience articles? So, the pros who make at living
at writing personal experience stories write about
some body else's tragedies and triumphs.[++] ~~Probably~~
the dean of personal experience story tellers ~~is~~ must be
Terry Morris, one-time president of the American
Society of Journalists and Authors, and proflific
magazine writers. She ~~switched,~~ abandoned about
1950, ~~from~~ writing shortstories in favor of human
interest magazine articles about people in crisis.
But she never abandoned her ~~f~~gift for telling a touching
story, so she sold her first two artgicles to
COSMOPOLITAN and McCALL'S early in 1951. Terry's
all-time favorite was "Please don't lose faith in Me"
                        from the viewpoint of
an as-told-to ~~dtd~~ article ~~by~~ the mother of a
schizophrenic son ~~that~~ McCALL''S ran it ~~in~~ July 1953;
we've reprinted the first page hearby~~/~~, so you can study
how a master handles domebody else's personal experience.

[++]Sometimes the person who lived the experience
gets the entire by-line. Other times, the actual author
is listed second:as told to....." Rarely, usually only
inarticles involving clelebrities, does the author get
the traditional by-line.

CHECKLIST FOR EDITING

At the risk of having you edit this book first, here's a condensation of the things to look for when editing manuscripts. It summarizes every important aspect of good writing that's been considered in this book.

The checklist is divided into three sections. Inspect the paper to see that all the elements of Checklist A are there. Then read the paper's body, using the questions in Checklist B as your guide. Finally, reread the entire paper slowly and carefully, with Checklist C's questions in mind. Eventually, you'll develop your own mental checklist as these considerations become second nature.

A. The paper's structure

    1. The title

        a. Does it still reflect all of your theme (both topic and purpose) or is it too narrow?

        b. Does it still reflect only your theme, or is it too broad?

    2. The lead

        a. Is it really a lead? Does it entice the reader?

        b. Does it appeal to intellect, emotions, or both?

        c. If it appeals to emotion, which one? If to intellect, with what device (question, shocking statement, contradiction etc.)?

        d. Did you find a better lead while writing the first draft?

        e. Does the lead pertain to the theme of the paper?

    3. The topic sentence

        a. Do you have one?

        b. Does it define the topic of the paper?

        c. Is it too broad or too narrow? (Check it against your final title.)

    d. What is the purpose of the paper? (To report, give directions, inform, or persuade?)

    e. How is the purpose stated or implied in the topic sentence?

4. *The body*

    a. Does it follow your outline?

    b. Can you find a more logical order?

    c. Are all the points in your outline covered?

    d. Did you think of new points that should be added?

    e. Are newly added points in their best places in the manuscript?

    f. What logical patterns do you use? (Time sequence, from general to specific, from least to most, etc.) See Chapter 8's checklist (210) for review if you're unsure.

    g. Do you stick to the same logical pattern all the way through the body? If not, do you have a good reason?

5. *The ending*

    a. Do you sum up, echo the lead, restate the purpose, or incite the reader to action?

    b. Whichever you do, does it sound satisfying?

    c. Are there any new ideas, facts, or opinions in the ending? If so, take them out.

6. *The readers*

    a. Is it assumed that readers are for or against the theme?

    b. Is it assumed that readers know the subject?

    c. What else is assumed about the readers? Is the assumption correct?

    d. Is opinion stated in the paper, or are structure, content, and words used to show point of view?

    e. Is everything included that the reader needs, and everything excluded that's not needed? (Have you thoroughly explained anything that may puzzle or confuse the reader?)

B: The content of the paper's body

1. The unsupported statements
   a. Indicate (with a checkmark) all the unquestioned truths in your paper, the statements that are so widely accepted you can say them without proof or support.
   b. Are you certain every truth checked is as readily believed by your readers as by you?
   c. If you end up with dozens of checkmarks, ask yourself, "What have I said that's new?"

2. The generalizations
   a. Is every generalization stated so that it says what you want it to say?
   b. Are its limits expressed when its supports don't make a strong case?
   c. Does it assume a fact that hasn't been proved?
   d. Does it lead to a conclusion you haven't discussed?
   e. Is it based on a conclusion you overlooked?
   f. Is every generalization supported with specifics?
   g. Do you provide enough evidence?
   h. Does the evidence really support it, or are you stretching?
   i. Do the specifics really lead to a different generalization? (Maybe they're in the wrong place in your paper.)
   j. Have you chosen the best supports for each generalization? Check your notes again.

3. The exposition
   a. Have you verified your facts and assessed them for accuracy, authenticity, credibility, plausibility, or corroboration? Have you expressed their limits?
   b. Is opposing evidence presented? If so, is it refuted?
   c. Is evidence used according to the principle of fair use? (Do you use another author's words or ideas only sparingly, with credit, and only if it's the best literary device to make your point?)

    d. Do you use statistics correctly, with credit, and have you evaluated their sources?

    e. If there are numbers the reader may not be able to grasp, are they made vivid?

4. *The quotations*

    a. Why have you quoted or paraphrased? (Are the exact words important or is the voice of authority needed?)

    b. Does the quotation say what you want it to say?

    c. Is it the only way to present the information your paper requires?

    d. Have you used quotation marks wherever you've borrowed more than a few words in a row, and given credit with identifying credentials or title?

    e. Are your authority's facts correct?

    f. Is his authority still intact?

    g. Is his statement within the parameters of his expertise? If not, have you labeled it opinion?

    h. Does the quotation or paraphrase represent accurately his meaning as well as his words?

    i. Has he changed his mind since then?

    j. Have you chosen only the best parts to quote, and paraphrased the rest in interesting, economical words?

    k. If you've used a primary source, have you indicated that, and have you identified the basis of your source's expertise?

    l. If it's a secondary source, have you also credited the place where you got your information?

5. *The anecdotes*

    a. Does every anecdote make the point you want to make?

    b. Does the point belong in the article?

    c. Is it a complete story in miniature with a beginning and an ending?

    d. Does it have a setting? Is the scene briefly described?

e.   Does it show real people and something happening?
f.   Does time pass or do people move about?
g.   Is it in past tense? Should it be?

C. The words, sentences, and paragraphs

1. *The paragraph*
   a.   Does each paragraph have a theme?
   b.   Have any extraneous themes crept in?
   c.   Is the topic phrase expressed? Where?
   d.   Does it clearly show the purpose of the paragraph?
   e.   Is each theme fully amplified? What techniques are used for amplification? Are there enough specifics to support each theme?
   f.   Do the ideas proceed in logical sequence? Would you change any sentences around?
   g.   Are there any gaps in the logical progression of ideas?
   h.   As a reader, do you feel any paragraphs are too long? Too short?

2. *The transitions*
   a.   Do the sentences flow into one another, or are any transitions too abrupt?
   b.   Do you use echoing words or phrases? Are they forced?
   c.   Are your punctuation transitions adequate and correct?
   d.   Do your transition words do what you want them to do (add, subtract, compare or contrast, etc.)?
   e.   Do you use transitional sentences and paragraphs to connect your major subtopics? Do they do the job well?

3. *The sentences*
   a.   Are sentences varied in structure and length?
   b.   Are parallel sentences used effectively? Is there too much parallelism?
   c.   Do the last words in sentences provide effective climaxes?

4. *The words*
   a. Are nouns and verbs varied, repeated only when emphasis is wanted?
   b. Is the mood of the words appropriate to the theme?
   c. Is simple present or past tense used, with the same tense throughout? If not, is there good reason?
   d. Are parallel phrases used to express parallel ideas?

5. *The basics*

The basics of writing words and sentences are covered thoroughly in the Checklist for Unit II at the end of Chapter 6. Turn to that page now for review. Then glance at the Checklist for Unit I at the end of Chapter 2 for one final overview of your paper.

CHAPTER 15
HOW TO DEVELOP A
STYLE OF YOUR OWN

*When we encounter a natural style
we are always surprised and
delighted, for we thought to see
an author and found a man.*
Blaise Pascal

All through school you've been studying great writers' styles—
the lush images of Hudson, the verbal economy of Thoreau, the
blunt language of Hemingway, the heavy prose of Faulkner. You
may have concluded that style is something a good writer works
for even more earnestly than communication. As a result, if
you're like the learning writers we've known and taught, you've
probably fastened onto the style of your favorite author and—
consciously or not—attempted to mimic it in your own prose.

That isn't the way to find a style of your own.

You already have a style. It may be suppressed in your
writing by vain efforts to resurrect Joyce or Lovecraft through
your fingertips, but fortunately it's there in your speaking pattern,
where you'll find it if you look and listen.

You do have a style of speaking that's just a little different
from anyone else's. You form your sentences a bit differently,
put your vocal accents where they feel right to you, find certain
rhythms more pleasing than others, choose a vocabulary that
reflects your upbringing and outlook on life. If the upbringing

has been in front of a TV set, your style may be hackneyed. If it's been rich in reading romantic novels, it may be lush and flowery. If science fiction novels daily levitated onto your desk, your speaking style will reflect that. If you studied in two languages, your style will be richer than that of those who've learned only in English. If you've been given leeway to think or to dream or to criticize a great deal, your style will show it. With each new year, each new experience, your style will become more distinctly your own.

Do you doubt that your speaking style is already just a bit different from everyone else's? Try phoning a long-standing friend, disguising your voice, and talking without announcing who's on the phone. See just how long it takes the friend to recognize you.

Writing style is speaking style transferred to the written page. It's practically as simple as that. The best way to find your style is to give little thought to it, but to write the way you speak. Style doesn't come with effort, but with relaxation. The better your command of writing skills, the more facility you have with words, and the less you have to think about mechanics, the more smoothly your writing will flow in your own particular voice. If you could hold conversations with Hudson, Thoreau, Hemingway, and Faulkner, you'd hear in their voices the echoes of their writing styles.

But we've oversimplified a bit, to make our point. Writing is really more than scribbled speech. It's speech reconsidered, thoughts that we've had a chance to dust and polish. Unlike our spoken words, which fly off and can't be caught to be reworded no matter how inexactly or intemperately phrased, our writing doesn't have to be shared until we feel it says exactly what we mean to say. Writing, then, is speech perfected, the voice we'd like to present to the world. Your writing style should be the way you wish you spoke all the time, a reflection of all the qualities you like most about yourself.

When you've succeeded in letting your natural writing style mature, you'll probably know it without being told. But maybe you'll be fortunate enough to have someone say to you, as coauthor Kesselman-Turkel remembers a colleague saying to her many years ago, "I could tell you wrote that even if I hadn't seen your name on it. It sounded like you."

Here are some guidelines that will help you find your style.

15.1 WRITE NATURALLY.

Spend time perfecting your outlines and doing your research so that you can write your first drafts quickly and naturally. Then devote plenty of time to editing with care and precision. Pursue the word that feels just right. Explore sentence constructions until you land on one that says what you feel needs saying, and says it in a way you enjoy listening to. When you type (or hand-write) your final draft, the words and phrases should flow easily from your head into your fingers and onto the paper. When you sense that you're speaking softly to a sheet of paper, you will know that your own unique style has matured.

15.2 WRITE HONESTLY.

Stick to ideas you understand, to words you can use in speaking, to a point of view you believe in. If you exaggerate, your reader will doubt the validity of your words. If you use humor or irony or satire as an affectation instead of only when the subject honestly calls for such an approach, you'll come off sounding inane or, worse, pompous. If you use words you're not sure of and haven't the ambition to check, you won't fool readers but may sound like a fool. If you try to explain or defend what you don't understand or believe in, your paper won't be argument but alibi.

15.3 WRITE FROM EXPERIENCE.

Don't stretch for images or figures of speech. Use those that come easily and naturally to mind, or the strain will show through and distract your reader from the important points you want to make. Know your subject thoroughly before you begin to write, and you'll think of plenty of fresh comparisons, contrasts, and insights to supply in your own natural style.

15.4 WRITE ALWAYS WITH THE READER IN MIND.

Though your ideas and attitudes remain the same, you choose your words just a little differently depending on whether you're speaking with parents, friends, teachers, or strangers. You must choose your written words, too, with the reader in mind. Politeness, interest, and congeniality all have their place in writing. Don't badger your reader, insult him, or bore him. Don't explain things he can be counted on to understand, and don't leave out an explanation unless you're sure none is needed. Don't be long-winded, but say what you have to say as succinctly as you know how.

George Orwell said, in his essay "Politics and the English Language," "If it is possible to cut a word out, always cut it out." That advice alone, if followed, will immensely improve your style. Your distinct pace—the rhythm and tone of your writing—will take over. You and the reader will communicate, which is the whole purpose of writing.

APPENDIX A

ILLUSTRATION II/1
Notes on editorial changes

Most of the changes were made to eliminate redundancies (see lines 2, 8, 9, 10, 19, 20, 21, 23, and 40 for examples), sharpen verbs (see lines 3, 17, 18, 20, 26, 48, and 49 for examples), and insert missing details (see lines 5, 7, 20, and 39).

In line 1, we have an example of where general wording is better than the more specific original words. The change makes the question much easier for the reader to remember, and since the rest of the paragraph spells out the specifics, only a generalization is needed in the topic sentence.

The sentence in line 7 states a new topic. Therefore it should begin a new paragraph. By eliminating most of the words in line 8, we shift the focus from the employee to the employer—but we've decided that nothing is lost in the shift. Do you agree or disagree? Notice that, by starting a new sentence on line 12, we point up the ironic information that was lost when the writer made it just the last of a string of details. This is the sort of playing with words that we enjoy most about editing.

We changed line 14 to say what the writer had meant to say.

Authors' Revisions of Illustration II/1

1 What ~~are~~ *makes* illegal [grounds for] discrimination? ~~The~~ *It depends on*

2 ~~grounds will differ with~~ the law, ~~but~~ most laws are based

3 on the Civil Rights Act of 1964, *which* prohibiting *a* discrimination

4 on the basis of race, color, sex, religion, creed or

5 national origin. Other laws ~~cover areas such as age,~~ *prevent discrimination based on*

6 handicap, sexual preference, ~~and~~ even student status.

7 ¶ Discrimination *by employers* can occur in many ways. ~~The following~~

8 ~~are~~ some *are:* ~~of the ways an employee can be adversely~~

9 ~~affected by employment discrimination:~~ failure ~~of the~~

10 ~~employer~~ to hire, ~~you,~~ failure to promote, *unwarranted* discharge,

11 denial of health or medical benefits, sexual harassment,

12 verbal harassment (for example, racial slurs), ~~and~~ *Even*

13 re*t*aliation for filing a discrimination complaint *is considered discrimination.*

14 In the often long and drawn-out interim ~~period after~~ *between the time*

15 you file a complaint and *the time* some action is taken, you may

16 forget the details of your complaint, *the* dates, *the* witness, etc. *and such.*

17 *To* ~~A~~ helpful ~~aid to~~ remembering *but* ~~is to~~ immediately start

18 your own file of the incident. ~~Have a~~ list of any

19 important dates involved in the charge. ~~This will help~~

20 ~~refresh your memory,~~ *Keep a file of pertinent* Documents ~~are also important.~~

21 ~~Any~~ letters ~~received~~ from your employer, ~~along with~~ progress

22 reports or evaluations of your work, ~~a copy of~~ your

23 employment contract, ~~and~~ letters ~~of correspondence~~ or

24 medical reports from your doctor (if disability or

The double insertion of *the* on line 16, and the elimination of *etc.* are grammatical corrections; the writer's parallel construction (details, dates, witnesses) begs the *the*s.

The word changes in lines 26 and 27 are prompted by common sense: you can't guess what the reader is thinking and it's unwise to try. The new paragraph isn't necessary for this one sentence because the previous paragraph covers time, work, and effort. But there is a new topic introduced in line 29; that should begin a new paragraph.

Notice that, on line 30, we inserted the answer to the question of line 29. Papers aren't quizzes for readers; if you pose a question, it's only fair to answer it. Some writers save their answers, thinking it builds suspense. The technique is dangerous, since it may instead simply annoy the reader.

Lines 30 and 33 have the same problem as line 26: they second-guess the reader. Out they go. Can you guess why we got rid of *large* in line 30? Did you notice that the idea in line 32 is really a subordinate idea for the previous sentence? Our clue was the word *settlements* in both sentences.

Notice the subtle change in emphasis that comes from changing line 34 to present tense: things that may not happen any more suddenly become things that are still happening. (Here we question whether the author is sure of her statement, or whether she wants to hedge with the word *rarely*.) We eliminated the phrase in lines 35 and 36 because it overlaps the information given in the writer's line 32 and, also being a lower number, detracts from the drama of *millions*. (If it had made an important point, we might have left it in.)

Did you make the change, in line 37, from the fuzzy generality to the more specific *complainants*?

Line 41 demonstrates the importance of comma placement in making your meaning clear. Between lines 39 and 45 we made one sentence out of three; notice that the change from separate sentences to parallel clauses makes the ideas easier for the reader to follow even though the sentence is double-sized. The change in line 47 is not needed grammatically; it is merely more pleasant to the ear than the two *unders* so close together.

Lines 48 through 50 do the reverse of 39 to 45; they make one sentence into two. We did it because we felt both ideas were

25   sickness is an issue in your complaint).

26   ~~You may think that~~ This ~~is~~ may use a lot more time, work

27   and effort than you bargained for, ~~and well it may be,~~

28   but if you hope to have the discriminatory act rectified

29   it's important to do these things. ~~you'll find a way to persist.~~ What is in it for you?

30   Probably very little, in terms of money. ~~You've heard about the~~ huge settlements ~~that large~~

31   companies have been forced into, sometimes running into millions, ~~made~~ for discriminating against a group

32   of employees. ~~Such settlements may run in the millions.~~

33   But ~~what you may not realize is that~~ these mammoth

34   settlements never rarely ~~didn't~~ go to single ~~one~~ individuals or even to a small

35   groups of individuals. ~~Six-figure settlements usually~~

36   ~~result from~~ In a class-action suits, and the money is sometimes

37   divided up between thousands of complainants. ~~class members.~~

38   In the majority of cases, ~~the only remedy sought~~

39   it is an individual ~~one~~ who is seeking the remedy. As an individual, you can

40   recover either ~~several types of damages. You can recover~~

41   money, in the form of back pay, or personal damages, and

42   attorney's fees (usually only recoverable under federal

43   law); or Non-monetary relief, ~~can be granted~~ in the form of reinstatement,

44   a promise of an interview for a job or promotion, or ~~an~~

45   admission of guilt by the employer. ~~Once again~~ different

46   laws provide ~~allow~~ for different remedies, so ~~and~~ you should check

47   to see whether the remedy you want is available within ~~under~~

48   the law you file under. In short, have ~~Having~~ a clear idea of what redress

49   you want and finding out how ~~such a remedy is available~~ you can obtain it.

50   This ~~to you~~ will save you frustration and disappointment.

equally important, and we wanted to punch each one home separately. Do you have a better change?

To line 51 we added the idea that patience is an *asset*; then, for full effect, we had to change around the placement of the subordinate clause. We edited the next sentence, beginning on line 55, for conciseness—but then we realized that the entire sentence ought to be either eliminated or elaborated, since it introduces a new idea. (Most writers, even professional ones, often get last-minute urges to add to the ideas in their papers. The difference between a good writer and a poor one is that the good writer edits the afterthought into the paper, in its proper place, with proper elaboration.)

Line 59 gets rid of the legalese (*were given broad mandates*) and substitutes an idea (*they are trying*); jargon in lines 60 and 61 (*discriminatory practices* and *remedies*) is also cut. Watch out for redundancies like *end or eliminate* in line 60. Writers who aim for precision sometimes fall into the trap of including two words whose differences in meaning are so subtle that the precision only distracts the reader.

Notice that the addition of *but* to line 62 takes what seems to be a completely new idea and puts it into the context of the paragraph.

If you didn't catch the paragraphing corrections, don't be concerned. Paragraphs are discussed in detail in Chapter 12. If you did make the changes, nice going!

APPENDIX B

Illustration 14.2 is an actual reproduction from the first-draft of this textbook. To find out what our editing changes were, compare it with the first two paragraphs in Section 1.1.

51 ~Perhaps~ one of ~the~ most important _your_ ... _assets will be_

52 ~remember~ when filing a complaint with a government

53 agency, ~is to be~ patient. Both the EEOC and state-

54 level equal rights agencies suffer from ✗ tremendous

55 backlog of cases. ~to be resolved.~ _unresolved_ [This is not because~,~ _of_

56 ~bureaucrats working for equal rights agencies are more~

57 _see note_ ~inept than those working in other agencies~, but ~is~ _unusual ineptness;_

58 rather ~the result~ of constraints beyond the agencies' _because_

59 control.] ~These agencies were given broad mandates~ to _They are trying_

60 end or eliminate discriminat~ory practices in society.~ _ion_

61 and ~aid~ victims, ~of discrimination by providing remedies.~ _help its_

62 _but_ _one of their_ ~Every~ ~agency~ decision, is open to ~question~ and attack _challenge_

63 in the courts.

APPENDIX C

HOW TO ACHIEVE A TEN-YEAR PAINT JOB

If you're ~~one of those~~ [like most] home-owners, ~~dreading~~

~~the next time~~ you [either] have to shell out a lot of

cash to get the outside of your house painted, or

go through the mess and agony of doing it yourself,

take heart! At least somebody has ~~scientifically~~

attacked the problem ~~with~~ scientific ~~acumen,~~ [ally] ~~accumulated~~

actual research data, [now] to show how best to paint ~~the~~ [your]

your aging castle. ~~and~~ best news of all, ~~they~~

~~say that~~ a properly done paint job should last for

10 years.

The U.S. Forest Products Laboratory/ (FPL) in Madison, Wisconsin, is affiliated

~~both~~ with the U.S. (Dept.) of Agriculture and the University

of Wisconsin. Its staff of 25 scientists, technicians,

and backup ~~staff~~ [personnel] conduct research into virtually

every aspect of wood and its thousands of uses. ~~The~~ [Its]

~~FPL's has/finally tackled~~ research [has] includes [a] ~~a thou~~

thorough study ~~of paint~~ not only [of] wood, but [of] types of

paint used to protect wood, reasons for/ [premature] paint failures,

~~how~~ paint ~~weathers~~ [weathering of] as it protects, and even ideal

painting techniwue s. When ~~they found~~ [FPL's researchers] ~~paint materials~~ [that ordinary paints]

~~lacking in several areas,~~ [performed poorly,] they develope[d] [better] formula~~tions~~

that are now commercially available.

~~Incidentally,~~ the ~~paint~~ techniques developed at FPL

for [painting or staining] wood siding ~~works on any~~ will prove valuable even

if your house is covered with ~~one of the other kinds~~ [non-wood]

~~of siding, that needs periodic painting or staining.~~

[left margin: put later on, in talking about how to paint]

APPENDIX D

How many of us can survive enough falls off 28-stor~~ie~~[y] buildings, or ~~can~~ recover from enough near-fatal illnesses, to make a living ~~at~~ writing personal experience articles? ~~So,~~ the pros who make a[/] living at ~~writing personal experience stories~~ [it] write about some~~body~~ else's tragedies and triumphs.[++] [Probably]

¶ the dean of personal experience story[]tellers ~~is~~ must be [our friend] Terry Morris, one-time president of the American Society of Journalists and Authors. ~~and proflific magazine writers,~~ [About 1950, Terry] ~~She switched,~~ abandoned ~~about~~ [short-story writing] ~~1950, from writing short stories~~ in favor of human interest magazine articles about people in crisis. [Her genius] ~~But she never abandoned her gift~~ for telling a touching story [carried over from fiction to non-fiction; and] ~~so~~ she sold her first two articles to COSMOPOLITAN and McCALL'S early in 1951. ¶ Terry's all-time favorite ~~was~~ [is] "Please don't lose faith in Me" from the viewpoint of an as-told-to ~~old~~ article [by] the mother of a schizophrenic son. ~~that~~ McCALL'S ran it [in] July 1953; we've reprinted the first page [nearby//] so you can study how a master ~~handles~~ [molds] somebody else's personal experience.

++Sometimes the person who [lived] the experience gets the entire by-line. Other times, the actual author is listed second:as told to.... ["] Rarely[,] usually only [for] ~~in~~ articles involving celebrities[,] ~~does~~ the author ~~get~~ [can] [count or a] ~~the~~ traditional by-line.

INDEX

Where there are numerous listings, numbers in italics refer to pages on which the terms are defined or otherwise discussed in depth.